THE "FALL" OF THE ARAB SPRING

Constitutional bargains are seen as cornerstones of democratic transitions in much of the world. Yet very few studies have theorized about the link between constitution-making and democratization. Shifting the focus on democratization away from autocratic regime break down, this book considers the importance of inclusive constitution-building for democratization. In this pathbreaking volume, Tofigh Maboudi draws on a decade of research on the Arab Spring to explain when and how constitutional bargains facilitate (or hinder) democratization. Here, he argues that constitutional negotiations have a higher prospect of success in establishing democracy if they resolve societal, ideological, and political ills. Emphasizing the importance of constitution-making processes, Maboudi shows that constitutions can resolve these problems best through participatory and inclusive processes. Above all, The "Fall" of the Arab Spring demonstrates that civil society is the all-important link that connects constitutional bargaining processes to democratization.

Tofigh Maboudi is an Assistant Professor of Political Science at Loyola University Chicago, who has studied Arab constitutions and constitutionalism for over a decade. Maboudi's research focuses on comparative constitutional studies, democratization, authoritarianism, and Middle East politics. His research has appeared in several journals including The American Political Science Review, Comparative Political Studies, and Political Research Quarterly. He is the co-author of *Constituents before Assembly: Participation, Deliberation, and Representation in the Worldwide Crafting of New Constitutions* (2017). Professor Maboudi has been a Visiting Scholar at the American Bar Foundation.

T0384532

COMPARATIVE CONSTITUTIONAL LAW AND POLICY

Series Editors

Tom Ginsburg *University of Chicago*
Zachary Elkins *University of Texas at Austin*
Ran Hirschl *University of Toronto*

Comparative constitutional law is an intellectually vibrant field that encompasses an increasingly broad array of approaches and methodologies. This series collects analytically innovative and empirically grounded work from scholars of comparative constitutionalism across academic disciplines. Books in the series include theoretically informed studies of single constitutional jurisdictions, comparative studies of constitutional law and institutions, and edited collections of original essays that respond to challenging theoretical and empirical questions in the field.

Books in the Series

Making We the People: Democratic Constitutional Founding in Postwar Japan and South Korea
Chaihark Hahm and Sung Ho Kim

Radical Deprivation on Trial: The Impact of Judicial Activism on Socioeconomic Rights in the Global South
César Rodríguez-Garavito and Diana Rodríguez-Franco

Unstable Constitutionalism: Law and Politics in South Asia
Edited by Mark Tushnet and Madhav Khosla

Magna Carta and Its Modern Legacy
Edited by Robert Hazell and James Melton

Constitutions and Religious Freedom
Frank B. Cross

International Courts and the Performance of International Agreements: A General Theory with Evidence from the European Union
Clifford J. Carrubba and Matthew J. Gabel

Reputation and Judicial Tactics: A Theory of National and International Courts
Shai Dothan

Social Difference and Constitutionalism in Pan-Asia
Edited by Susan H. Williams

Constitutionalism in Asia in the Early Twenty-First Century
Edited by Albert H. Y. Chen

Constitutions in Authoritarian Regimes
Edited by Tom Ginsburg and Alberto Simpser

Presidential Legislation in India: The Law and Practice of Ordinances
Shubhankar Dam

Social and Political Foundations of Constitutions
Edited by Denis J. Galligan and Mila Versteeg

Consequential Courts: Judicial Roles in Global Perspective
Edited by Diana Kapiszewski, Gordon Silverstein, and Robert A. Kagan

Comparative Constitutional Design
Edited by Tom Ginsburg

The "Fall" of the Arab Spring

DEMOCRACY'S CHALLENGES AND EFFORTS TO RECONSTITUTE THE MIDDLE EAST

TOFIGH MABOUDI

Loyola University Chicago

CAMBRIDGE
UNIVERSITY PRESS

Shaftesbury Road, Cambridge CB2 8EA, United Kingdom

One Liberty Plaza, 20th Floor, New York, NY 10006, USA

477 Williamstown Road, Port Melbourne, VIC 3207, Australia

314–321, 3rd Floor, Plot 3, Splendor Forum, Jasola District Centre, New Delhi – 110025, India

103 Penang Road, #05–06/07, Visioncrest Commercial, Singapore 238467

Cambridge University Press is part of Cambridge University Press & Assessment, a department of the University of Cambridge.

We share the University's mission to contribute to society through the pursuit of education, learning and research at the highest international levels of excellence.

www.cambridge.org
Information on this title: www.cambridge.org/9781009010320

DOI: 10.1017/9781009023382

First published 2022
First paperback edition 2024

A catalogue record for this publication is available from the British Library

ISBN   978-1-316-51932-5   Hardback
ISBN   978-1-009-01032-0   Paperback

To Ghazal

For your love and support, for keeping me motivated, and for the many hours you spent reading multiple drafts of each chapter

Contents

Figures

Tables

Acknowledgments

This book builds on my doctoral dissertation at American University (AU). I am particularly grateful to my advisor, Todd Eisenstadt, for his invaluable insights and guidance throughout the process of writing this book. Todd's office door has always been open to me, and several years after leaving AU, he remains a mentor, a co-author, and a dear friend. I am also deeply grateful to my dissertation committee members, Zachary Elkins, Ryan Moore, and Diane Singerman, for their insightful comments and constructive criticisms. My special thanks go to Diane for her meticulous and extensive feedback, encouragement, and unconditional support from the first day I started the graduate program at AU. I would also like to thank Carl LeVan for reading my dissertation and for his constant constructive comments and practical advice. I have also been fortunate to receive feedback on different parts of this work from Nathan Brown, Donald Horowitz, Hélène Landemore, Ben Manski, Gabriel Negretto, Bruce Rutherford, and Antoine Yoshinaka.

My doctoral dissertation focused mostly on constitution-making processes in Tunisia, Egypt, and Morocco. As the post–Arab Spring events, including those related to constitutional reforms, evolved over the years, so did the scope of my research for this book. Over these years, I have received extensive feedback on different parts of the book from several of my colleagues at Loyola University Chicago, all of whom deserve thanks: Claudio Katz, David Doherty, Robert Mayer, Vincent Mahler, and Peter Sanchez. I am especially thankful to Claudio, Vince, and Peter for reading, editing, and commenting on multiple chapters of this book. I have also enjoyed able research assistance from several graduate students at Loyola University Chicago: Muhammet Asil, Rebecca Ely, Ratri Istania, and Paul Olander. Rebecca's help in preparing the manuscript is particularly appreciated.

This research carries undeniable costs. For financial support, I am thankful to Loyola University Chicago and the Office of Provost at AU. The Jacques Berque

Centre for Studies in Social Sciences and Humanities in Morocco, the Tangier American Legation Institute for Moroccan Studies (TALIM), and the Center for the Study of Islam and Democracy (CSID) in Tunis facilitated my travel and work in Morocco and Tunisia. Mahmoud Hamad, Wissam Benyettou, and the Arab Association of Constitutional Law were generous in offering their resources and assistance. I am also grateful to Ellen Lust for putting her resources at my disposal during my 2014 research in Tunisia. Yahia Benyamina provided invaluable insights about Algeria. Parts of this book were written while I was a visiting scholar at the American Bar Foundation, for which I am thankful to Tom Ginsburg and Ajay Mehrotra.

Scholarly dialogue with several colleagues helped guide this work. I benefited from discussions with participants of the 2018–2019 American Political Science Association's Middle East and North Africa Workshop, including Ahmed Jazouli, Asma Nouira, and Peter Schraeder. Special thanks go to the organizers of the workshop, Ahmed Morsi and Andrew Stinson. I presented parts of this book at George Washington University, University of Illinois at Chicago, and the University of Texas at Austin. I also benefited from discussions at United States Institute of Peace, National Endowment for Democracy, and the World Bank, for which I am grateful to Susan Stigant, Amira Maaty, and Daniel Lederman, respectively.

My family deserves endless thanks. I dedicate this book to my wife, Ghazal, not because she is my soulmate but because of her contributions to this book; Ghazal meticulously read every single word of this book several times, providing editorial and substantive suggestions. A simple dedication does not do her justice: I am forever indebted to her for her unwavering support and dedication. I am also thankful to our daughter, Sabrina, for brightening my days, for waking me up every morning at 5 o'clock to work, and for forgiving my absence during the most joyous years of her life. To my best friends, Amin and Shahin, who share my intellectual passion: "No winter lasts forever; no spring skips its turn." (Hal Borland)

Finally, I would like to thank the anonymous reviewer and the editors of Comparative Constitutional Law and Policy series for their comments and suggestions. Some of the chapters or sections in this book are reworking of the following articles:

Maboudi, Tofigh. 2020a. "Participation, Inclusion, and the Democratic Content of Constitutions." *Studies in Comparative International Development* 55 (1): 48–76.
Maboudi, Tofigh. 2020b. "Reconstituting Tunisia: Participation, Deliberation, and the Content of Constitution." *Political Research Quarterly* 73 (4): 774–789.

Introduction

The wave of popular uprisings engulfing the Middle East and North Africa in 2010 and 2011 – commonly known as the Arab Spring – created a unique momentum for democratization in a region known for "robustness of authoritarianism" (Bellin 2004) and "non-constitutionalism" (Brown 2002). Despite four regime breakdowns, these uprisings failed to bring democratic change to the region. A plethora of studies have attempted to explain the failure of the Arab Spring in democratizing the region; however, focusing on elite negotiations or structural explanations of authoritarian regime durability, this literature has overlooked the importance of constitutional processes (see, e.g., Kamrava 2014; Lynch 2014; Brownlee, Masoud, and Reynolds 2015; Elbadawi and Makdisi 2017; Ketchley 2017; Volpi 2017). Ten years into the Arab Spring, no major study has theorized about the link between constitution-making and democratization. This book shifts the focus away from autocratic regime breakdown and structural mechanisms of democratic transition to a constitution-building approach to the study of democratization and popular uprisings in the Arab world.

The popular uprisings in the Arab world, which started in Tunisia and quickly spread to several countries in the Middle East and North Africa, instigated a wave of constitution-making in the region. Since the uprisings, seventeen constitutional events took place in eleven Arab nations including five new constitutions adopted in Morocco (2011), Syria (2012), Egypt (2012 and 2014), and Tunisia (2014) and two other constitutional reform processes, which failed to produce or adopt a permanent constitution (Libya (2017) and Yemen (2015)). Furthermore, six nations amended their constitutions including Jordan (2011, 2014, and 2016), Oman (2011), Bahrain (2012 and 2017), Saudi Arabia (2013), Algeria (2016 and 2020), and Egypt (2019).

The Arab Spring was a wake-up call not only for the leaders but also for more than 300 million people living under those constitutions, which for

1

decades were merely instruments for authoritarian control rather than institutions for the enforcement of rule of law and the protection of people's rights. Searching for new social contracts, protesters in Egypt, Tunisia, Algeria, and other countries concentrated on finding constitutional remedies for the ills of Arab polities. This "constitutional sophistication of demonstrators" came as a surprise to Arab executives who often view their people as lacking political sophistication (Brown 2013, 44). Those leaders who were not overthrown by the protesters hastened to make constitutional reforms in an effort to pacify the situation. Morocco was the first to adopt a new constitution only six months after the start of the demonstrations. Less than two years into the Arab Spring, however, it became clear that these constitutional reforms would not make meaningful changes to the status quo. With the exception of Tunisia, the search for new social contracts failed; authoritarianism remained robust; and the hope for constitutionalism faded away.[1] Why was Tunisia the sole Arab country that succeeded in adopting a democratic constitution? More broadly, what role do constitutional negotiations play in establishing democracy?

Recently, scholars of participatory and deliberative democracy suggest that inclusive constitution-making processes are most likely to generate "smart" and "epistemically superior" outcomes (see Landemore 2017). This call for "direct democracy" in constitution-making processes, or what Chambers (2004, 153) labels "the democratization of popular sovereignty," not only emphasizes the legitimacy of the process but also predicts that more participatory and inclusive constitution-making processes yield more democratic outcomes (Pateman 1970).

Building on these normative assumptions, several empirical studies have focused on examining the relationship between constitution-making and a vector of outcomes, such as constitutional durability (Elkins, Ginsburg, and Melton 2009) and legitimacy (Moehler 2008), conflict resolution (Widner 2005), and democratization (Eisenstadt, LeVan, and Maboudi 2015). While some of these studies find robust empirical evidence linking participatory or inclusive constitutional processes and democratic outcomes (Eisenstadt, LeVan, and Maboudi 2015; Eisenstadt and Maboudi 2019), several

---

[1] While this book was being prepared for print, Tunisia was witnessing a political crisis. On July 26, 2021, President Kais Saied dismissed the prime minister and suspended the parliament, jeopardizing the future of democracy in the sole "successful case" of the Arab Spring. Less than two months later, Saied suspended parts of the constitution to grant himself the power to unilaterally reform the constitution. As discussed in Chapter 3 of this book, while the constitution stipulated the creation of a Constitutional Court as the ultimate arbiter of constitutional disputes, the Parliament – caught up in years of partisan disputes – failed to appoint its share of judges. And when Saied suspended the parliament, there was no Constitutional Court to stop his unconstitutional power grab.

others remain skeptical about a causal link (Horowitz 2013; Saati 2015). The empirical evidence is, thus, inconclusive at best. Moreover, this growing field has not succeeded in establishing a convincing direct causal mechanism through which constitution-making processes affect specific democratic outcomes. Building on theories of democratization, political institutions, comparative constitutionalism, and participatory and deliberative democracy, this book seeks to explain the role of constitutions and constitution-making processes in democracy-building.

More specifically, I seek to explain in the following pages of this book that there is reasonable evidence to believe that democratic constitution-making processes enhance the democratic content of constitutions and that democraticity of constitutions facilitates democratization. Eisenstadt et al. (2017a), in a manuscript that appeared in this series, *Constituents Before Assembly: Participation, Deliberation, and Representation in the Crafting of New Constitutions*, show that broad participation by individuals or groups is critical if new constitutions are to enhance the level of democracy in any country. Extending that idea, I argue that the mechanism through which constitution-making processes lead to democratization is the participation of institutionalized, organized, and independent civil society organizations (CSOs) in the new constitutional negotiations.

In advancing these claims, the book proceeds in seven chapters. Chapter 1 lays out the theoretical groundwork of the book. In the chapter, I offer a conceptualization of democratic processes, democratic constitutions, and democratization. I also conceptualize constitutions and constitutional functions and changes. I will then present my argument that builds on three propositions. First, constitutional negotiations have a higher prospect of success in establishing democracy in transitioning states if they resolve social, ideological, and political dilemmas. Second, constitutions can resolve these problems best through a participatory and inclusive process. Third, the link that connects constitution-making processes to the resolution of these dilemmas is civil society. Without the engagement of civil society during constitutional moments, new constitutions can face hurdles in establishing democracy. In other words, the missing link that connects constitution-making processes to successful democratization is a strong and independent civil society that can shape and steer constitutional debates. Through constitutional fora, conferences, roundtables, and focus groups, CSOs play a vital role in steering constitutional debates and generating public interest and awareness beyond the polarizing issues within the society.

The empirical evidence for this thesis derives from cross-national statistical analyses and comparative case studies. In Chapter 2, I use an original worldwide data set of 195 constitutions adopted in 118 countries from 1974 to 2015 as well as an original data set of all constitutions in the Middle East and North Africa from 1861 to 2020 to study the impact of the process of drafting constitutions on their democratic content. A recent study finds a positive relationship between public participation in constitution-making and the protection of minority rights (Fruhstorfer and Hudson 2021). Another study, however, shows that the identity of groups present at the constitutional bargaining table matters more for democracy than mere public participation (Eisenstadt and Maboudi 2019). Building on the extant literature and using cross-national, time-series analyses, the chapter suggests that both individual-level participation and group inclusion improve the democratic content of constitutions by guaranteeing more rights. Particularly, I build on participatory and deliberative theories of democracy, not only to conceptualize and operationalize democratic processes and democratic constitutions but also to emphasize the importance of constitution-making processes for democracy. Differentiating between individual-level participation and group-level inclusion as two democratic, albeit distinct, forms of democratic processes, the chapter offers robust statistical evidence that greater inclusion and participation are associated with an increased number of democratic provisions in constitutions, specifically de jure constitutional rights, indicating that broad participatory and inclusive processes can improve the democraticity of constitutions.

Next, Chapters 3–6 employ case studies from all recent constitutional reforms in the Arab world to establish a causal mechanism for the cross-national statistical pattern discovered in Chapter 2. Specifically, Chapter 3 focuses on pathways of success by showing that the successful democratic transition in Tunisia was facilitated by a constitution that addressed both social and ideological cleavages as well as human rights and unresolved political dilemmas. In the chapter, I first provide an overview of the process of constitution-making and democratic transition in Tunisia. The chapter then shows that in order for new constitutions to facilitate democratic transitions, both participation and inclusion in the process are necessary. I use empirical evidence from a statistical content analysis of the public input and constitutional drafts, as well as interviews from Tunisia, to establish a causal mechanism for the cross-national patterns found in Chapter 2. The statistical analysis of a data set of more than 2,500 citizen proposals and the content of three constitutional drafts show that 43 percent of public proposals were included in the final draft of the Tunisian constitution. The results also demonstrate that public input related to rights and freedoms is more likely to generate change in the constitution than other public proposals. Furthermore, empirical evidence from field research and interviews with drafters of the Tunisian constitution, leaders of different political parties, CSOs, and constitutional law experts show that public participation and the inclusion of a wide range of interest groups in the constitutional bargaining process both legitimized the constitution and improved its democratic quality. Next, the chapter explains the role of civil society in shaping the public sphere of constitution-making and steering constitutional discussions. CSOs in Tunisia fulfilled three core functions. They acted as a third-party arbiter of constitutional and political disputes among different groups. Different CSOs also acted as watchdogs, ensuring the integrity and transparency of the process. Third, they created a public sphere for constitutional debates by offering an inclusive venue for citizens to engage in the constitution-making process. Finally, the chapter shows that as inclusive and participatory processes inevitably broaden the constitutional debate, properly steering the discussion becomes crucial for a successful democratic transition. More specifically, democratization is more likely to be on the horizon when constitutional debates and negotiations encompass both democratic political institutions and social and ideological issues.

Chapters 4 through 6 turn attention to pathways of constitutional failure in facilitating democratic transitions and examine when political choices (in the process or constitutional design) and intractable differences (such as lack of strong and independent civil society or the prevalence of ethnoreligious divisions) yield such constitutional failures. Chapter 4 focuses on the process of constitution-making and cases in which a non-inclusive process leads to either constitutional failure or democratic backsliding. The first type of process leading to the failure was the "populist" process where the general public was massively mobilized to participate in the constitution-making process, but the process did not ensure the inclusion of citizens' input, partly because the process was non-inclusive and partly because an institutionalized and independent civil society did not exist to channel their voices (Egypt 2012). The second type was the "window-dressing" process where severely contested regimes unwilling to democratize initiated constitutional reforms, which only appeared inclusive or participatory by allowing a small group of moderate opposition groups to participate (e.g., Jordan 2011, Morocco 2011, Egypt 2014, and Algeria 2016). The third failed pathway was through "closed" constitution-making processes where input from the general public was not sought, nor were major interest groups and CSOs offered a seat at the table. This included cases where an ethnic minority ruled against the majority's will (Bahrain 2012 and Syria 2012), where a stable authoritarian regime was under no public pressure for democratization (Oman 2011 and Saudi Arabia 2013), and where constitutional reform was a crucial step to strengthen the incumbent's grip over power (Egypt 2019). The last failed pathway of constitution-making processes included "conflict" constitutions, which involved a non-inclusive process in ethnically or regionally divided nations. As the cases of Yemen (2015) and Libya (2017) show, in such circumstances, the process of crafting the constitution only exacerbates the existing conflict.

Next, Chapter 5 focuses on civil society and its role in fortifying democratic constitutions as well as on elements that present a threat to constitutional success. It highlights how civil society was undermined and why CSOs failed to play a more consequential role in constitution-making and democratiza-tion. It first examines why the characteristics of the constitution-making process matter if civil society is to succeed in its democratizing role. As the cases of Jordan, Morocco, and Algeria show, when the process is not inclusive, CSOs cannot fulfill their democratizing role. The chapter also looks at both endogenous and exogenous factors impacting civil society's failure, which persist across the region. The first endogenous factor hindering the work of most CSOs in the region is the lack of organizational capacity. In Egypt (2012), for instance, lack of political experience and negotiation skills as well as a unified agenda hindered the CSOs' public outreach efforts. The second endogenous factor leading to civil society's failure is the CSOs' lack of public legitimacy. The chapter also examines two exogenous factors that contribute to civil society's failure in playing a more prominent role in democratization. First, using the cases of Yemen and Libya, I discuss the negative impact of societal cleavages and conflict on the work of civil society. Second, I explore the negative impact of undemocratic forces, such as the military or inter-national intervention in Egypt and Bahrain.

The last empirical chapter explores how the content of new constitutions hinders democratization by focusing on five particular types of nondemocratic and nonconsensual constitutional designs, which emerged during the Arab Spring. In Chapter 6, I first examine cases where constitutions failed to limit the arbitrary powers of the monarchs (Morocco and Jordan) by utilizing a constitutional design that lacks textual clarity, adopting contradictory provi-sions, and creating parallel institutions, which would leave the door open for future manipulations through illiberal constitutional interpretations. Similarly, in countries such as Algeria and Egypt, the constitutions remained undemocratic, despite adopting executive term limits, because they failed to address the lack of checks and balances and constraints on the executive's powers. The other three failed pathways of constitutional design were specific to countries that were deeply divided across different lines. When these divisions resurfaced during the moments of constitutional negotiations, the "non-consensual" constitutions that emerged failed to properly address them. First, in countries where an ethnoreligious minority is ruling against the majority's will (Bahrain and Syria), new constitutions failed to institutionalize power-sharing. Second, where regional cleavages, rivalries, and grievances were prominent issues as in Yemen and Libya, federalist and region-based power-sharing constitutional arrangements failed to prevent conflict. Lastly, where a country was deeply divided across ideological and identity lines (as was Egypt in 2012), the winner-takes-all approach to constitutional drafting alienated at least half of the population, leading to the failure of the constitution and, subsequently, the democratic transitional process.

In Chapter 7, I compare and contrast Tunisia's successful pathway to constitution-making and democratization to the failed pathways in other Arab nations. I conclude the book with a discussion of lessons learned from the failure of the Arab Spring to democratize the region. The chapter contends that despite being a failed democratization project, the Arab Spring created a new repertoire for change in an exceptionally authoritarian region. The mistakes and bad choices and decisions made then will continue to live as lessons learned by people who for the first time were empowered to bring about democratic change from below. As the recent public protests and renewed interests in constitutional reforms in Iraq and Lebanon (2019–2020) and the overthrow of authoritarian leaders and constitutional changes in Algeria and Sudan (2019) show, grassroots movements for constitutionalism and democratization are still alive and quite powerful, and the lessons learned from the Arab Spring will no doubt have an everlasting impact on contentious politics in the Arab world.

Constitutions, Civil Society, and Democratization in the Arab World

Constitutional reforms almost always occur in the context of crises or some sort of "exceptional circumstances," including regime changes (Russell 1993, 106; Elster 1995, 370). Since the Third Wave of democracy, constitutional reforms have become an essential part of democratic transition. As a result, constitutional negotiations – and renegotiations – are intertwined with transitional arrangements. Over one-fifth of all new constitutions since the Third Wave have been drafted during moments of transition. Similarly, every single Arab country with significant protests during the Arab Spring went through some kind of constitutional change in response to the uprisings. Yet, only in Tunisia, the birthplace of the Arab Spring, the constitutional reform process led to democratization. What was exceptional about Tunisia and its constitutional reform?

The Tunisian political scene was nowhere near an ideal environment for democratic transition. In effect, transitional negotiations broke down several times, most notably in June 2013 as a result of a controversial draft constitution (known as "the June Constitution") and the assassinations of secular political leaders. In the wake of the breakdown of these negotiations, the General Union of Tunisian Workers (l'Union Générale Tunisienne du Travail, or UGTT) joined forces with three other civil society organizations (CSOs), including the Tunisian Union of Industry, Trade and Handicrafts (UTICA), the Tunisian Bar Association, and the Human Rights League, and hosted the national dialogue with leaders of different political groups (Chayes 2014). These four associations, which later came to be known as the National Dialogue Quartet, convinced the political parties participating in the dialogue to sign a Road Map document, which outlined the formation of a new nonpartisan government, an independent electoral commission, and modification of the June Constitution. The result of this national dialogue was a consensual constitution approved by 93 percent of the votes in the

Tunisian National Constituent Assembly (NCA) and a successful democratic transition. The 2015 Nobel Peace Prize awarded to the Tunisian National Dialogue Quartet for their role in the constitution-making and peacebuilding in Tunisia marked the progressive nation as a role model for democratic transition in a region that is often characterized as hostile to democratic norms.

The National Dialogue Quartet, and more broadly the Tunisian CSOs, played three key roles in constitutional renegotiations. First, they acted as a watchdog over the Constituent Assembly, ensuring the transparency and integrity of the constitutional process. Second, CSOs were actively engaged in steering the constitutional debate by creating a public sphere for constitutional discussions through constitutional fora, conferences, round tables, and organized protests. Lastly, they acted as an independent, third-party arbiter of constitutional and political disputes. In these capacities, CSOs paved the way for democratic transition by ensuring that the constitution reflects the aspirations of the Tunisian society for democracy and equality. The influential role of civil groups was made possible through an inclusive and participatory process, which allowed all major social groups to actively engage in the constitution-making and, more broadly, in the transitional process.

By contrast, in Egypt, where the stakes were arguably much higher, efforts to weld the opposition parties into a more coherent democratic force for change failed, partly due to a weakly institutionalized and unorganized civil society undermined by decades of authoritarian domination. A participatory process, similar to that in Tunisia, took place in Egypt as well, and, in terms of sheer numbers, even more people participated and were engaged in the constitutional debate. Nevertheless, in contrast to Tunisia's experience, the popular participation in Egypt was less effective in changing the constitution. Massive protests, boycotts, and withdrawals from the Constituent Assembly just a few days before the constitutional referendum showed that the 2012 Egyptian Constitution was not what many groups in the country wished for. Eventually, on July 3, 2013, General El-Sisi, the Egyptian army chief, capitalized on this broad dissatisfaction with the constitution and the Muslim Brotherhood government and led a coup d'état to remove the country's first democratically elected president and suspended the constitution. With a revolution, a military coup, a counterrevolution, and two constitutions adopted in just two years, the Egyptian transitional process held the most dramatic series of events of the Arab Spring (Mednicoff 2014).

Why did the Tunisian constitution-making process facilitate democratic transition while the Egyptian process failed to bring about democratic change? Previous studies suggest several factors were important for the failure of democratic transition in Egypt, such as a politically powerful military (Barany 2011), a relative imbalance of power between political forces including Islamists and non-Islamists (Brownlee et al. 2015), lack of a clear design for transition (Brown 2013), weak CSOs as well as lack of a progressive Islamist leadership (Stepan and Linz 2013), and the country's global and geopolitical importance (Mednicoff 2014). While these factors may explain the failure of constitution-making and the broader transition in Egypt, they fall short of offering a general explanation for the success or failure of constitutions in establishing democracy across other cases. As the cases of Egypt and Tunisia show, constitutional negotiations have increasingly become intertwined with transitional negotiations; yet, the relationship between the two processes has largely remained understudied in the context of the Middle East. The question remains, what role do constitutional negotiations play in democracy-building?

Building on theories of democracy and the recently developed conjectures in comparative constitutionalism, this book examines the circumstances under which constitutions facilitated or failed to facilitate democratic transition during the largest wave of popular movements in the twenty-first century in the Middle East and North Africa (MENA). The core argument of this book is that constitutional negotiations facilitate democratic transitions if they succeed in designing a constitution capable of resolving societal cleavages and the political ills prevalent in society. CSOs can help bring about such constitutions if they are engaged in constitutional negotiations through an inclusive and participatory process. Before expanding on this argument, I first briefly discuss the concept of democracy, followed by the conceptualization of constitutions, as well as constitutional functions and changes. I then present my thesis and conclude the chapter with a brief overview of the Arab Spring upheavals and constitutional changes in the Arab world.

DEMOCRATIC PROCESS, DEMOCRATICITY, AND DEMOCRATIZATION

The causal link that I seek to establish in this book is that a democratic process leads to a democratic constitution, which itself leads to democratization. We should, as such, differentiate between democratic processes, democratic constitutions, and democratic outcomes (i.e., democratization). To make this distinction, we should first ask what democracy is. That is, what characteristics a country should have to be counted as a democracy?

As Coppedge (2012, 11) suggests, one of the most difficult challenges in studying democratization lies in conceptualizing democracy. Indeed, democracy is one of the most contested concepts in political science. A minimalistic definition of democracy entails a system of government in which rulers are selected through competitive elections (Schumpeter 1942). The more contemporary applications of this electoral conception overlap with Dahl's concept of polyarchy. Dahl (1998) identifies five criteria for democracy including effective participation, equality in voting, gaining enlightened understanding, exercising final control over the agenda, and inclusion of adults. Dahl (1998), however, develops these utopian criteria in the context of the government of very small and voluntary associations. And while he argues that these criteria can also be applied to the government of a state, he acknowledges that no association can realistically meet all these criteria (Dahl 1998, 42).

In some of his earlier works, Dahl (1971) establishes the minimum, attainable threshold for what he calls polyarchal democracy, that is, modern large-scale democratic government. Dahl's concept of polyarchy has two dimensions, including contestation and inclusiveness, which to some degree parallels the Schumpeterian concept of electoral democracy. Dahl's polyarchy, however, is more elaborate and has six institutional requirements including: "(1) elected officials; (2) free, fair, and frequent elections; (3) freedom of expression; (4) alternative sources of information; (5) associational autonomy; and (6) inclusive citizenship" (Dahl 1998, 85). Dahl's concept of democracy, while not accepted by all political scientists, is a well-known starting point for many scholars who offer alternative definitions of democracy (Coppedge 2012).

As Coppedge (2012, 12) argues, while there are numerous definitions of democracy, almost all can fit into one of the six overlapping models of democracy: socioeconomic, people's, participatory, representative, liberal, and deliberative democracy. Since people's democracy is limited to some communist regimes, deliberative democracy is still in an experimental phase, participatory democracy is still limited to some Western countries and only to a limited extent, and socioeconomic equality is not considered in many cultures as necessary or event relevant to democracy, these models of democracy lack the generalizability necessary to compare democratic regimes (Coppedge 2012). However, all democratic states today enshrine some form of representative democracy ranging from "popular sovereignty," which emphasizes the rule of the majority, to "liberal democracy," which emphasizes limits on the powers of the majority (Coppedge 2012).

Going back to the question of what constitutes a democratic state, I adopt a liberal representative definition of democracy to determine whether a country has transitioned to democracy. On the one hand, to distinguish between democracies and hybrid regimes, we cannot use a minimalistic, Schumpeterian definition. On the other hand, we cannot operationalize democratic regimes or democratization using utopian characteristics such as Dahl's (1998) five criteria that are "unattainable." Neither can we use models with limited generalizability and applicability to transitioning states, such as participatory or deliberative definitions. While I build on participatory and deliberative models of democracy to conceptualize and operationalize democratic constitution-making processes, I believe we cannot use these models to determine whether a country has transitioned to democracy.[1] Indeed, as previous studies show, participatory and deliberative decision-making processes, including participatory budgeting or participatory and deliberative constitution-making, do improve a country's level of democracy down the road (Eisenstadt et al. 2017). However, we cannot argue that a country is really "a deliberative democracy," even though elements of participatory or deliberative decision-making processes might to some extent be at work. By contrast, we can call a state "a liberal representative democracy" if it meets the minimum institutional requirements. Besides guaranteeing basic human rights, liberal representative democracy should limit the tyranny of the majority by guaranteeing some fundamental rights to minority groups. It should also limit the government's arbitrary use of power by "creating constitutional checks on executive, legislative, and judicial powers" (Coppedge 2012, 13). Democratization can, thus, be achieved when there is a shift toward rule of law and constitutionalism (i.e., the limit on the arbitrary use of power) and when the government guarantees protection of rights, including minority, group, and associational rights.

Democratization in this sense is more likely to be achieved when representatives of major political and societal interests are involved in the constitutional bargain during the transition, highlighting the importance of democratic constitution-making processes. Building on participatory and deliberative models of the democratic theory, I argue that a democratic constitution-making process has two main features, including being inclusive and participatory. Theories of deliberative democracy contend that democratic authenticity requires substantive and real public participation and deliberation (Dryzek 2000), which empowers citizens, particularly the marginalized in society (see Chambers 2003). As will be discussed in the next chapter, democratic authenticity in constitution-making is most likely to be realized through inclusive and participatory processes where major

---

[1]   See Chapter 2 for a detailed discussion on the conceptualization and operationalization of democratic constitution-making processes.

societal, political, and interest groups, including civil society and citizenry, are allowed to take part in the constitutional bargain.

A genuinely inclusive and participatory process is more likely to lead to consensual and democratic constitutions in transitioning states than noninclusive processes. That is, nondemocratic processes – including window-dressing and populist processes that only *appear* inclusive and participatory – cannot democratize constitutions or generate societal consensus over the constitutional terms. But what constitutes a democratic constitution? Carey (2009) argues that constitutional ideals have three characteristics including democracy, temperance, and durability. Democracy refers to the kind of ideals one expects to see in the constitution such as the inclusiveness property of constitutions and the degree to which they reflect the popular consensus. Thus, for Carey (2009), democracy is the most prominent constitutional ideal. Temperance refers to constitutional properties that limit the power of officeholders and encourage moderation and deliberation through establishing checks and balances. Lastly, durability refers to constitutional stability over time.

Refining and expanding Carey's constitutional ideals, Landemore (2016) considers nine criteria for a "good constitution," including formal qualities, Gordian Knot factor, rights-heaviness, democraticity, temperance, deliberative capacity, value fitness, adaptability, and minimal expected durability. Landemore (2016, 79) argues that a good constitution should "(1) be a clear, concise, logically coherent document; (2) offer reasonable procedural solutions to foreseeable political conflicts; (3) protect and entrench rights of various kinds, first and foremost human rights, as well as (4) entrench democratic principles – centrally political equality and majority rule." Such a document should also "delineate (5) a temperate political system, characterized by (6) deliberative capacity … [and] contain (7) values and principles that are representative of citizens' preferences while allowing for (8) the possibility of change over time and yet retaining (9) a decent (sufficient) life expectancy" (Landemore 2016, 79).

Indeed, not all democratic constitutions are "good" constitutions. Building on Landemore (2016), I argue that, at a bare minimum, a democratic constitution should entail democraticity, rights-heaviness, and temperance. Democraticity refers to the overall democratic quality of the constitution. Such a quality includes several important components, such as the degree to which a constitution reflects the popular consensus and the degree to which a constitution promotes government transparency. Landemore's democraticity is similar to Carey's democracy ideal of the constitution with one difference. Contrary to Carey (2009), who considers various constitutional rights under the democracy ideal, Landemore (2016) proposes a separate category for consideration of rights: rights-heaviness. By rights-heaviness, Landemore (2016) refers to both the quantity and quality of constitutional rights. For Landemore, the minimum threshold for a good constitution is the entrenchment of basic human rights. Most undemocratic constitutions, however, also include basic human rights, which have become a common fixture of all constitutions (Elkins et al. 2014b). Democratic constitutions, as such, should guarantee a wider array of rights including basic human rights as well as association and group rights, such as minority group's rights. Lastly, democratic constitutions should limit the government's arbitrary use of power by institutionalizing checks and balances.[2]

I argue that these democratic characteristics of the constitution-making process and the content of constitutions can explain the successful and failed pathways of democratization during the Arab Spring. Without a democratic process, a democratic constitution is less likely to materialize. It matters who sits – and who does not sit – at the constitutional negotiation table. When large segments of society are not represented in the constitutional bargain, the constitution is less likely to protect their interests. Without popular consensus, protection of group rights, and constrained governments, new constitutions will fail to facilitate democratization.

There is then a clear link between what I define as a democratic regime and the characteristics of democratic constitutions. In other words, democratization cannot be achieved without constitutional democraticity, rights-heaviness, and temperance. These democratic characteristics of constitutions, in turn, depend to a large extent on the democratic features of constitution-making processes (i.e., participation and inclusion). Constitutions, as such, play an important role in establishing democracy. Not all constitutions, however, function as democratizing tools.

CONSTITUTIONS AS CONTRACTS

Constitutions fulfill different functions in democratic and authoritarian settings. In authoritarian regimes, for example, Ginsburg and Simpser (2014) argue that constitutions serve four key purposes. They can function as an "operating manual" to offer a means of binding authoritarians so that members of the ruling coalition do not act outside of the prescribed norms. Similarly, constitutions can be "billboards" that advertise autocrats' policy statements, "signaling the intentions of leaders within the regime to those

---

[2]   Chapter 2 builds on these three criteria to operationalize democratic constitutions.

outside of it." Alternatively, when serving as "blueprints," constitutions describe societal aspirations rather than political institutions as they exist. Lastly, under the "window-dressing" function, "the text is designed to obfuscate actual political practice" (Ginsburg and Simpser 2014, 6–8). Besides these four functions, constitutions in authoritarian settings can help formalize pacts among different competing groups (Ginsburg and Moustafa 2008) or legally change publicly undesirable policies (Moustafa 2007). They can also provide the legal basis for leaders' political, social, and economic plans (Negretto 2013). Many rulers find it less costly and more legitimate to enforce their wishes through constitutional amendments, as was demonstrated by Singapore's ruling party's move to constitutionally suppress opposition parties (Silverstein 2008) or the Algerian government's constitutional amendment in 2008 to remove presidential term limits (Goui 2015).

As Ginsburg and Simpser (2014) argue, authoritarian leaders may seek to implement constitutional change for several reasons. Through constitutional reforms, authoritarians seek to control their challengers within the ruling coalition, signal intentions of reform (whether genuine or not) to regime critics (domestic and international), and, perhaps, bargain over transitions of power and future regime prospects. Whatever the case, societal pressures for liberalization, as O'Donnell and Schmitter (1986) and Przeworski (1991) argue, constitute part of the reason for authoritarian constitutionalism. Authoritarians need stability, aim to distribute risk, and also seek information to control actors inside and outside their coalition through sanctions, and constitutions can deliver these ends for them.

In democracies, by contrast, constitutions serve two simultaneous functions: they enable the government to rule while at the same time constraining it. Achieving these constitutional objectives, needless to say, has proven to be a challenge, especially for new democracies. In James Madison's (Federalist Paper #51) words, "[i]n framing a government which is to be administered by men over men, the great difficulty lies in this: You must first enable the government to control the governed; and in the next place, oblige it to control itself." A central question in democratic theory concerns the mechanisms by which the rules and institutions (especially those identified in the constitution) that constrain a government are maintained and enforced (Ordeshook 1992, 138). In the last few decades, at least two models have emerged to address this concern, which, following their central arguments, can be labeled as "contractual" and "self-enforcing" models.

In the first model, constitutions are conceptualized as contracts between the state and society or even among citizens (Brenan and Buchanan 1985). This view was built on the modern social contract theory, which regards the state as a social contract among men (and women) (Hobbes 1968; Locke 1988; Rousseau 1997). Several economists employed this conceptualization in the 1980s to answer important questions regarding the limits on the exploitative power of governments and the problem of maintaining the constitutional contract (see, e.g., Buchanan and Faith 1987; Aranson 1988; Grossman and Noh 1988; Epple and Romer 1989; Wagner 1987). Niskanen (1990, 57), for example, suggests that a constitution is a unique form of "contract among various parties to form a government in which the government – the object of the contract – has the dominant power to interpret the rules and resolve any disputes in its favor." An effective constitution, as such, is a "set of rules that serve the interests of the current dominant coalition" (Niskanen 1990, 58). The constitution or its specific rules and provisions are maintained as long as the benefits of maintaining the set rules exceed the costs for the dominant coalition.

Scholars have raised several criticisms of these contractual or, as Grossman and Noh (1988) call them, "proprietary" government models. The major criticism focuses on how such a contract and its terms are defined and enforced (Ordeshook 1992). The conventional explanation is that the Supreme Court, as a third party, interprets or enforces the constitution. But, as critics point out, this explanation only pushes the problem back a step as now we must ask how social groups enforce the rules and regulations that define the Supreme Court's (or any other third party's) jurisdiction (Niskanen 1990; Ordeshook 1992). There are several other reasons why a third-party justification is not an adequate explanation. As Niskanen (1990) notes, there is no plausible theory to explain why the Supreme Court should have the authority or the incentive to play this role. The American Constitution itself does not empower the Supreme Court as the arbiter of constitutional disputes between different branches. Moreover, the Supreme Court is specific to the United States (although it has become more popular across the world in the last few decades), and in many countries, the highest court does not have any constitutional role (Niskanen 1990).

Partly as a response to these criticisms, a new literature, using a game-theoretic approach, has emerged that conceptualizes constitutions not as "contracts" but as "devices" by which organized social groups coordinate to achieve particular outcomes (see, e.g., North and Weingast 1989; Przeworski 1991; Ordeshook 1992; Weingast 1997). A constitution endures only if it is self-enforcing (Ordeshook 1992), and to be self-enforcing, it should overcome the coordination problem (Weingast 1997). The coordination problem is similar to a Prisoner's Dilemma game; the only difference is that the game is played repeatedly indefinite number of times (Ordeshook 1992). There are multiple equilibria in an iterated Prisoner's Dilemma game, which can resolve the dilemma to each player's satisfaction. This multiplicity of equilibria is the key here because it implies that the only way players (i.e., citizens, groups, or political entities) can achieve a mutually agreeable outcome is to coordinate their strategies. In other words, it is the repetition of the game, rather than the exogenous enforcer (third party) that allows the establishment of outcomes as equilibria. If each person (or player) believes that the other will abide by the rules, then both players have the incentive to act accordingly. As such, the agreement (constitution) will be self-enforcing (Ordeshook 1992, 147).

Building on both "contractual" and "self-enforcing" models, Elkins et al. (2009) follow the rationalist approach in institutional studies to introduce their "theory of renegotiation." Following the "contractual" model, they define constitutions as a specific type of contract and call "bargains," which are meant to endure. Unlike the "contractual" model, however, constitutional bargains are not enforced by a third party (although constitutional courts can resolve ambiguities down the road); rather, they are self-enforcing (Elkins et al. 2009, 76–77). "A constitution will be maintained only if it makes sense to those who live under its dictates," they write, "so a crucial quality of any successful constitution is that it will be self-enforcing" (Elkins et al. 2009, 7). The model of Elkins et al. also assumes that a constitutional bargain, once adopted, will endure as long as there are no endogenous or exogenous shocks that would alter the cost–benefit analysis for groups considering remaining in or exiting from the bargain.

Constitutions, as such, change when those under its rule find it less costly (and more beneficial) to alternate the rules. Given the costs associated with constitutional renovations, constitutional change becomes more likely when the constitution no longer serves its purpose. In such circumstances, the cost of maintenance and enforcing the constitution becomes much higher than its benefits. Constitutional renegotiation can be initiated by any party in the bargain, which anticipates higher future costs than benefits. It can be initiated by the incumbent, winners, or authoritarian leaders (which we can collectively refer to as "top-down" processes) or alternatively by the opposition, losers, or grassroots movements ("bottom-up" processes).

Prior to the Arab Spring, the majority of constitutions in the Middle East were drafted through a top-down process. Constitutional bargains were, thus, limited in their scope and purpose. If we understand constitutions as "the basic legal framework for governing" and constitutionalism as "ideologies and institutional arrangements that promote the limitation and definition of means of exercising state authority," then the general purpose of constitutions in the Arab world was defining state authority and organizing power without necessarily limiting it (Brown 2002, 8–12). For Nathan Brown (2002), such "nonconstitutionalist" constitutions have three functions. First, they are "symbolic," that is, constitutions have become so common that it is difficult to imagine state sovereignty without a constitution (written or non-written). Second, they can be "ideological," as many constitutions go into length to proclaim the basic ideology of the state. And finally, nonconstitutionalist constitutions can be "enabling," making lines of authority and succession clear but not restricting the actions of leaders. Thus, constitutions in the region were historically drafted not for the sake of constitutionalism but for extra-constitutional purposes. And as Brown notes, democracy cannot exist without constitutionalism. The Arab Spring uprisings, however, changed the cost–benefit calculation of several Arab leaders and forced them to enter new constitutional bargains.

CONSTITUTIONAL RENEGOTIATIONS
IN A NONCONSTITUTIONAL WORLD

Eleven Arab countries in the MENA changed their constitutions after the 2011 popular uprisings. The failure of Arab constitutions in establishing the rule of law and constitutionalism over a long period, along with increased constitutional knowledge in the public sphere, precipitated a call across the region to renegotiate constitutional bargains.

Since the twentieth century, Arab constitutions have faced many challenges, from colonial rule to independence wars and modernization, all of which threatened their stability. Rather than perishing, these constitutions endured by changing forms. They selectively borrowed constitutionalist language from European constitutions, establishing democratic institutions such as political parties, parliaments, and courts, but modified them to serve authoritarianism (Brown 2013). The outcomes of these selective borrowings were Frankenstein-style constitutions that were neither democratic nor authoritarian. They allowed multicandidate presidential elections, for example, but made it extremely difficult for anyone but the incumbent to qualify or win. Constitutions were rich in "escape hatches" that allowed the executive to breach provisions of the bargain repeatedly. Over time, constitutional modifications resulted in more authoritarian than democratic constitutions and created strong, unchecked executive authority across the region (Brown 2002).

Constitutions were, as such, not "making sense" anymore for people who lived under their mandate. They did not limit the executive power or enforce the rule of law. But CSOs and other democratic forces were too weak to challenge the state for a new constitutional bargain. It was not until the late 1970s and early 1980s when a public sphere for constitutional talks was formed. Economic and political liberalizations in the 1970s and 1980s led to more freedom of speech across the region. Opposition press emerged in countries like Egypt. Media with higher professional standards and greater ability to cover news, such as Aljazeera, entered the market which, through the expansion of satellite receivers, created new competitors against authoritarian state-owned media that once had the monopoly of controlling the news feed. Furthermore, nongovernmental organizations (NGOs), think tanks, and universities started to hold discussions and conferences on trending political issues (Brown 2013). Expansion of postsecondary education, along with increased internet penetration and social media, made the general public more aware of a host of political matters.

The development of these public and political spheres contributed to the emergence of a common framework for assessing major political problems in the Arab world in the wake of the 2011 uprisings. As Brown argues, "[The Arab Spring upheavals] have been premised, in large part, on the proposition that the ills of Arab politics need a constitutional solution" (2013, 41). It is no accident that the majority of protesters concentrated on rule of law, dignity, and government harassment. From Western Sahara to the Levant to the Arabian Peninsula, protesters were more organized than before, and rather than having a wide range of demands, they surprisingly focused on their constitutions. With their nations in search of new social contracts or new pacts that could protect them from the state itself, Arab leaders had no choice but to negotiate new constitutional bargains. But these new constitutional bargains mostly failed to change the status quo, as they did not lead to more accountability, rule of law, or constitutionalism. Less than a decade into these new bargains, it seems that most Arab constitutions have failed to deliver what they promised. Why did these constitutional bargains fail in resolving the problems that prompted them in the first place?

CONSTITUTIONS AND DEMOCRATIZATION: THE MISSING LINK

This book suggests that the inclusion of different organized groups in constitutional processes leads to democracy. Groups participating in constitutional (re)negotiations need to coordinate their strategies to achieve a mutually beneficial equilibrium, which is a Magna Carta that successfully resolves social, ideological, and political dilemmas and is deemed "fair" by all groups. The key assumption here is the iteration of the game. To overcome the coordination problem inherent in a repeated game, groups participating in constitutional (re)negotiations must learn to participate and to choose "voice" over "exit" (Hirschman 1970). This in turn would instigate trust among these groups, leading to compromise, and subsequently democracy (Axelrod 1984). In other words, the success or failure of constitutional (re)negotiations in establishing democracy depends to a large extent on whether they can resolve the ideological and political dilemmas prevalent in societies with social or religious divisions and a legacy of authoritarianism. The resolution of these dilemmas requires public and inclusive constitutional debates. Constitutions should not be silent on ideological issues that divide society or leave the door open for the executives' abuse of power. Constitutional renegotiations provide a unique opportunity for transitional states to engage in public debates on these issues and build trust among the relevant parties. The question is why such comprehensive debates did not take place in most Arab polities.

The answer lies in the inclusion or lack thereof of CSOs at the bargaining table. Through constitutional fora, conferences, roundtables, and focus groups, CSOs play a vital role in steering constitutional debates. And through organizing protests, gatherings, and national dialogues, they are the dominant democratic force in shaping the public and political spheres. Most CSOs are dedicated advocates of human rights, social and individual equality and justice, and strong democratic institutions, including an independent judiciary (which could protect them from future retaliations). And when they are institutionalized, organized, and financially and bureaucratically independent, they can steer constitutional debates in the direction that not only can resolve social and ideological cleavages but also can concentrate on other urgent issues such as human rights and democratic institutions. We should, however, note that even with the presence of an institutionalized civil society, some constitutional negotiations still do not succeed in resolving ideological and political cleavages. The reason is a vector of unfavorable exogenous factors including the dominance of nondemocratic forces such as the military and the prevalence of ethnoreligious or regional divisions that can polarize civil society and render it ineffective in steering constitutional debates.[3]

CSOs, however, can play the abovementioned roles as much as they are allowed to be or succeed in forcing themselves into being part of the constitutional negotiations. An inclusive and participatory constitution-drafting process can guarantee access to civil groups. The main function

---

[3]   We should differentiate between ideological cleavages and religious divisions in the region. While the former concerns cleavages and polarization across ideological lines, for example, between Islamists and non-Islamists, the latter is about the divisions mostly between Shias and Sunnis in the Arab world.

of inclusive processes is to signal a credible commitment by the incumbent (or the majority group). Allowing the main segments of society to take part in constitutional negotiations in a transparent manner increases the cost of breaching particular provisions of the bargain for any party. Through inclusive processes, participating groups learn democratic negotiations and compromise. More likely than not, the result of these democratic negotiations is a binding agreement that is viewed as "fair" by most groups and, hence, has a higher prospect of success in institutionalizing the rule of law.

In sum, the argument in this book builds on three propositions. First, constitutional negotiations have a higher prospect of success in establishing democracy in transitioning states if they resolve social, ideological, and political dilemmas. Second, constitutions can resolve these problems best through a participatory and inclusive process. Third, the link that connects constitution-making processes to the resolution of these dilemmas is civil society. Without the engagement of CSOs during constitutional moments, new constitutions can face hurdles in establishing democracy. In other words, the missing link that connects constitution-making processes to successful democratization is a strong and independent civil society that can shape and steer constitutional debates. In the next sections, I elaborate on each of these three propositions.

Social and Political Ills and the Constitutional Design

Scholars of the MENA often use the term "Arab exceptionalism" in reference to the resistance of the Arab world to democratic values and progressive ideas (see, e.g., Stepan and Robertson 2004; Angrist 2012). The Arab world is a "nonconstitutional world" because constitutions have historically suppressed democratic values and ideas (Brown 2002). The result has been a series of social and political challenges or ills, which, as discussed above, led to widespread calls for constitutional remedies in the aftermath of the Arab Spring. Only when constitutions addressed all of these issues, a pathway for democratization was opened. These challenges can be divided into two groups: political and societal ills. Political institutions that contribute to strong, unchecked executives constitute the most important political challenges in the Arab world (Brown 2013). Also, ethnoreligious, regional, and ideological cleavages were among the most divisive social issues, which created heated debates and social tensions in several Arab Spring cases (Brown 2017). As this book seeks to show, none of the Arab constitutions, with the exception of Tunisia's, could attenuate these political and societal issues. The failure of most Arab constitutions in addressing these issues can be traced to the lack of an institutionalized, organized, and independent civil society, which is an important force in establishing democracy and democratic consolidation down the road.

Political Ills of Authoritarianism: Unchecked Executives

Constitutions in the Arab world are arguably "nonconstitutionalist" because they have failed to limit the executives' arbitrary use of power, protect citizens and groups' rights, and build societal consensus over divisive issues. That is, most Arab constitutions rank exceptionally low on Landemore's (2016) demo-craticity, rights-heaviness, and temperance. Over the past several decades, this nonconstitutionalism resulted in a series of political and societal challenges or ills, which ultimately led to widespread calls for constitutional reforms in the aftermath of the Arab Spring. The most important political issue for constitutions drafted in the wake of the Arab Spring was how to avoid political institutions, which empower strong men without constitutional constraints. Constitutional texts in the Arab world have historically created exceptionally strong executives with virtually no constraints. Egypt's Mubarak, for example, ruled without any constitutional constraints from 1981 to 2011 under an emer-gency law he issued after the assassination of his predecessor, Anwar Al-Sadat. In the wake of the Arab Spring and the fall of dictators, one after another, political debates emerged about the way constitutions could prevent another strong man from coming to power. Several questions took the central stage. What is the best political system for increased executive accountability? How to institutionalize an independent judiciary. How to institutionalize executive constraints and term limits.

A major political debate, which emerged in a few countries, including Tunisia, was regarding the structure of a new political system. Indeed, one of the most important institutional designs concerns the executive and legisla-tive powers and whether they should be combined or separated (Samuels 2007). Three forms of separation of power can be distinguished including parliamentarism, presidentialism, and semi-presidentialism. There is a vast scholarship on whether these forms are associated with specific outcomes. For example, Linz (1990) contends that presidentialism is associated with *regime* instability, while Cheibub (2007) argues that parliamentarism is associated with *government* instability. Presidential systems are also believed to enjoy more national accountability but less legislative accountability (Shugart and Carey 1992).

Surprisingly, given the history of strong, nondemocratic presidents and the consequences of political systems, most constitutional bargains did not address the issue and, instead, retained the old political system. The issue of presidentialism was only fiercely debated in a few countries, including Tunisia. In fact, this was the single most important issue on which political parties resisted compromise (Marks 2014). Ennahda – a moderate Islamist party with a plurality of seats in the NCA – and its members who experienced years of imprisonment and exile under a strong presidency, insisted on adopting a parliamentary system. Opposition groups, on the contrary, believed that a presidential system could give them a higher chance of defeating the more organized Ennahda party in the executive elections. In the end, both groups agreed on a mixed, semi-presidential system.

Another major political problem that most post–Arab Spring constitutions did not resolve was the independence of the judiciary. Courts in the Arab world were historically subordinated to the executive office (Brown 2002). Even in Egypt, where the courts enjoy semi-independence, they have been unable to effectively challenge executive authority. While some political debates took place during the recent constitutional negotiations, the status quo did not change drastically. The only exception was Tunisia, where heated debates in the NCA led to new provisions that guarantee a strong and independent judiciary.

Without institutionalizing a balance of power or independent judiciary, most Arab constitutions failed to limit the executives' arbitrary use of power. In some monarchies, including Morocco and Jordan, the kings adopted constitutions that did not limit their powers by utilizing a constitutional language that lacked textual clarity, adopting contradictory provisions, and creating parallel institutions, which left the door open for future manipulations through illiberal constitutional interpretations. In some Arab republics, including Algeria and Egypt, where protesters focused on executive term limits, despite adopting executive term limits, the constitutions remained "nonbinding," allowing strongmen to manipulate the constitutional order without even lifting term limits and stay in power for years to come.

In sum, with the exception of Tunisia, Arab constitutions remained exceptionally undemocratic, filled with "escape hatches," strong executives, and subordinate courts. Most constitutional bargains in the aftermath of the recent upheavals failed to establish democracy and constitutionalism because the constitution-making processes were noninclusive and nonparticipatory, shutting out voices from different political and societal groups including CSOs.

Social Ills of Authoritarianism: Ethnoreligious and Ideological Cleavages

Writing democratic constitutions is even a greater challenge for societies with an authoritarian legacy that are also deeply divided. These divisions can be across ethnolinguistic, religious, regional, or even ideological lines such as secular versus religious identities. For several decades, these cleavages have been muted under authoritarian state repression across the region. However, when authoritarian regimes fell or initiated constitutional reforms to extend their rule, these cleavages gradually moved to the top of national debates.

When there are competing visions for the identity of the state and when there are clashing societal norms and values, innovative constitutional solutions become inevitable if the conflict is to be avoided. Without consensual constitutional solutions, these disagreements will be inflated. Subsequently, constitutional negotiations, instead of becoming instruments of compromise, become a major source of conflict and escalating societal tensions (Lerner 2011). What constitutes an appropriate constitutional resolution to address these societal ills depends to a large degree on whether that society is segmented along ethnoreligious or geographical lines or whether competing identities are the major source of divisions.

Ethnoreligious or regional cleavages were indeed the most important challenge for several Arab countries including Bahrain, Syria, Libya, and Yemen. When ethnoreligious and regional divisions are the major source of discord, power-sharing can function as the institutional mechanism for preventing conflict and enhancing democracy. A rich body of literature has suggested a variety of such power-sharing institutional arrangements including federalism, consociationalism, different electoral systems (such as proportional representation), as well as constitutional guarantees for special group rights. Each of these institutional arrangements, depending on the source of societal divisions, can provide a power-sharing solution for those deeply divided societies. None of the four countries mentioned previously could constitutionalize consensual power-sharing arrangements, mostly because the constitutional negotiation processes were noninclusive.

Power-sharing arrangements are, however, less relevant in societies that are deeply divided across ideological or identity lines. The constitutional solution for ideologically polarized societies is to avoid a winner-takes-all approach. Rather, the constitution should be satisfying enough for all groups to accept. In other words, the constitutional design should be the second-best choice for most groups. To achieve this, the constitution should adopt an "incrementalist" approach, that is, using broad, vague, and often contradictory language in order to avoid a clear interpretation that might please one societal group but alienate the others (Lerner 2011).

Arab polities are divided across several ideological lines, the most important of which is perhaps the polarization between Islamists and non-Islamists (Brown 2017). During the post–2011 constitutional renegotiations, the role of religion in society became a source of societal and political polarization in several countries. For example, in Egypt, the major public debate over the new constitution was the issue of Sharia (Maboudi and Nadi 2016). Some of the major controversial issues that emerged in these constitutional renegotiations were whether Islam should be the religion of the state, whether Islamic Sharia is *a* or *the* source of legislation, whether constitutions should criminalize blasphemy, whether *takfir* (and other forms of religious calls for violence) should be banned, and the extent to which constitutions should guarantee and protect freedom of religion for minorities.

The major challenge that parties in the constitutional bargain faced was how to acknowledge the importance of religion in society while restricting its influence over the state. While most Islamists wanted the constitution to make strong statements about the role of Islam in state and society, most seculars attempted to limit this role. To address this challenge, the Tunisian constitution-makers used an "incrementalist approach" and intentionally formulated contradictory and vague provisions on several controversial issues pertaining to the role of religion and Islamic Sharia. By contrast, the Egyptian constitution drafters under the Muslim Brotherhood government took a very different approach. Rather than using an intentionally vague and contradictory language on controversial issues dividing the Egyptian society in order to avoid a winner-takes-all outcome, the constitution in its entirety had a more Islamist tone and alienated the non-Islamists' vision about the identity of state and society. When constitutional negotiations have clear losers and winners, there is no incentive for the losers to remain in the bargain, and as such, rebellion or new constitutional bargains will become an inevitable solution down the road.

In the section that follows, I suggest that the main reason these political and societal challenges were not resolved was because of a lack of strong and independent civil society. When strong and independent CSOs form an influential coalition in constitutional negotiations, constitutions are more likely to constrain the executive's unchecked powers and adopt more progressive rights and power-sharing institutions. By contrast, when weakly institutionalized and unorganized civil groups are shut out of constitutional bargaining, what emerges is a constitution that cannot address prevailing political or social issues.

The Role of Civil Society

The civil society thesis is a relatively newly developed conjecture in democratic theory, which, since the early 1990s, has attempted to explain the post–Cold War democratic transitions, specifically in Eastern Europe and Latin America (Yom 2005). The theoretical foundations of the role of civil society, however, go back to Tocqueville (1969), who suggested that civic associations are essential to stable and effective democratic institutions. Another influential work is Almond and Verba's study of the civic culture (1963), which examines differences in democratic governance across five nations using surveys of political attitudes under the rubric of civic culture. Building on these two classic studies, Putnam (1993) develops one of the first theoretical arguments for the role of civil society in a democratic society. Putnam's (1993) core argument is that differences in the present-day institutional performance of the various regions of Italy can be traced back to differences in patterns of civic engagement that extend back to the early Middle Ages. Giving Tocqueville his assent, Putnam (1993, 182) writes, "Tocqueville was right: Democratic government is strengthened, not weakened, when it faces a vigorous civil society."

The civil society thesis received a mixed response of admiration, skepticism, and criticism. Some scholars criticized Putnam's argument over the decline in democratic participation and civic engagement in established democracies and in particular in the United States (see Ladd 1996).[4] Levi (1996) argues that Putnam's work fails to establish the mechanism through which participation in civil society produces social capital and democratic-minded citizens. Tushnet (2000) refers to a paradox at the heart of the civil society thesis, which the extant literature has not yet explained in a satisfactory manner. That is, while the institutions of civil society are expected to function as a check on the government, they are themselves regulated and constituted by the government. For Tushnet (2000, 382), the civil society thesis failed to explain how exactly civil society institutions can be sources of influence on the government when the threat of government regulations endangers their existence. Perhaps the strongest criticism of the civil society thesis came from Fiorina (1999, 396), who argued that "civic engagement may not necessarily be a good thing." For Fiorina, civic engagement and political participation in the United States is on the rise, and it is the main cause of a decline in political trust. This is because, Fiorina argues, "the transition to a more participatory democracy increasingly has put politics into the hands of unrepresentative participators—extreme voices in the larger political debate" (1999, 409)

Building on the critics of the civil society thesis, including Fiorina (1999), several Middle East scholars argue that the emphasis on civil society as

---

[4]   In another seminal study, *Bowling Alone*, Putnam (2000) writes explicitly on the decline of civil society in the United States.

a democratizing force in the region is overrated (Wiktorowicz 2000; Yom 2005). While there is some validity to these criticisms with regard to most parts of the Middle East, the role of CSOs in the region has shifted in the past two decades. A more recent scholarship, focusing mostly on labor unions in Tunisia, emphasizes the importance of CSOs for democratization (see, e.g., Angrist 2013; Bishara 2014; Beining 2016; Netterstrøm 2016). This proliferation of studies on civil society in the region is part of a broader and growing literature that explores the role of civil society in the breakdown of autocratic regimes around the globe (see, e.g., Lewis 1992; Stepan 2001; Bunce 2003). The mechanism through which civil society instigates democratic transitions seems simple and straightforward. Years of political repression under authoritarian rule trigger activism among CSOs, such as unions, syndicates, movements, and associations, which demand liberal reforms. Under the pressure for liberalization, the ruling elites are forced into bargains and soon transitional pacts ensue (Diamond 1999). Democratic transitions, however, are not as straightforward as O'Donnell and Schmitter's (1986) pacted transitions suggest, and CSOs play a more complicated role in democratic transitions than these studies presume.

I argue that civil society is the critical link between constitutional bargains and democratization. A limited, albeit very important, number of studies systematically explore the role of civil society in successful constitutional experiences. One of the most influential works is Andrew Arato's (2000) book examining the impact of different constitution-making methods on democratic constitutions and institutional outcomes in transitioning states. Arato (2000) differentiates between civil society as movements and civil society as institutions, arguing that civil society movements that are weakly institutionalized may interfere with the emergence of workable political parties which are crucial for new democracies. CSOs, as such, facilitate democratic constitutions only if they are institutionalized, particularly during moments of transition. This institutionalization in turn facilitates democratic consolidation (Linz and Stepan 1996).

Strong and independent CSOs, thus, have several key roles. They contribute to the emergence of workable political parties (Arato 2000). Also, in the absence of strong political parties, CSOs can translate popular participation into democratic constitutional text (Hudson 2020). When institutionalized, they can steer public debates on constitutions. As Putnam (1993, 90) contends, "[p]articipation in civic organizations inculcates skills of cooperation as well as a sense of shared responsibility for collective endeavors. Moreover, when individuals belong to 'cross-cutting' groups with diverse goals and members, their attitudes will tend to moderate as a result of group interaction and crosspressures." These "skills of cooperation" and "moderate attitudes" are crucial for successful democratic transitions. To play these functions, however, CSOs should be institutionalized, organized, and independent from state pressure, a quality that very few CSOs in the region possess, including the Tunisian UGTT.

Civil Society in the Arab World

Tunisia's "democratization through constitutionalism," which was the way regimes transitioned in the Third Wave in Eastern Europe and Latin America (1973 until about 2000), may prove exceptional worldwide in the present era of authoritarian backsliding. Tunisia, in contrast to other Arab Spring cases, such as Egypt, is distinguished by strong and independent CSOs like labor unions. The Tunisian Bar Association, the Tunisian League for Human Rights, the UTICA, and the UGTT, for example, are among the oldest and most organized CSOs in the whole region and played a significant role in Tunisia's recent transition toward democracy and won accolades for stewarding the country's democracy through constitutionalism (Chayes 2014).

The Egyptian state, by contrast, subordinated CSOs, rendering them incapable of channeling people's demands for democracy. As Stepan and Linz (2013) argue, associational life and civil groups play an important role in the destruction of authoritarian regimes and the construction of democracy. Although several Egyptian CSOs were successful in mobilizing protesters against President Hosni Mubarak, they were less effective in shaping the country's transition (Meisburger 2012). The existence of independent and strong interest groups in Tunisia, however, allowed Tunisians to participate, in a way Egyptians could not; even though the social media participation of Egyptians, who "liked" the 2012 constitution in record numbers on Facebook, was unprecedented (Maboudi and Nadi 2016).

The case of Egypt is typical in the region, where the proliferation of associational life since the 1990s has mostly been a function of authoritarian regimes' strategy for controlled liberalization under pressure from Western countries and international organizations (Yom 2005). The MENA nations, which are often said to base political identities on ethnic and tribal clans and "the politics of the belly" (Jean-François 1993), are better described as having a weak civil society. The region's lag in democratization (Norton 1993, 1995), the robustness of its authoritarianism (Bellin 2004), and its economic underdevelopment (Kuran 2004) can be (at least partially) attributed to the weakness of civil society. Timur Kuran, like many other economists, argues that weak civil society in the region is the unintended consequence of institutions historically rooted in Islam, particularly "the strict individualism of Islamic law and its lack of a concept of corpora [written laws] which hindered organizational development and contributed to keeping society weak" (2004, 71). This is, however, not to say that Islamic law contradicts the formation of civil society and interest groups but rather that Islamic institutions (both formal and informal) had monopolized associational life for centuries, hindering the development of nonreligious CSOs in most parts of the region (Yom 2005). As anthropologists and historians indicate, mosques have historically been sources of social, political, educational, and even medical activities in the region (Al-Sayyid 1995). More recently, however, there has been a boom of volunteer and professional organizations in the Middle East, and Islamists comprise only a portion of these groups (Antoun 2000). Women's movements transcending particular religious interests were the cornerstones of the 2009 Green Movement in Iran and the 2011 Jasmine Revolution in Tunisia. And while the business groups in Egypt and Jordan have strongly represented economic interests, students' movements in Morocco have forced the state to take unprecedented steps to improve the socioeconomic status of the youth.

The success of civil society in translating societal demands into constitutional language does not, however, lie in the sheer number of these organizations. While before the Arab Spring, Egypt, Morocco, Algeria, Lebanon, and the Palestinian territories had the largest per capita CSOs (Yom 2005, 16), for the most part, these institutions were "more an instrument of state social control than a mechanism of collective empowerment" (Wiktorowicz 2000, 43). CSOs can translate social demands into a constitutional language only when they have political weight and function in favorable circumstances. The Tunisian UGTT, in that sense, is a unique organization in the Arab world. The union is considered one of the most important political players in Tunisia, particularly after the fall of Ben Ali's regime, which in alliance with other CSOs could steer the constitutional debate and effectively act as a third-party mediator when negotiations reached a deadlock. What can then explain the failure of UGTT's counterparts in other countries to act as effective third-party mediators and champions of people's will? I argue that several factors can render civil society ineffective.

First, without an inclusive and participatory process, civil society cannot play its democratizing role. Noninclusive processes keep civil society out of the constitutional bargain and subsequently weaken their role in the democratic transition. Inclusive processes, by contrast, provide an opportunity for civil society to be part of the constitutional bargain. Though necessary, inclusive and participatory constitution-making is not a sufficient criterion for the success of civil society in its democratizing role. Besides constitution-making features, several other factors may create obstacles for civil society. At the onset of the Arab Spring, most CSOs faced various endogenous and exogenous challenges, which undermined their work.

Most youth, women, and diaspora movements suffered from the lack of organizational capacity and essential political skills and training. Moreover, many of the established unions and NGOs that possessed organizational capacity were struggling with the lack of public legitimacy due to either state co-optation or foreign donors' influence. Besides these two endogenous challenges, most CSOs faced exogenous hurdles to their work. None of these groups were protected by formal or informal institutions such as constitutional guarantees or political norms, making them vulnerable to states' repressive apparatus. That is, they were not institutionalized. To make matters even worse, these weakly institutionalized CSOs had to operate in hostile political environments rife with ethnic, religious, regional, and ideological polarization as well as military and regional interventions.

Indeed, the predominance of regional divisions in Yemen and Libya and ethnoreligious divisions in Syria negatively affected the emergence of a strong civil society that could facilitate the constitutional bargain and democratic transition processes in these nations. Similarly, domestic and foreign military campaigns in Egypt and Bahrain muted civil society and rendered it ineffective. By contrast, when these exogenous and endogenous challenges do not exist, an organized, independent, and institutionalized civil society can emerge to steer the constitutional bargain in a direction that may resolve the social and political ills of authoritarianism.

Participatory and Inclusive Processes

I consider next the mechanism through which civil groups help consolidate democracy in nations where they operate by focusing on their participation in constitutional deliberations. As Landemore (2012) contends, we can differentiate among three forms of participation. The first is deliberative, emphasizing the centrality of "epistemic competence" (Landemore 2012, 254). The second form is participation through mere aggregation, where "strength in numbers" drives non-elite participation. The third form of participation, which is less optimal than formal deliberation but perhaps normatively superior to sheer aggregation, is elite bargaining and pacts. This approach is the form of interest group politics popularized by O'Donnell and Schmitter (1986) and also used later by Higley and Gunther (1992) and Brownlee (2007). In Landemore's (2012) view, bargaining is an inferior form of participation to formal deliberation because it leaves the door open for "strategic" communication, whereby actors are not sincere about their preferences.

Building on Landemore (2012), I argue that deliberation is the main mechanism through which CSOs can fortify democracy by moderating the constitutional discussion. However, this book argues that successful deliberation takes place through two distinct paths: individual-level participation and organized group inclusion. Indeed, without inclusion, civil society cannot be part of the constitutional debate, and without participation, it cannot create a public sphere for constitutional discussions. Going back to the self-enforcing thesis, both inclusion and participation are important for securing the necessary conditions for a self-enforcing constitution. An *inclusive* process guarantees a "fair" constitution, which is beneficial to most groups in the society. And a *participatory* process, following propositions of participatory constitution-making models, can create a consensus among citizens and a constituency of citizens that are willing to defend and support the terms of the constitutional bargain, which will exponentially increase the cost of reneging on constitutional limits.

It is, therefore, important to first differentiate between *inclusion* and *participation*.[5] With a few exceptions, including Horowitz (2013) and Eisenstadt and Maboudi (2019), most previous studies have either combined participation and inclusion or use the two terms interchangeably to refer to the same phenomenon. Participation refers to the inclusion of the mass or the general public in any stage of constitutional reforms processes. The most common form of public participation in constitution-making involves the popular vote (to elect a constituent assembly) and referenda (to vote on the final draft of the constitution). Most citizens get involved in constitution-making through these passive means, both of which are representative forms of democracy. But neither is educative: They provide only minimal levels of information and create at best a minimal sense of constitutionalism or constitutional attachment in the society. However, there is another – more active – form of public participation, rare although it may be, which is closer to the concept of direct democracy. Public deliberation on the content of constitutions can lead to democratically superior outcomes (Landemore 2017). What can be more democratic than people coming together to debate their own constitution and share its authorship? Yet, public deliberation is the least common type of public engagement in constitution-making. Only 12 percent of constitutions written since the Third Wave of democracy incorporated public deliberation.[6] Most constitutional processes are participatory only in

---

[5] Chapter 2 extensively discusses these two concepts and how they are measured in this study.
[6] Chapter 2 discusses some potential reasons for why public deliberation is still uncommon in constitution-making.

the final stage of constitutional ratification through plebiscite (50 percent of cases). Even then, public participation can – and often does – serve functions other than a genuine form of democracy.

More often in authoritarian or hybrid regimes, but sometimes in democracies as well, political elites mobilize public participation for either window-dressing or populist ends. Public participation quickly turns into a political tool, rather than an expression of the people's will. Such processes focus more on giving the impression of participation than creating a public sphere for constitutional discussions. In this situation, CSOs (even if allowed to take part) and their work will most likely have little or no effect on engaging the public with constitutional bargaining. Moreover, by mimicking the characteristics of inclusive and/or participatory reforms, window-dressing and populist constitution-making processes can pose a danger to democratic movements.

Inclusion and participation, thus, should not be treated as the same. While participation entails individual decisions, as citizens individually try to make a change, inclusion aggregates individual voices into groups and associations that can better organize and channel people's voices at the constitutional negotiation table. For Horowitz (2013) and Eisenstadt and Maboudi (2019), this collective strength is the primary reason why inclusive processes are more successful in democracy-building than mere participation. Yet, inclusion and participation are not mutually exclusive, and a democratic constitutional process could and should entail both. Indeed, while inclusion matters significantly, without meaningful public participation, CSOs cannot improve the people's constitutional knowledge and engage them in the constitutional bargain. Empirical evidence, although limited, points to the importance of both inclusion and participation. Eisenstadt et al. (2015, 2017a) and Fruhstorfer and Hudson (2019) find empirical evidence that participation, especially in the early stages of constitution-making, yields more democratic outcomes. Both studies, however, combine inclusion and participation in one estimate. Eisenstadt and Maboudi (2019), by contrast, show that when participation and inclusion are measured separately, inclusion matters most for post-constitutional levels of democracy. In Chapter 2, I show that public participation also matters for the content of constitutions: More participation leads to more democratic provisions, especially individual and group rights, in constitutions.

Constituent assemblies (more precisely, coalitions with the majority of seats) may have several motives for initiating an inclusive and participatory process, but perhaps the most important one is to make credible commitments to the minority groups in the assembly. As the process of constitutional renegotiation in Egypt (and the subsequent overthrow of the Muslim Brotherhood government by the military and angry protesters) shows, participation and inclusion raise the cost of reneging on the constitutional bargain. This increased cost functions as insurance for the minority groups in the bargain.

A Mutually Reinforcing Mechanism

The three components of this thesis – constitutional design, civil society, and process – are most likely to be mutually reinforcing. Inclusive and participatory processes are likely to empower CSOs to take a meaningful part in the constitutional debate. At the same time, it is likely that a strong and independent civil society will increase the pressure for a more inclusive process. Indeed, more inclusion increases the number of interest groups with a wider range of "ideal points," which exacerbates the coordination problem (Elkins et al. 2009), making it more difficult for civil society to work toward creating a national consensus on the most important constitutional issues. As will be discussed in Chapter 3, to overcome this challenge, anti-gridlock mechanisms should be institutionalized in the constitutional negotiation process.

It is especially important for civil society to create public interest and awareness about constitutional issues beyond those pertaining to ideological cleavages, which already mobilize large segments of society. Without these efforts, even with participatory processes, the general public will probably be less engaged in constitutional discussions. If, on the contrary, CSOs create a public sphere for constitutional debate, the constitutional design is more likely to address the concerns raised in these public fora. A constitutional design that addresses the social and political challenges is very likely to enhance democracy, which in turn, generates further inclusion and participation.

I acknowledge that there is a certain level of endogeneity to this argument. Given the cross-national nature of this study and the interaction of several endogenous and exogenous elements, this degree of endogeneity is unavoidable. Through a combination of robust statistical analysis and empirical case studies from the Arab Spring, however, I seek to show that the impact of this endogeneity on the major findings is likely to be minimal. The remainder of this chapter offers a very brief introduction to the Arab Spring uprisings and events that led to constitutional renegotiations in the MENA.

THE ARAB SPRING: CONSTITUTIONAL
CONTINUITY AND CHANGE

The most common narrative on the popular uprisings in the Arab world (the Arab Spring) is that the sequel of upheavals started on December 17, 2010, when a twenty-six-year-old street vendor, Mohamed Bouazizi, set himself on fire in front of a local municipal office in the city of Sidi Bouzid in central Tunisia after his property was confiscated by local officials (Brownlee et al. 2015). This action led to massive protests in Sidi Bouzid. President Zine El Abidine Ben Ali, the Tunisian dictator, initially ignored the protests, then called them riots. He finally recognized the severity of the circumstances and paid a visit to Bouazizi at the hospital, but his visit was too little too late. Bouazizi died a few days later, and his shocking death triggered massive protests across the country against unemployment, corruption, and government brutality. Under mounting pressure, President Ben Ali was forced to flee the country after the military refused to use force to put down the protests. A relatively peaceful democratic transition followed Ben Ali's departure, leading to the promulgation of the most progressive Arab constitution in January 2014.

The revolution in Tunisia spreads rapidly across the MENA. In Egypt, hundreds of thousands of protesters gathered in Tahrir Square and other squares around the country and demanded the departure of their own dictator, President Hosni Mubarak. Seeing Mubarak as a liability, the powerful Egyptian military forced the president to resign only eighteen days after the protests started. Soon it became clear that although Mubarak resigned, the military was less willing to give up power. The sweeping electoral victory of the Muslim Brotherhood and deep divisions between the Islamists and non-Islamists resulted in a controversial constitution in 2012, which led to mass protests against the democratically elected President Mohamed Morsi. The military capitalized on popular dissatisfaction with the Muslim Brotherhood government, staged a coup, and paved the way for a new constitution in 2014. The relatively democratic constitution of 2014 did not survive long, and in 2019, the Egyptian parliament approved a bill to amend the constitution, changing the length of presidential terms to six years with two-term limits. This change allows current President El-Sisi to potentially remain in office until 2030.

In Morocco, a group of youths (later named the February 20 Youth Movement) organized a mass protest in Rabat, Casablanca, and other cities on February 20, 2011 (Benchemsi 2012). Demonstrators called for major reforms including a new, more democratic constitution. In response to the protests, King Mohammed VI gave a rare, televised speech, known as the "March 9 speech," promising a "comprehensive constitutional change" featuring "the rule of law," an "independent judiciary," and an "elected government that reflects the will of the people through the ballot box," making Morocco the first nation to change its constitution in response to the Arab Spring uprisings (Banani 2012, 11–15). In another relatively poor monarchy, Jordan, the protests started as early as January 2011. The fate of Jordan was very similar to that of Morocco. Protesters concentrated on unemployment, inflation, corruption, and real constitutional and electoral reforms to make the Hashemite kingdom a true constitutional monarchy. Like his Moroccan counterpart, King Abdullah II of Jordan was able to skillfully manage the situation by a series of constitutional changes in 2011, 2014, and 2016, which provided nothing but mere lip service to democracy.

In Yemen, violence escalated fast, as President Ali Abdullah Saleh was unwilling to give up power until he narrowly escaped an assassination attempt in June 2011. He eventually signed a power transition plan, prepared by the Gulf Cooperation Council (GCC), to relinquish power in November 2011. Yemen seemed to be on track for democratic transition with the appointment of Abdrabbuh Mansur Hadi as the interim president who took office in February 2012. But shortly after a draft constitution was introduced in January 2015, the Shia Houthis from the less affluent south, who were excluded from the constitutional renegotiation, rebelled and occupied the presidential palace. Soon, Saudi Arabia formed a Gulf coalition against the Houthi rebels, pushing Yemen further into a civil war, which has so far claimed thousands of lives.

In Syria, like Yemen, an armed rebellion against the regime was met with a violent response from the state and armed international intervention, which fueled the civil war. Unlike in Yemen, however, the Syrian protesters from Raqqa, a poor Sunni town and the birthplace of the uprisings, did not initially chant *Erhal* (Leave!) and were only demanding more rights and greater equality. From January to March 2011, the protests were minor and mostly concentrated in Daraa and other small Sunni-populated towns. Syria's Alawi Shia dictator, President Bashar Al-Assad, however, reacted to these protests with an iron fist. In mid-March, major protests erupted in Daraa and Damascus in response to the Baathi government's brutal crackdown of peaceful protests, such as the incarceration and torture of fifteen young students who were writing anti-government graffiti, including the thirteen-year-old Hamza Al-Khateeb, who was tortured and killed by the regime. A few months later, the rebel Free Syrian Army was created on July 29, 2011, marking the transition into an armed insurgency. President Al-Assad made some late promises for change, including a new constitution adopted in 2012, which did not make any changes to the authoritarian status quo. The rise of the terrorist organization Islamic State of Iraq and Syria (ISIS) on the one hand, and increasing support from Iran, Hizbullah (the Lebanese paramilitary group), and Russia, on the other, eventually kept Al-Assad in power.

In the Gulf region, major protests erupted only in Saudi Arabia and Bahrain. In Saudi Arabia, in addition to constitutional reforms in 2013, King Abdullah moved quickly with co-opting the protesters by financial promises, including the creation of jobs for the youth, and managed to control the situation. Unlike the rest of the Gulf region, however, the protests in Bahrain were considered strategically important for regional and global powers, including Saudi Arabia and the United States. The small, Shia-majority island ruled by a minority Sunni dynasty is a close ally to Saudi Arabia and hosts the US Fifth Fleet in the Persian Gulf. Iran, which supports the Shia Bahraini, has historical claims over the island. Therefore, when the protests began among the Shia population for justice and equality, they were met with a government crackdown with the help of the Saudi militia. Despite Bahrain Emir's pledges for democratic reforms, constitutional changes in 2012 and 2017 did little in changing the status quo or satisfying popular demands for equality and justice.

Among all Arab leaders, Libya's Muammar Qaddafi had the worst fate. In Libya, uprisings started in February 2011 after security forces opened fire on a protest in the city of Benghazi. With the military remaining loyal to Libya's dictator, protests soon turned into a blood bath. After the UN Security Council authorized all necessary means to protect civilians in March 2011, NATO intervened by attacking Qaddafi's forces and military strongholds. After four decades in power, Qaddafi was captured and killed by a group of rioters in August 2011. The National Transitional Council (NTC), which led the revolt, became the de facto government of Libya between 2011 and 2012 and adopted an interim constitution (Constitutional Declaration) in 2011. Article 30 of this constitution called for the election of a national legislative body, the General National Congress (GNC), in less than a year. The to-be-elected GNC was tasked with appointing a committee to draft a permanent constitution in sixty days and submit the draft for approval in the GNC, with subsequent ratification coming through a public referendum. Political turmoil and concerns over the proportional make-up of the GNC, however, led the NTC to amend the Constitutional Declaration only a few days before the legislative elections (Gluck 2015). The outbreak of violence, with some 300 militia groups fighting each other, regional divisions, and lack of any constructive negotiations have so far prevented the creation of a permanent constitution that binds Libyans together.

To the western borders of Libya, protests started in Algeria from late December 2010 and continued until early 2012. The massive protests around the country had similar causes including unemployment, inflation, corruption, restrictions on freedom of speech, and poor living conditions. The Algerian government responded with a series of reforms and suppression of the protests. The first major reform was the lifting of the state of emergency in February 2011. During the initial months of the uprisings, President Bouteflika, Algeria's ruler since 1999, announced that he would initiate a series of democratic reforms in the country. Bouteflika appointed his minister of state and senior advisor, Ahmed Ouyahia, to undertake the constitutional reform process. After five years of consultations behind closed doors, constitutional amendments were introduced and approved by both legislative chambers in February 2016. The constitutional reform package included seventy-four amendments and thirty-eight new provisions. The most important change was made to Article 74, which since 2008 lifted a two-term limit on the presidency so as to allow Bouteflika to run for a third and fourth term. The 2016 constitution reinstated the presidential term limit, although it allowed Bouteflika to finish his fourth term in 2019 and to run for a fifth term if he wished. Although eventually the status quo did not change and Bouteflika weathered the uprisings, the 2016 revised constitution embodies more civil rights and liberties than its predecessors, including the recognition of the role of women and youth in society, freedom of the press, and more linguistic rights for the Imazighen minority (Maboudi 2019, 568–569).

Lastly, in a usually forgotten case, the Kingdom of Oman, minor protests had a significant impact on political and economic reforms. The demonstrations started with about 200 protesters gathering on January 17, 2011, against rising prices of goods, corruption, and low wages. The protests increased, on and off, until they peaked in April. The government managed the protests by initiating a number of social, political, and economic reforms including constitutional amendments in October 2011 and increasing the minimum wage. Although the status quo did not change and the position of Sultan Qaboos, the King of Oman, remained very strong, those small protests were strong enough to bring about reforms that were ignored for years in the kingdom.

As this brief overview shows, the Arab Spring uprisings were closely tied to constitutional reforms throughout the Arab world. While a number of these constitutional reforms did change the status quo, most failed in bringing about meaningful reforms. Nonetheless, this wave of constitutional reforms is unprecedented in a region, which boasts constitutional stability. As Table 1.1 shows,

TABLE 1.1 *History of constitutions in the Middle East and North Africa*

Country	Number of Constitutions	Earliest Constitution	Number of Constitutions since 1974	Average Durability of Constitutions
Afghanistan	6	1923	3	11.5
Algeria	3	1963	2	12
Bahrain	1	1973	0	14
Egypt	7	1882	2	12.5
Iran	2	1906	1	55
Iraq	3	1925	1	17
Israel	1	1958	0	57
Jordan	2	1946	0	34.5
Kuwait	2	1938	0	27
Lebanon	1	1926	0	82
Libya	2	1951	0	29
Morocco	4	1962	1	13
Oman	1	1996	1	19
Qatar	1	2003	1	12
Saudi Arabia	1	1992	1	23
Syria	5	1950	1	9
Tunisia	3	1861	1	19
Turkey	7	1876	1	15.5
United Arab Emirates	1	1971	0	44
Yemen	2	1970	1	14
Total	55	–	17	–
Mean	2.75	–	0.85	26

Source: Author's estimation based on Brown (2002) and Comparative Constitution Project data set (Elkins et al. 2009)

the average duration of the fifty-five constitutions adopted in the region from 1861 to 2019 is twenty-six years, which is seven years longer than the global average age of constitutions (Elkins et al. 2009). The most durable constitution in the region is the Lebanese Constitution of 1926, a constitution that was suspended and reinstated twice by the French colonial administration (Brown 2002, 71).[7]

What has changed since the first Arab constitution in 1861? As Nathan Brown (2002) noted in his seminal book, *Constitutions in a Nonconstitutional World*, while constitutions and constitution-making have evolved in the region over the

[7] It was first suspended for two years between 1932 and 1934 and again between 1939 and 1943.

last century and a half, these constitutional renovations have not brought constitutionalism and rule of law to the Arab world. There was some hope that the constitutional wave of the Arab Spring might eventually establish constitutionalism and democracy in the region. But that dream very soon faded away as authoritarianism withstood the popular pressure for democratic reforms. The new constitutional order in the Arab world, with the exception of Tunisia, could not remedy the social and political ills that triggered the unprecedented uprisings in the region. This outcome was partly because of noninclusive and nonparticipatory processes and partly because of a lack of strong and independent civil society. The next chapter evaluates the relationship between democratic constitution-making processes and the democraticity of the constitution using empirical evidence from two cross-national studies.

2

Democratizing the Parchments

The Impact of Process on the Democratic Content of Constitutions

Over the past four decades, constitutional reform processes have generally become more inclusive and participatory.[1] In an effort to legitimize the constitutional process, for example, the 1987–1988 Brazilian assembly solicited more than 61,000 citizen proposals for the constitution (Benomar 2004, 89). In similar efforts, the Constitution of Kenya Review Commission collected more than 37,000 citizen proposals in 2002–2003 (Cottrell and Ghai 2007, 11), and the 2012 Constituent Assembly of Egypt received more than 113,000 public comments and suggestions for the constitution (Maboudi and Nadi 2016). While such extensive forms of public inclusion in the writing of constitutions sometimes serve as window-dressing, when genuine, they often play an important role in legitimizing the process and the constitution (Wing 2008). Still, the impact of process on the content of constitutions has remained understudied. With the exception of a few case studies (e.g., Maboudi and Nadi 2016; Hudson 2018), empirical evidence on the impact of public deliberation – through inclusive and participatory processes – on the content of constitutions is limited. Does the process of drafting constitutions matter for the democratic content of constitutions? Does it matter who is at the table when negotiating constitutional terms and provisions?

Historically, constitution-making has been viewed as an elite affair, ever since the Federal Convention deliberated on the American Constitution in 1787. It has been conventionally argued that elites are better informed, more committed to democratic values, and could be trusted more with safeguarding the general good than the masses. Recently developed conjectures in the literature of participatory and deliberative democracy, however, contend

---

[1] A recent study, for example, shows that over 70 percent of constitutions promulgated from 1974 to 2015 incorporated some form of mass public participation in the process (Eisenstadt, LeVan, and Maboudi 2017a).

that inclusive constitution-making processes are more likely to generate "smart" and "morally superior" outcomes (see Landemore 2017). This call for "direct democracy" in constitution-making processes, or what Chambers (2004, 153) labels "the democratization of popular sovereignty," not only emphasizes the legitimacy of the process but also predicts that more participatory and inclusive constitution-making processes yield more democratic outcomes (Pateman 1970). This book offers empirical evidence in support of these theories, arguing that inclusive and participatory constitutional negotiations are likely to result in democratic constitutions, which attenuate unresolved social and political problems prevalent in society. Participatory and inclusive processes open up the space for civil society organizations to get involved in the constitutional debate. Civil society organizations, in turn, can act as representatives of the public, ensuring its interests and demands are reflected in the constitution, thus ensuring a more democratic constitution.

This chapter provides empirical evidence for the first part of this thesis, showing the impact of process on the democratic content of constitutions. First, using an original data set and statistical analysis of all 195 constitutional reform processes in 118 countries from 1974 to 2015, this chapter examines the impact of public participation and group inclusion in constitution-making processes on improving the democratic content of constitutions. This study distinguishes between public participation and group inclusion, which are often used interchangeably in the extant literature, and uses two original measures for individual-level public participation and aggregate-level group inclusion in constitution-making processes, which are premised on the participatory and deliberative theories of democracy. The findings from the statistical analysis demonstrate that participatory processes are more likely to result in constitutions with more democratic provisions. Inclusive processes, by contrast, have statistically significant correlations only with increased number of rights in the constitution. The results also show that when we examine the impact of participation and inclusion during different stages of constitution-making, participation and inclusion in the *origination* stage (rather than *deliberation* or *ratification* stages) are more consequential for the democratic content of constitutions. Second, using another original data set of all constitutions in the MENA from 1861 (when Tunisia adopted the first modern constitution in the region) to 2020, I show that participatory and inclusive processes have a positive impact on the democratic content of MENA constitutions. Taken together, these findings offer empirical support for participatory and deliberative theories of democracy and their call for giving all citizens and societal groups an equal opportunity and the right to participate and influence the outcome (Chambers 2004; Pateman 2012).

In this chapter, I first review the representative, participatory, and deliberative theories of democracy and discuss the two hypotheses this chapter raises.
The "participation" hypothesis states that constitutions drafted via broad
participatory processes are more likely to secure democratic provisions.
Similarly, the "inclusion" hypothesis posits that constitutions drafted through
broad inclusive processes are more likely to secure democratic provisions.
These hypotheses will be evaluated in two steps using original data sets from
across the world and MENA. In the first step, I introduce the "participation"
and "inclusion" variables, discuss the measurement of the democratic content
of constitutions, and then present the results from the global study. In
the second step, I briefly present the regional data set and the results using
that data set. Finally, a discussion of the main findings and their implications
for our understanding of theories of democracy and participatory constitution-
making will be presented.

PARTICIPATION AND INCLUSION IN THE CRAFTING
OF NEW CONSTITUTIONS

Historically, the constitution-writing task was reserved for a select group of
highly trained and well-informed elites who, it was argued, were more committed to democratic values than the masses and could better serve the general
good. Edmund Burke (1999) famously suggests that the mass lacks a "mature
judgment" and "enlightened conscience" to be trusted with complicated
issues such as the constitution. James Madison (1961) similarly argues in
Federalist No. 10 that "the public voice, pronounced by the representatives
of the people, will be more consonant to the public good than if pronounced
by the people themselves, convened for the purpose." The role of representation for Madison, as such, is "to refine and enlarge the public views." By
contrast, John Adams (2000) contends, in *Thoughts on Government*, that
a representative assembly should be "in miniature an exact portrait of the
people at large." This notion of representation as a "mirror image" of the
society was an expression of fairness and equality for the anti-federalists and an
objection to the elitism of the Madisonian "filtering" metaphor (Fishkin
2009).

More recently, Pitkin (1967) identifies four views of representation including formalistic, descriptive, symbolic, and substantive representation. Much
of the discussion on representation during the Cold War was informed by
Pitkin's emphasis on formal procedures of authorization and accountability,
or what she calls 'formalistic representation' (Plotke 1997). The literature on
representation has evolved in several directions since the Cold War, and the

formalistic conception of representation is no more satisfactory, partly due to several transformations in the domestic and international context of political representation. Increasingly, interest groups, civil society organizations, non-governmental actors, and international advocacy groups have taken steps in standing, speaking, and acting for "underrepresented" people within a country, which has resulted in innovative ways of conceptualizing representation (Warren and Castiglione 2004).

In the context of constitutional reform processes, formalistic representation implies that a group of representatives, preferably authorized by people via an upstream election and accountable to their constituency via a downstream referendum, should be tasked with constitution-making. This emphasis on representative processes with public authorization or accountability is in line with Elster's "hourglass model" that prescribes broad upstream and downstream consultation but a deliberation and drafting process that is limited to a select group of drafters (Elster 2012). For Elster, if a constituent assembly is legitimate (authorized by popular election) and citizens are allowed to approve the document (and as such hold their representatives accountable), then public consultation during the drafting process is not necessary.

The failure of various democratization efforts with their emphasis on formalistic representation during the Second Wave of democracy, however, called into question the effectiveness of representative processes for democratic outcomes. Third Wave of democracy and the normative concerns related to the "crisis of representation" associated with delegative and competitive models of democracy (Avritzer 2012) led to unprecedented innovations in public participation in different political processes – which were once reserved for elites – including participatory constitution-making. As Wampler (2012, 667) notes, "the direct incorporation of citizens into complex policy-making processes is the most significant innovation of the third wave." Eisenstadt et al. (2017a), for example, show that more than two-thirds of constitutions promulgated since the Third Wave of democracy have incorporated some form of direct citizen input from voting in constitutional plebiscites to participating in constitutional workshops, focus groups, national conferences, and other forms of public deliberation.

Parallel to these innovations in direct citizen participation in constitution-making processes, recently developed conjectures in theories of participatory and deliberative democracy have laid the foundation for justifying direct public input in constitution-making. Developed mostly in response to rising criticism of the traditional democratic institutions (Barber 1984; Avritzer 2012), theories of deliberative democracy contend that a Burkean elite delegation with no public input can threaten the foundations of democracy as rule by the people (Mansbridge et al. 2012, 14). On the contrary, democratic authenticity requires substantive and real public participation and deliberation (Dryzek 2000), which empowers the marginalized groups in society (see Chambers 2003).

These recent studies in the literature of participatory and deliberative democracy suggest that the people should be involved in the formulation and writing of the constitution for several reasons. First, inclusive and participatory processes are educational and developmental tools for citizens to practice democratic skills and procedures (Pateman 1970, 42). Increased public participation and group inclusion in decision-making processes can also function as a self-enforcing mechanism, preventing the government's abuse of power (Smith 2009). Second, public participation and group inclusion can generate smart and epistemically superior outcomes (Landemore 2013). Translated to constitution-making processes, this literature suggests that constitutional provisions proposed by more participatory and inclusive constituent assemblies are more democratic than those generated by a select group of elites (see Landemore 2017).

These participatory and deliberative models, however, have been criticized on several grounds. Some scholars suggest that constitution-making is an elite affair (Elster 1995; Horowitz 2008, 2013) that should be protected from the often-disruptive mass involvement (Arato 1995; Elster 2000; Sunstein 2001). Moreover, several studies have warned against the dangers of direct public participation in constitutional processes. "Participatory distortion" can result in self-selected groups with extremist views to dominate the public deliberation domain (Verba et al. 1995).[2] Participation in constitutional reform processes can also run the danger of populism and manipulation of the people by interest groups and elites (Ghai 2012).[3] Furthermore, participation increases the number of veto players that can make reaching consensus more difficult (Tsebelis 2002).

Despite the warnings about the potential dangers of public participation and reservations about the effectiveness of participatory and deliberative processes, a few empirical studies suggest that participatory and inclusive processes resulted in the inclusion of various provisions on social and economic justice and corruption in Kenya (Cottrell and Ghai 2007), human rights in South Africa (Sarkin 1999), civil rights such as the right of the disabled

[2] For Verba et al. (1995), participatory distortion is the difference between those that participate (e.g., voters in an election) and the total population of those who could participate (e.g., eligible voters).
[3] As will be discussed in Chapter 3, fear of populism was among the main reservations the Tunisian opposition had against opening the constitutional process to public debate.

people in Colombia (Brett and Delgado 2005), rights of indigenous people in Guatemala (Marulanda 2004), and women's rights in Uganda (Hart 2003). One comparative study of twelve cases shows that overall increased participation yields more provisions on human rights protection (Samuels 2006). These studies suggest that public participation and group inclusion can increase both the legitimacy and the democratic content of constitutions (Bannon 2007). Although these findings are important, the empirical evidence has remained inconclusive and the propositions mostly normative. Most importantly, however, these studies either lump participation and inclusion together (Eisenstadt et al. 2015) or use them interchangeably (Landemore 2017). This study, however, calls for a clear distinction between public participation and group inclusion in the constitution-making.

The main difference between participation and inclusion is in how public will is translated into policy outcomes. A participatory process calls for the direct involvement of individual citizens to protect their own rights in the constitution (Hart 2003). An inclusive process, however, is not a mere aggregation of individual participation. An inclusive process entails the inclusion of interest group advocates for societal positions (such as civil society organizations) as a necessary condition for the fashioning of a new constitutional order in all regimes, whether democratic or authoritarian. As Eisenstadt and Maboudi (2019) also argue, in procedural terms, formal advocacy for ideas and issues may in fact be more important than widespread support for those issues. Horowitz (2013, 293), for example, noted the need for inclusion of all major interest groups within the constitution-drafting coalition, as Indonesia's 2002 "slow, consensual, insider-driven process allowed the careful creation of new institutions and the creation of understandings among legislators." In addition to this call for inclusion, Moehler (2008) demonstrated that while participation in the 1995 Ugandan constitution-reforming process provided civic education, it also made citizens cynical. Moehler's findings revealed that views of local leaders, rather than mere public participation, drove citizen views of the constitution's legitimacy.

Inclusion, as such, is very close to Dahl's notion of pluralism. Dahl explains pluralism as the array of groups beyond the electorate that contribute positions and resources to the governmental framework. Pluralism assures wide representation to a broad array of groups; however, it also slows down policy-making, as groups adverse to political processes obstruct implementation of adverse policies (Dahl 2005, 1–8). Inclusion, as such, might slow down policy-making, but the articulation of different interests yields more democratic outcomes. Nonetheless, the breadth of inclusion and the articulation of different ideas are different from public participation and, as Horowitz (2013) argues, matter more for democratic outcomes.

This study, thus, distinguishes between public participation and group inclusion and uses two original measures for individual-level public participation and aggregate-level group inclusion in constitution-making processes, which are premised on the participatory and deliberative theories of democracy. Using a cross-national analysis of 195 constitutions from 1974 to 2015, as well as an analysis of all MENA constitutions since 1861, this chapter examines the impact of these two choices of constitutional process on the democratic content of constitutions.

HYPOTHESES

If the argument on the "epistemically superior outcome" of more inclusive constitutional processes is correct, then we should expect that constitutions drafted by an inclusive constituent assembly and with broad public participation have more provisions on (1) democratic political institutions (where the executive is accountable to the legislature, and the judiciary is independent); (2) various individual, group, and political rights and freedoms; and (3) transparent political processes (such as independent electoral commissions) than constitutions without such processes. As such, the following two hypotheses are raised:

H 2.1: *Constitutions drafted via broad participatory processes are more likely to secure democratic provisions than constitutions drafted without participation.*

H 2.2: *Constitutions drafted via inclusive processes are more likely to secure democratic provisions than constitutions drafted without inclusion.*

Both hypotheses speak to the deliberative and participatory theories of democracy that emphasize the importance of participatory and inclusive processes for democratic outcomes (Fishkin 2009). If the participation hypothesis is corroborated, it would provide empirical evidence for normative contentions that participatory processes yield democratically superior outcomes (Widner 2008; Wing 2008). It would show that after all, the general public is also committed to democratic values. The second hypothesis, by contrast, speaks to the studies that emphasize the inclusion of different societal groups and interests in constitutional processes rather than mere public participation (Horowitz 2013). Any evidence in support of the inclusion hypothesis would suggest that any participation must be fully channeled to assemble a constitution that resonates with the participants and that constitution-making is a political process and, as such, requires advocates with credibility derived from powerful entrenched interests, the popular will, or some combination of these. I test these hypotheses in two stages using a global data set and a data set of MENA constitutions.

DATA AND ANALYSIS

This study builds on a previous work (Eisenstadt et al. 2017b) to quantify the design of constitution-making processes across 195 constitutions that have been drafted from 1974 to 2015. In their Constitutionalism and Democracy Database of 138 constitutions, Eisenstadt et al. (2017b) measure the poly-archic nature of constitution-making processes in three stages of *origination*, *deliberation*, and *ratification*.[4] Their "process" variable is a measure of inclusiveness of constitutional processes in those three stages, and it has three dimensions including the extent to which elites are included, the extent to which the general public is allowed to participate, and the transparency of the process.

This book distinguishes between public participation and group inclusion as two separate (but not mutually exclusive) measures of constitution-making processes, which should not be lumped together or used interchangeably. I introduce two new measures for individual-level public participation and aggregate-level group inclusion in constitution-making processes, which are premised on the participatory and deliberative theories of democracy. Participation, in this study, refers to the degree to which the general public is involved (participates) in different stages of constitution-making processes. Inclusion, on the other hand, refers to the extent to which major political and social groups in the society are included in the process.[5] Colombia 1991, Ecuador 2008, and Tunisia 2014 are a few examples of constitutional reform processes that were both participatory and inclusive. China 1982, Saudi Arabia 1992, and Somalia 2012, on the other hand, are a few cases where the process was neither participatory nor inclusive. In-between, there is a range of cases that are either inclusive (e.g., Portugal 1976) or participatory (e.g., Egypt 2012).

---

[4] The first stage of constitution-making is *origination* in which constitution drafters are elected or appointed. The second stage, *deliberation*, includes deliberation and the actual writing of the constitution. The last stage, *ratification*, covers the mechanism of approving the constitution draft (Eisenstadt et al. 2017a).

[5] Major groups here include all relevant political parties, blocs, and movements, interest groups, civil society organizations, as well as ethnic, religious, or linguistic groups. A process is considered inclusive if all of these groups are present and non-inclusive if major groups are systematically excluded.

A constitution-making process can be inclusive without being participatory. An illustrative case in point is the Portuguese constitution-making process (1975–1976) where the process was not participatory but inclusive. Following the April 1974 military coup led by the Movement of the Armed Forces, the Portuguese citizens elected the Constituent Assembly tasked with drafting a new constitution in April 1975. However, the people were not invited to provide feedback on the content of the constitution (during the deliberation stage), and the document was ratified without a public referendum. Although nonparticipatory, the process was inclusive as all major groups (from the left-wing Communist Party to the central-left Socialist Party and the far-right Social Democratic Center) were part of the constitutional negotiations in all stages of the constitutional process (Magalhães 2015, 438–440).[6]

While estimating the level of public participation is easier, measuring inclusion is more complicated. How, exactly, do we determine whether groups are represented in the process? This study measures the inclusion variable as the absence of exclusion. "Negatively" measuring noninclusion (or partial inclusion through boycotts) is more straightforward than "positively" measuring inclusion. This is due to the extensiveness of available information on boycotts and other forms of constitution refusals by major political and social groups. For example, since all major non-Islamist groups and political parties in Egypt (2012) boycotted the constitution, the process is coded as noninclusive.

We should also distinguish between self-exclusion and forced exclusion as two broad forms of noninclusive constitutional processes. Self-exclusion, which is when a group voluntarily decides not to participate, although it is allowed to, is usually in the form of boycotts, withdrawal from the process, or other forms of vote-holding. Voluntary exclusion can be viewed as either a strategic move (often to press a matter on the majority in constituent assemblies) or a protest (when a group believes its participation will not yield the desired outcome). The inclusion variable considers both forms of exclusion (i.e., self-exclusion and forced exclusion) and treats them the same. In other words, the inclusion variable does not differentiate between the various functions or degrees of scope and breadth of exclusion. Rather, when any of these conditions exist in a case, this study counts that case as a noninclusive process. This is because differentiation among causes of exclusion is difficult for some cases. But even without being able to code

[6] Portugal (1976) has a score of 2 (on a 0–6 scale) in the *participation* measure of this study and is coded as "mixed." However, its score of *inclusion* is 6 (on a 0–6 scale), and it is coded as "inclusive."

self-exclusion (as in Egypt's April 6 Youth Movement), as distinct from authoritarian group exclusion (as in Morocco's February 20 Youth Movement), the inclusion variable reflects whether constitutional processes are representative of all relevant societal groups and interests. Having explained the empirical difficulties of measuring inclusion and the logic of how this chapter addresses these, in the section that follows, I discuss in more detail how I operationalize inclusion and participation.

Operationalizing Participation and Inclusion

The *participation* variable estimates the extent to which the general public is involved in the three stages of origination, deliberation, and ratification.[7] For each stage, the level of public participation is coded 0 (nonparticipatory), 1 (mixed), or 2 (participatory). The *participation* variable then aggregates the measures of these three stages. It ranges from 0 (no public participation at all) to 6 (genuine public participation in all three stages). I then recoded the *participation* variable to create three ordered categories of "participatory," "mixed," and "nonparticipatory." Table 2.1 below shows the coding rules for components of the *participation* variable. As this table shows, a participatory process in the origination stage entails a popular election of the constitution-drafting body, and participation in the ratification stage entails a public referendum on the constitution. A participatory process in the deliberation stage, however, requires public deliberation and direct citizen input on constitutional proposals, which reflects the deliberative model of democracy and its emphasis on participation beyond merely voting or delegating authority (Fishkin 2009).

As Figure 2.1 shows, most constitutions from 1974 to 2015 were drafted with limited public participation in the first two stages. Only twenty-nine constitutions were written using participatory means in the origination stage. In the deliberation stage, only twenty-three constitution-making processes used extensive public input. However, almost 50 percent of the cases (96 constitutions) were participatory in the ratification stage.

---

[7] To measure levels of participation and inclusion, two coders coded all 195 constitution-making processes, and a third coder coded only the cases where the first two coders differed (9 percent of the cases). Coders consulted several sources including William S. Hein & Company (2012), Widner (2004), Institute for Democracy and Electoral Assistance's Constitutionnet.org, Comparative Constitutions Project (CPP), Economist Intelligence Unit country reports, and the *CIA World Factbook*. A few cases, such as Afghanistan or Somalia, required additional research from peer-reviewed area studies journals.

TABLE 2.1 *Coding criteria for participation variable*

		Stage of Process		
		Origination	Deliberation	Ratification
Level of Participation	Participatory	Constituent Assembly (CA) or other constitution-drafting bodies directly elected by citizens	Extensive public input is sought from the general public.	Constitution is ratified via public referendum.
	Mixed	Constitution-making body appointed by the parliament, *or* from within parliament, *or* a national conference, *or* only partially elected by citizens	Broad public input is not directly sought but people are informed through media, *or* only constitution education workshops are held, *or* only civil society is consulted.	Constitution is ratified by an elected Constituent Assembly, *or* the public referendum is strongly influenced or manipulated by the state.
	Nonparticipatory	Appointed body to write the constitution	There is no public input or education of any kind.	Constitution is ratified by a decree *or* by an appointed body.

Next, the inclusion variable measures the degree to which different groups in the society are included in the three stages of origination, deliberation, and ratification. For each stage, the level of inclusion is coded 0 (noninclusive), 1 (mixed), or 2 (inclusive). The *inclusion* variable then aggregates the measures of these three stages. It, therefore, ranges from 0 (noninclusive in all stages) to 6 (inclusive in all three stages). Finally, I recoded the *inclusion* variable to create three ordered categories of "inclusive," "mixed," and

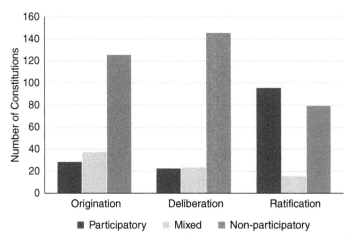

FIGURE 2.1 Level of participation in different stages of constitution-making processes

"noninclusive."[8] Table 2.2 shows the coding criteria for this variable. The hallmark of the "inclusive" origination stage is the inclusion of representatives from all major groups, whether elected or appointed, in the constitution-drafting body. This is different from a "participatory" origination stage, which requires a constituent assembly directly elected by citizens, because an inclusive body can also be appointed. A case in point is Zimbabwe (2013), where after the disputed and violent elections of March and June 2008, all major political parties agreed to set up a Parliamentary Constitution Select Committee (COPAC) representing all stakeholders to draft a new constitution. The Zimbabwean COPAC was "inclusive" but not elected by the people (Hodzi 2013). An inclusive origination process, however, does not always follow by inclusion in the deliberation and ratification stages. If a political party or group dominates the assembly, it might act in an exclusionary manner, by imposing its views and failing to engage in constructive deliberation with the opposition. Egypt (2012) is an example of such processes that is coded "inclusive" in the origination stage but "mixed" in the deliberation stage. Egypt is coded "noninclusive" in the ratification stage because all non-Islamist groups withdrew from the Constituent Assembly,

---

[8] The additive approach to categorizing participation and inclusion variables suggests that this study treats each stage as equally important. Although a previous study (Eisenstadt et al. 2015) suggests that participation in the origination stage is more important for democracy, this book assumes that democratic constitutions require public participation and the inclusion of different societal groups in all three stages of constitution-making.

TABLE 2.2 *Coding criteria for inclusion variable*

		Stage of Process		
		Origination	Deliberation	Ratification
Level of Inclusion	Inclusive	The CA is directly elected by citizens, *or* an appointed body that represents all major groups in the society is tasked with writing the constitution.	All major groups participate in the deliberation and writing the constitution.	Constitution is approved by a representative body (appointed or elected) without any boycotts.
	Mixed	An elected or appointed body that only represents some of the major groups in the society is tasked with drafting the constitution.	A specific group including the head of state or military influences the process, *or* the majority party in the CA acts exclusionary, *or* radical groups are excluded.	A representative body ratifies the constitution, but the vote is influenced by the head of state or military, *or* a small group of representatives boycotts the vote.
	Noninclusive	A nonrepresentative body is appointed to write the constitution.	The deliberative body excludes major groups in the society.	Constitution is verified by a dominant group, party, or the head of state *or* a large group of representatives boycotts the vote.

did not ratify the constitution, and boycotted the referendum (Maboudi and Nadi 2016).

As Figure 2.2 demonstrates, most constitutions from 1974 to 2015 were noninclusive (major political parties or groups were excluded from the process). Only twenty-nine constitutions were inclusive in the origination stage, thirty-seven in the deliberation stage, and forty-seven in the ratification stage. In other words, constitutional processes were more inclusive in the ratification and deliberation stages than in the origination stage.

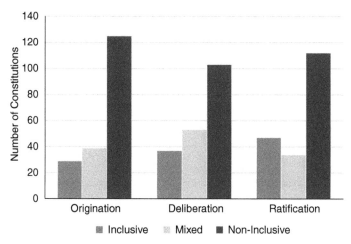

FIGURE 2.2 Level of inclusion in different stages of constitution-making processes

Take, for example, Zambia where the economic crisis in the 1980s, the collapse of the Soviet Union, and growing popular dissatisfaction with the ruling United National Independence Party (UNIP), forced President Kenneth Kaunda to call for constitutional reform aimed at introducing multi-party elections after twenty-seven years of authoritarian (and mostly single-party) rule (Widner 2004). In September 1990, President Kaunda appointed a twenty-two-member Constitutional Review Commission (CRC) headed by a veteran lawyer, Patrick Mphanza Mvunga. The "noninclusive" CRC soon toured the country, collected public feedback, met with different parties, and drafted a report of constitutional recommendations. From the onset, the CRC (also known as the Mvunga Commission) was opposed by the main opposition party, the Movement for Multi-Party Democracy (MMD), which boycotted the commission in protest to UNIP's domination of the process. A breakthrough came in July 1991 when Zambia's National Organization of Churches mediated a committee of ten delegates (five from the incumbent UNIP and five from the opposition MMD) to negotiate changes to the constitution. These negotiations led to an agreement over the content of the constitution, and a draft was submitted to the Zambian Parliament, which approved the constitution in August 1991 (Widner 2004). Because of the boycotts and the UNIP's dominance over the process, the Zambian constitutional reform process is coded "mixed" in the deliberation stage. However, since the constitution was approved by an elected body, the ratification stage is coded "inclusive." Table 2.3 shows the descriptive statistics for participation and inclusion variables. As the data shows, the average levels of inclusion and

TABLE 2.3 *Descriptive statistics of participation and inclusion variables*

	Constitution-Making Stage	Range	Mean	SD
Participation	Origination	0–2	0.50	0.74
	Deliberation	0–2	0.36	0.69
	Ratification	0–2	1.00	1.00
	Aggregate Participation	0–6	1.86	1.66
Inclusion	Origination	0–2	0.50	0.74
	Deliberation	0–2	0.66	0.78
	Ratification	0–2	0.66	0.85
	Aggregate Inclusion	0–6	1.82	2.24

participation are very similar across all cases, despite meaningful differences among individual cases.

The cases of Zambia, Zimbabwe, and Egypt show that participation and inclusion are not interdependent, that is, participatory processes do not necessarily yield inclusion, and vice versa. However, as Table 2.4 shows, in approximately half of the cases, the overall levels of participation and inclusion are similar. As the table shows, still, the majority of constitutions (59 constitutions including China 1982, Saudi Arabia 1992, and Somalia 2012) are drafted via noninclusive and nonparticipatory processes. Finally, the only case from 1974 to 2015 that is participatory but noninclusive is Egypt 2012, which will be discussed in the following chapters.

Measuring the Democratic Content of Constitutions

This chapter focuses only on de jure constitutional provisions and the raw number of democratic provisions specifically, rather than the de facto democratic quality of constitutional provisions. To estimate the democratic content of constitutions, I use the CCP database, which records the characteristics of national constitutions from 1789 to 2013 (Elkins et al. 2014a).[10] From this data set, I use ten binary variables that illustrate different characteristics of constitutions as proxies for democratic content of constitutions. Although issues covered in constitutions across the world vary widely, they all include a few

---

[10] The CCP data set includes all independent states from 1789 to 2013, but the current release covers only 52 percent of those country-years, which is 105 (out of 195) observations in this study. Using the CCP codebook rules, two coders independently coded the content of the missing constitutions in my data set, and a third coder coded only the cases where the first two coders differed.

TABLE 2.4 *Participation and inclusion in constitutional reform processes,* 1974–2015[9]

		INCLUSION			Total
		Noninclusive	Mixed	Inclusive	
PARTICIPATION	Nonparticipatory	59	14	0	73
	Mixed	50	31	23	104
	Participatory	1	2	13	16
	Total	110	47	36	193

main subjects including provisions relevant to government configurations as well as rights and freedoms (Elster 1993, 175). I also included a third category for the "political transparency" provisions in constitutions. As Table 2.5 shows, the dependent variables encompass these three main categories in the text of constitutions, which also reflect some of the major social and political ills in the Arab world as discussed in the previous chapter.

The choice of these three categories and their proxy variables are based on the three components of democratic constitutions discussed in Chapter 1, including temperance, rights-heaviness, and democraticity (see Landemore2016). First, democratic constitutions should limit the power of the executive by empowering other institutions including the legislature and the judiciary (Lijphart 2012). Thus, the first category of outcomes (Political Institutions) estimates whether such independent institutions exist. The *executive accountability* variable measures whether the legislature has the power to hold the executive accountable. And the *judicial independence* variable estimates whether the constitution guarantees the independence of central judicial institutions. As we have seen in Chapter 1, executives who are not accountable to anyone and courts that are subordinate to the executive are among the most important authoritarian features of Arab constitutions.

Second, protection of rights and freedoms is another requirement for democratic constitutions (Elster 1993), but there is no standard way for categorizing constitutional rights. For example, Elkins et al. (2014b) categorize rights, based on their occurrence in national constitutions, into "common" rights (such as freedom of expression) that occur in more than 50 percent of national constitutions and "rare" rights (such as the right to affordable housing) that appear in less than 50 percent of all national constitutions. A better

---

[9] Data on levels of participation and inclusion are missing for two observations.

TABLE 2.5 *Description of dependent variables*

Category	Variable	Description	Coding
Political Institutions	Executive Accountability	Does the legislature have the power to interpellate members of the executive branch?	1 if "yes"
	Judiciary Independence	Does the constitution contain an explicit declaration regarding the independence of the central judicial organ(s)?	1 if "yes"
	Expression	Does the constitution provide for freedom of expression or speech?	1 if "yes"
Rights and Freedoms	Religion	Does the constitution provide for freedom of religion?	1 if "yes"
	Party Formation	Does the constitution provide for a right to form political parties?	1 if "yes"
	Minority Quota	Does the constitution stipulate a quota for the representation of certain minority groups in the first (or only) chamber?	1 if "yes"
	Human Rights Commission	Does the constitution contain provisions for a human rights commission?	1 if "yes"
	State of Emergency	Does the constitution provide for suspension or restriction of rights during states of emergency?	1 if "no"
Transparency	Elections Oversight	Does the constitution provide for an electoral commission or electoral court to oversee the election process?	1 if "yes"
	Public Minutes	Is a record of the deliberations of the legislature published?	1 if "yes"

way is perhaps to distinguish rights as political, civil, social, and economic, pertaining to their desired goals. Historically, core rights included liberty of conscience, property and personal security rights, and freedoms of expression and association. More recently, however, constitutional rights have assumed two new roles. On the one hand, they are designed to protect minority groups, and on the other hand, they guarantee material welfare (Elster 1993).[11] Therefore, the second category (Rights and Freedoms) consists of six variables as proxies for constitutional provisions for core civic rights and freedoms (freedom of *expression* and *religion* variables), political and minority protection rights (*party formation* and *minority quota* variables), and institutions protecting rights (variables for *human rights commission* and ban on restricting rights during a *state of emergency*).

Finally, transparency is another important characteristic of democratic constitutions, especially those crafted after the Third Wave. Transparency of political processes is inherent in democratic values, and it is necessary for government accountability and a democratic polity (Dahl 1971; March and Olsen 1994). Hence, it is important for a constitution to ensure that various political processes are as transparent as possible. The last category (Transparency) uses two proxy variables, *election oversight* and *public minutes*, to measure whether a constitution includes provisions regarding transparency.

Using the above variables, I created three indices for the democratic content of constitutions. First, the *political institutions* index is created by aggregating *executive accountability* and *judiciary independence*. This variable ranges from 0 where the executive is not accountable to the legislative and the judiciary is not independent to 2 where both conditions exist. Second, *rights and freedoms* index is created from the sum of *expression, religion, party formation, minority quota, human rights commission,* and *state of emergency* variables.[12] This variable ranges from 0 where none of these right and freedom provisions exist to 6 where all six provisions exist. The *transparency* index is created from the sum of *election oversight* and *public minutes* variables. It ranges from 0 where neither of the provisions exists in the constitution to 2 where the constitution provides both. Lastly, the *democratic content* index is created from the aggregation of all variables. It ranges from 0 (no democratic provision exists at all) to 10 (all democratic provisions exist). On average, each constitution in the data set has 5.3 democratic provisions (with a standard deviation of 2 provisions).

[11] As many established democracies do not have guarantees of social welfare in their constitutions, this study does not use them as proxies of democracy.
[12] Since the *state of emergency* variable is a negative measure of rights, I recoded it so that 1 indicates a constitution that does not allow for suspension or restriction of rights during states of emergency.

Control Variables

The tests in this study control for several variables that could have significant consequences for the democratic content of constitutions and/or the design of the process. Certain polities might be more inclined to allow a participatory and inclusive process and simultaneously end up with a 'democratic' constitution. In other words, it can be argued that it is not participation or inclusion that is affecting the constitution but some characteristics of the country that foster an inclusive process and democratic constitutions. Several control variables intend to control for these features. First, I lag the dependent variables using the previous constitution. Studies have shown that constitutions are not written on a blank canvas and that for the most part, constitutions resemble their predecessors (Elkins et al. 2009, 57). The normative assumption is that countries with democratic constitutions are more likely to utilize inclusive processes when reforming their constitutions and end up with a new democratic document. Several democratic backsliding cases, however, contradict this prediction. Take, for example, Turkey's 2017 constitutional reform process that has replaced a democratic constitution with a semi-authoritarian document whose main purpose is to extend President Erdoğan's tenure in office. In my data set, 169 constitutions have predecessors, and the remaining twenty-six cases are first constitutions in newly established states. As Table 2.6 shows, constitutions have become slightly more democratic over time. Overall, while constitutions promulgated from 1974 to 2015 have on average about five of the ten democratic provisions (first column), their predecessors have about four of those provisions (second column).

This study also controls for the level of democracy that could impact both the process of constitution-making and the content of a constitution. The *democracy* variable uses the average Polity IV democracy score for three years before the constitution promulgation. This variable ranges from –10 (strongly autocratic) to +10 (strongly democratic). The *domestic crisis* variable controls for recent major civil conflicts including revolutions, strikes, riots, and demonstrations since constitutions are often part of postwar peace-building, and this can influence the impetus for inclusiveness as well as the political stakes of public deliberation (Roeder and Rothchild 2005; Miller and Aucoin 2010). A natural log of Banks and Wilson's (2014) conflict variable is used for measuring the average domestic crisis for three years before the constitution promulgation. Next, ethnic fractionalization could impede democratization by breeding parochialism (Horowitz 1985) or facilitate it by enabling civil society mobilization (Bessinger 2008). Thus, the *ethnic division* variable controls for ethnolinguistic fractionalization using Alesina et al.'s (2003) data. This

TABLE 2.6 *Descriptive statistics of outcome variables*

Variable	Constitutions Promulgated from 1974 to 2015	Predecessors of Constitutions Promulgated from 1974 to 2015
Political Institutions Index	Mean: 1.55 SD: 0.65 N: 180	Mean: 1.42 SD: 0.73 N: 117
Rights and Freedoms Index	Mean: 3.32 SD: 1.33 N: 180	Mean: 2.31 SD: 1.19 N: 133
Transparency Index	Mean: 0.77 SD: 0.65 N: 180	Mean: 0.66 SD: 0.54 N: 117
Aggregate Democratic Content	Mean: 5.32 SD: 2.06 N: 180	Mean: 4.10 SD: 2.06 N: 133

variable ranges from 0 indicating ethnic homogeneity to 1 indicating significant fractionalization. This study also controls for *democratic* and *authoritarian transition* using the Polity IV democracy score. A five-point increase or decrease in Polity's democracy score in any year in the last three years before promulgation indicates a democratic or authoritarian transition, respectively. I also control for the level of development with a natural log of *GDP per capita*. Next, as larger countries may be less likely to democratize due to population density or other factors (Teorell 2010), a natural log of *population* variable is included. These last two variables are based on the World Bank's World Development Indicators (2013). Lastly, this study controls for time using waves of constitution-making. I do not include the year as a covariate because it assumes a linear effect of time. However, democracy and constitution-making often come in waves. In my data set, I identified two such waves. The first constitutional wave (1974–1979) resulted in 41 new constitutions, and the second wave (1990–1997) led to 69 new national constitutions. In other words, 110 constitutions in my data set of 195 constitutions were written during these waves. Two binary variables are used to control for whether the constitution was promulgated during any of these two waves.

STAGE I: MODEL SPECIFICATION AND RESULTS

Using the global data set specified previously, this section tests whether overall increased participation and/or inclusion increases the overall democratic content of constitutions, including democratic provisions pertaining to

political institutions, rights and freedoms, and transparency. Since all the
indices are ordered categories, an ordered probit model is used for all of the
outcomes. The general statistical ordered probit model is:

$$Y_i^* = \beta_1 Participation_i + \beta_2 Inclusion_i + \beta_3 Z_i + \epsilon_i, \qquad (2.1)$$

where Y^* is the latent (unobserved) dependent variable (democratic content of
constitutions). *Participation$_i$* and *Inclusion$_i$* are the main procedural features
of the constitution-writing process, and Z_i is a vector of covariates including lag
of the dependent variable (the content of previously in-force constitutions),
democracy, ethnic division, domestic crisis, authoritarian and democratic
transition, GDP per capita, population, and constitutional waves. Table 2.7
shows the results of the statistical analysis.

In all the models increased, overall participation contributes to the democratic content of constitutions, indicating that as the degree of public involvement in a constitution-making process increases, the constitution is more
likely to include provisions on democratic political institutions, various citizens' rights and freedoms, and transparent political processes. The inclusion
variable, however, shows mixed results in different models and is statistically
significant only for *Rights and Freedoms*. Among control variables, the content
of the previous constitution (*Predecessor Content*) is the most significant
predictor of the democratic content of constitutions. The results show that
countries in which the previous constitution was democratic are more likely to
adopt constitutions that secure several democratic provisions pertaining to
political institutions, citizens' rights and freedoms, and transparent political
processes. The level of democracy and ethnolinguistic fractionalization also
have a statistically significant relationship with the democratic content of
constitutions, showing that democratic or ethnically diverse countries are
more likely to adopt democratic constitutions. Lastly, the results show that
constitutions written during both constitutional waves have a negative correlation with the number of democratic provisions. For the first constitutional
wave (1974–1979), this relationship is significant for *Rights and Freedoms*,
Transparency, and *Democratic Content* outcomes. That is, constitutions
promulgated in the early years of the Third Wave of democracy have fewer
democratic provisions than other constitutions in the data set. For the second
constitutional wave (1990–1997), this relationship is slightly significant only for
the transparency outcome.

In the next step, I test the impact of participation and inclusion in
each stage of constitution-making on the democratic content of constitutions to explore whether there is a particular stage at which participation

TABLE 2.7 *The impact of participation and inclusion on the content of constitutions*

Variable	Political Institutions	Rights and Freedoms	Transparency	Democratic Content
Participation	1.01***	0.65***	0.74***	1.17***
	(0.28)	(0.23)	(0.25)	(0.21)
Inclusion	−0.29	0.28*	−0.23	−0.19
	(0.24)	(0.17)	(0.20)	(0.15)
Predecessor Content	0.36*	0.07	0.85***	0.13**
	(0.19)	(0.09)	(0.29)	(0.05)
Democracy [t-3]	−0.01	0.04*	0.00	0.04*
	(0.03)	(0.02)	(0.03)	(0.02)
Ethnic Division	0.42	0.15	1.25**	1.28***
	(0.57)	(0.43)	(0.54)	(0.42)
Domestic Crisis$_{ln}$	0.05	−0.02	0.05	0.03
	(0.05)	(0.04)	(0.05)	(0.04)
Democratic Transition	0.22	0.31	−0.10	0.06
	(0.51)	(0.23)	(0.54)	(0.31)
Authoritarian Transition	−0.57	−0.48	−0.72	0.20
	(0.57)	(0.35)	(0.67)	(0.52)
GDP per capita$_{ln}$	0.22	−0.07	−0.04	−0.19
	(0.16)	(0.12)	(0.14)	(0.12)
Population$_{ln}$	0.04	0.08	0.03	0.14**
	(0.10)	(0.07)	(0.09)	(0.07)
Constitutional Wave	−0.34	−0.74**	−0.74*	−1.02***
(1974–1979)	(0.40)	(0.29)	(0.38)	(0.31)
Constitutional Wave	−0.30	−0.14	−0.54*	−0.19
(1990–1997)	(0.35)	(0.23)	(0.30)	(0.25)
Observations	96	110	96	110

Robust standard errors are provided in parentheses. ***$p < 0.01$, **$p < 0.05$, and *$p < 0.1$.

or inclusion is the most consequential. The results from Table 2.8 show that while participation in the *origination* and *ratification* stages is statistically significant, inclusion is statistically significant only in the *origination* stage. The results indicate that participation and inclusion in the *origination* stage are more consequential for democratic constitutions than in any other stage.

The results from Tables 2.7 and 2.8 provide strong empirical support for Hypothesis 2.1, indicating that constitutions drafted via broad participatory processes are more likely to secure democratic provisions than nonparticipatory

TABLE 2.8 *The impact of different stages of participation and inclusion on the content of constitutions*

Variable	Democratic Content	Democratic Content
Participation (Origination)	0.34**	
	(0.16)	
Participation (Deliberation)	0.20	
	(0.17)	
Participation (Ratification)	0.51***	
	(0.11)	
Inclusion (Origination)		0.35*
		(0.19)
Inclusion (Deliberation)		−0.43
		(0.36)
Inclusion (Ratification)		0.39
		(0.31)
Predecessor Content	0.13**	0.11**
	(0.05)	(0.05)
Democracy [t-3]	0.03	0.04*
	(0.02)	(0.02)
Ethnic Division	1.02**	1.25***
	(0.43)	(0.43)
Domestic Crisis$_{ln}$	0.04	0.02
	(0.04)	(0.04)
Democratic Transition	−0.01	0.01
	(0.34)	(0.30)
Authoritarian Transition	0.18	−0.04
	(0.49)	(0.55)
GDP per capita$_{ln}$	−0.19	−0.15
	(0.12)	(0.11)
Population$_{ln}$	0.12*	0.14**
	(0.07)	(0.07)
Constitutional Wave (1974–1979)	−1.01***	−1.19***
	(0.31)	(0.28)
Constitutional Wave (1990–1997)	−0.25	−0.21
	(0.25)	(0.24)
Observations	110	110

Robust standard errors are provided in parentheses. ***$p < 0.01$, **$p < 0.05$, and *$p < 0.1$.

processes. The results also support Hypothesis 2.2, at least to some extent. The findings from these two tables show that while overall inclusion has a statistically significant relationship with increased rights and freedoms provisions in constitutions, inclusion in the *origination* stage of constitution-making is more consequential for the overall democratic content of constitutions. This finding supports recent studies that suggest that the *origination* stage is the most crucial stage of constitution-making for democratic outcomes (Eisenstadt et al. 2015; Fruhstorfer and Hudson 2019).

Endogeneity and Robustness Checks

The results from Table 2.7 stand several robustness analyses. First, I estimate a pared-down model using only the main predictors without any controls to see whether the results change with a larger sample. The results in Table 2.9 show that we observe the same effect for participation as in the model with covariates. That is, similar to the main estimated model in Table 2.7, while aggregate participation is correlated with the overall democratic content of constitutions, aggregate inclusion is not.

Second, I estimate the main model without the lag of the dependent variable. This chapter lags the dependent variables using the previous constitution. This, however, excludes new states from the analysis. It is empirically important to know whether such states are particularly democratic since they are unburdened by previous constitutions. Table 2.10 below shows that the results are very similar to the main model; indicating that even when we include new states in the analysis, we observe the same effects.

Next, I interact participation and inclusion and test the same model. Table 2.7 shows that participatory processes, in contrast to nonparticipatory processes, render more democratic constitutions, independent of how inclusive the process is. However, it could also happen that the positive effects of participation are contingent upon the inclusiveness of the process, and vice versa. To test this, an interaction term is added. Table 2.11 shows that the

TABLE 2.9 *Large sample model*

Variable	Democratic Content
Participation	1.07^{***}
	(0.16)
Inclusion	0.03
	(0.10)
Observations	179

Robust standard errors are provided in parentheses. $^{***}p < 0.01$, $^{**}p < 0.05$, and $^{*}p < 0.1$.

TABLE 2.10 *The impact of participation and inclusion on the content of constitutions (including new states)*

Variable	Democratic Content
Participation	1.07^{***}
	(0.18)
Inclusion	-0.06
	(0.12)
Democracy [t-3]	0.04^{***}
	(0.02)
Ethnic Division	0.45
	(0.33)
Domestic Crisis$_{ln}$	-0.02
	(0.03)
Democratic Transition	-0.25
	(0.21)
Authoritarian Transition	0.38
	(0.36)
GDP per capita$_{ln}$	-0.16^{*}
	(0.08)
Population$_{ln}$	0.10^{*}
	(0.06)
Constitutional Wave (1974–1979)	-0.54^{**}
	(0.27)
Constitutional Wave (1990–1997)	-0.28
	(0.19)
Observations	160

Robust standard errors are provided in parentheses. $^{***}p < 0.01$, $^{**}p < 0.05$, and $^{*}p < 0.1$.

interaction term is not statistically significant, indicating that the impact of participation is not contingent upon the inclusiveness of the process, and vice versa.

I also used ordinary least squares (OLS) and Poisson regressions as a robustness measure. Table 2.12 reports the results for the Democratic Content outcome, using OLS and Poisson regressions. I should, however, acknowledge one caveat as a result of applying the OLS model to the data. Since the outcome in this chapter ranges from 0 to 10 and it does not have negative values, the distribution will be positively skewed, which violates OLS's assumption of a normal distribution. It is also likely that an OLS model will produce negatively predicted values, which is theoretically impossible. Nonetheless, as one can see, the results for both OLS and Poisson

TABLE 2.11 *The impact of participation and inclusion on the content of constitutions (with interaction term)*

Variable	Democratic Content	Democratic Content
Participation	1.17***	1.05**
	(0.21)	(0.41)
Inclusion	−0.19	−0.35
	(0.15)	(0.50)
Participation X Inclusion		0.08
		(0.22)
Predecessor Content	0.13**	0.13**
	(0.05)	(0.05)
Democracy [t-3]	0.04*	0.04*
	(0.02)	(0.02)
Ethnic Division	1.28***	1.29***
	(0.42)	(0.43)
Domestic Crisis$_{In}$	0.03	0.03
	(0.04)	(0.04)
Democratic Transition	0.06	0.06
	(0.31)	(0.31)
Authoritarian Transition	0.20	0.21
	(0.52)	(0.52)
GDP per capita$_{In}$	−0.19	−0.18
	(0.12)	(0.12)
Population$_{In}$	0.14**	0.13**
	(0.07)	(0.07)
Constitutional Wave (1974–1979)	−1.02***	−1.02***
	(0.31)	(0.31)
Constitutional Wave (1990–1997)	−0.19	−0.19
	(0.25)	(0.25)
Observations	110	110

Robust standard errors are provided in parentheses. ***$p < 0.01$, **$p < 0.05$, and *$p < 0.1$.

models are not significantly different from the main model, pointing to the robustness of the empirical findings.

The results from Table 2.7 and the additional statistical analyses presented above show that public participation and the content of previous constitutions are the only statistically significant predictors of the democratic content of constitutions in all models. It can be argued, however, that the same factors that propel society to adopt more participation or inclusion in a constitutional process may lead to more democratic provisions in the constitution itself. One of these important factors is the country's level of democracy. More

TABLE 2.12 *The impact of participation and inclusion on the content of constitutions (OLS and Poisson models)*

Variable	(OLS) Democratic Content	(Poisson) Democratic Content
Participation	1.57***	0.29***
	(0.28)	(0.05)
Inclusion	−0.20	−0.04
	(0.20)	(0.03)
Predecessor Content	0.18**	0.03**
	(0.08)	(0.01)
Democracy [t-3]	0.04	0.01
	(0.03)	(0.01)
Ethnic Division	1.50**	0.27**
	(0.63)	(0.12)
Domestic Crisis$_{ln}$	0.03	0.01
	(0.06)	(0.01)
Democratic Transition	0.14	0.04
	(0.46)	(0.08)
Authoritarian Transition	0.06	0.00
	(0.76)	(0.12)
GDP per capita$_{ln}$	−0.23	−0.04
	(0.19)	(0.03)
Population$_{ln}$	0.19*	0.03*
	(0.10)	(0.02)
Constitutional Wave (1974–1979)	−1.42***	−0.31***
	(0.49)	(0.11)
Constitutional Wave (1990–1997)	−0.13	−0.03
	(0.36)	(0.06)
Constant	0.16	0.72
	(2.52)	(0.47)
Observations	110	110

Robust standard errors are provided in parentheses. ***$p < 0.01$, **$p < 0.05$, and *$p < 0.1$.

democratic countries, with already democratic constitutions, are more likely to have participatory and inclusive processes and write more democratic constitutions. While this is true in many cases, several robustness checks show that the results are not driven by levels of democracy. To clarify the relation between the constitutional process and democratic content of the constitution, I first split the data into democratic and authoritarian regimes, estimating whether increased participation and/or inclusion in either regime

TABLE 2.13 *Participation, inclusion, and content of constitutions in democracies and dictatorships*

Variable	Democratic Content Autocracies	Democratic Content Democracies
Participation	1.09***	2.40***
	(0.23)	(0.73)
Inclusion	−0.04	−0.78*
	(0.18)	(0.44)
Predecessor Content	0.12*	0.18
	(0.06)	(0.13)
Ethnic Division	1.16***	2.94***
	(0.43)	(1.10)
Domestic Crisis$_{ln}$	−0.00	0.11
	(0.04)	(0.08)
Democratic Transition	0.44	−0.47
	(0.48)	(0.49)
Authoritarian Transition	0.25	−1.13**
	(0.64)	(0.48)
GDP per capita$_{ln}$	0.02	−0.77***
	(0.14)	(0.27)
Population$_{ln}$	0.18**	−0.09
	(0.08)	(0.14)
Constitutional Wave (1974–1979)	−0.92***	−2.51***
	(0.35)	(0.96)
Constitutional Wave (1990–1997)	−0.05	−0.88**
	(0.30)	(0.45)
Observations	79	32

Robust standard errors are provided in parentheses. ***$p < 0.01$, **$p < 0.05$, and *$p < 0.1$.

type increases the overall democratic content of constitutions.[13] If the results are driven by the level of democracy, we would not expect participation to be a significant predictor of democratic content of constitutions in dictatorships.

The results in Table 2.13 show that regardless of the regime type, participation remains a significant predictor of the democratic content of constitutions. In both democracies and nondemocracies, citizen participation has a positive

[13] The measure for regime type variable is based on Cheibub, Gandhi, and Vreeland's Democracy-Dictatorship index (2010).

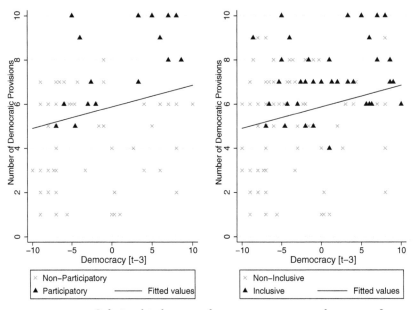

FIGURE 2.3 Relationship between democracy, process, and content of
constitutions

and significant correlation with the number of democratic provisions in
constitutions. Similarly, as Table 2.13 shows, there is a positive and slightly
significant relationship between the content of previous constitutions and the
number of democratic provisions only in autocracies.

Table 2.13 shows that despite the normative assumption, the level of
democracy is not a strong predictor of the content of constitutions.
Figure 2.3 also points to the same conclusion. The graphs show that the
most authoritarian countries (score of –10 in Polity IV index) on average
have 5 (out of 10) democratic constitutional provisions, while the most
democratic states (score of +10 in Polity IV index) on average have 7
democratic constitutional provisions. In other words, moving from –10 to
+10 on the Polity scale results in only a 20 percent increase in democratic
provisions of a given constitution. It also shows that constitutions drafted
with participatory or inclusive processes have more democratic provisions
than those with nonparticipatory or noninclusive processes, regardless of
their pre-implementation level of democracy.

Lastly, I use changes in the content of the constitution as the dependent
variable. The *Content Change* is an ordered categorical variable that indicates

TABLE 2.14 *Participation, inclusion, and change in the content of constitutions*

Variable	Democratic Content Change
Participation	0.56***
	(0.17)
Inclusion	0.06
	(0.14)
Democracy [t-3]	0.00
	(0.02)
Ethnic Division	−0.06
	(0.33)
Domestic Crisis$_{ln}$	−0.03
	(0.03)
Democratic Transition	0.12
	(0.25)
Authoritarian Transition	0.19
	(0.47)
GDP per capita$_{ln}$	0.01
	(0.08)
Population$_{ln}$	−0.02
	(0.06)
Constitutional Wave (1974–1979)	0.04
	(0.25)
Constitutional Wave (1990–1997)	0.24
	(0.18)
Observations	158

Robust standard errors are provided in parentheses. ***$p < 0.01$, **$p < 0.05$, and *$p < 0.1$.

whether the constitution has more, less, or a similar number of democratic provisions, compared to its predecessor. Table 2.14 shows the results for the impact of constitutional processes on change in the democratic content of constitutions. The results are similar to all other models, showing a positive and significant relationship between participation and change in the democratic content of constitutions. In other words, participatory processes are more likely to result in increased number of democratic provisions.

These statistical results cannot completely insulate the findings from the problem of endogeneity. I acknowledge that endogeneity exists and that the estimates are likely to be biased. However, the robustness tests suggest that such biases are unlikely to be large. In many societies, the level of democracy is an important predictor of both procedural features of constitution writing and the democratic content of constitution. The robustness tests, however, show that plausible alternative explanations such as level of democracy cannot systematically explain all the empirical findings and that regardless of regime type and level of democracy, increased participation in constitution-making processes is associated with more democratic provisions.

In sum, the results from the first section offer strong empirical evidence that participatory constitutions are more democratic in content than constitutions made with limited or no public input. This finding speaks to the democratic theory by offering empirical evidence that public participation in constitution-making processes can help ensure democratic constitutions. The statistical analysis also demonstrates that while, at the aggregate level, inclusion is a statistically significant predictor only of the number of constitutional provisions related to rights and freedoms, the inclusion of different groups and interests in the *origination* stage is statistically important for the overall democratic content of constitutions. Next, I evaluate this relationship particularly in the region.

STAGE II: EVIDENCE FROM THE MIDDLE EAST

To further examine the relationship between the process and democratic content of constitutions in the context of the MENA, I constructed an original data set of all constitutional changes in the region (including amendments) from 1861 when Tunisia adopted the region's first modern constitutions to 2020.[14] The data set comprises about 1,500 country-year observations.[15] Since 1861, 217 constitutional events occurred across twenty-three countries in the region. As Figure 2.4 shows, the majority of constitutional events in the region were amendments (129 events). During the same period, forty-nine new constitutions and thirty-two interim constitutions were adopted, while six constitutions were reinstated after being suspended for a while.

I constructed the same main variables that were used in the first step of the empirical analysis. The outcome is the democratic content of constitutions, which is based on the variables specified in Table 2.5. The main predictors, participation and inclusion, were also coded based on the criteria specified in

---

[14]   I used the CCP database (Elkins et al. 2014a) and Brown (2002) to construct this data set.
[15]   While the empirical analysis in the first stage was based on a "constitution" data (with 195 observations), here, I use "country-year" data (with 1,484 observations).

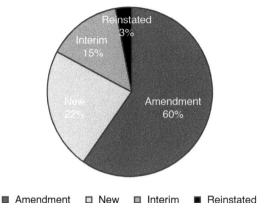

FIGURE 2.4 Constitutional events in the Middle East and North Africa, 1861–2020

Tables 2.1 and 2.2, respectively.[16] Next, I estimated an ordered probit model similar to the base model specified in the first stage of the empirical analysis.

As Table 2.15 shows, the results from the regional analysis confirm the findings from the global data. Both Participation and Inclusion variables have a positive and statistically significant relationship with the Democratic Content of Constitutions in the region. There is also a positive and statistically significant correlation between levels of democracy and the democratic content of constitutions. In general, the empirical evidence from the MENA is very similar to those from across the world.

In sum, evidence from MENA further confirms the robust empirical findings from across the world. Overall, the cross-national statistical analyses lend strong empirical support for the participation and inclusion hypotheses. That is, participatory and inclusive constitution-making processes are more likely to yield democratic constitutional parchments than nonparticipatory or noninclusive processes.

CONCLUSION: PARTICIPATION, INCLUSION, AND DEMOCRATIC CONSTITUTIONS

Among 195 constitutions adopted between 1974 and 2015, at least 70 percent have incorporated some degree of public input, showing a global trend in

---

[16] Similar to the case in the global analysis, two coders coded the process of all constitutional events in the region, and a third coder coded only the cases where the first two coders differed (12 percent of the cases). Coders consulted the same sources used in the global analysis.

TABLE 2.15 *Participation, inclusion, and the democratic content of constitutions in MENA*

Variable	Democratic Content
Participation	0.74^{***}
	(0.07)
Inclusion	0.09^{**}
	(0.04)
Democracy	0.09^{***}
	(0.01)
Domestic Crisis	0.00^{**}
	(0.00)
GDP per capita$_{ln}$	-0.10^{*}
	(0.06)
Population$_{ln}$	0.04
	(0.06)
Year	0.01
	(0.01)
Observations	540

Robust standard errors are provided in parentheses.
$^{***}p < 0.01$, $^{**}p < 0.05$, and $^{*}p < 0.1$.

participatory and inclusive constitution-making processes. The MENA shows a similar trend with over 52 percent of constitutional changes during the same period incorporating some form of public input. Theories of participatory democracy suggest that citizen participation is a necessary condition for democratically legitimate political processes and that all citizens and societal groups should be given an equal opportunity to participate and influence the outcome (Pateman 2012). Skepticism, however, remains as to the extent to which these participatory and inclusive processes are important for the democratic content of constitutions. Using original measures of participation and inclusion in 195 constitution-making processes from across the world from 1974 to 2015 and in all MENA constitutional changes from 1861 to 2020, this study shows that increased public participation and group inclusion can improve the democratic content of constitutions.

More specifically, the statistical analysis in this chapter points to two major findings. First, there is strong evidence that overall increased participation in constitution-making processes is associated with improvements in the democratic content of constitutions. This, however, does not mean that participation improves every single provision in the constitution or that all participatory processes are successful in generating democratic constitutions. Rather, public participation, in general, is more likely to generate a democratic outcome. Second, evidence from across the world shows that while the overall inclusiveness of the process is a significant predictor of only rights and freedoms in the constitution, inclusion in the *origination* stage of the constitution-making process is a statistically significant predictor of the overall democratic content of constitutions. In other words, the inclusion of different societal groups and interests early on in the process is more likely to yield constitutions that can resolve the social and political challenges within society. Moreover, evidence from the MENA indicates that inclusion is in fact a statistically significant predictor of the democratic content of constitutions across the region. A few cases illustrate these two conclusions.

Colombia (1991) and Tunisia (2014) are both examples of participatory and inclusive processes leading to more democratic constitutions. After the assassination of Colombian presidential candidate Luis Carlos Galán in 1989, which resulted in a students' movement calling for a referendum "for peace and democracy," a constituent assembly election was held in December 1990 after a national plebiscite on the assembly itself, in which the public overwhelmingly supported the election of a constituent assembly. After the plebiscite, the Supreme Court ruled that the assembly could not be limited in its scope and capacity. Although some major insurgents like the Revolutionary Armed Force of Colombia and the National Liberation Army were excluded, the demilitarized April 19 Movement (M-19) leftist insurgents were able to participate and won 19 (out of 70) seats in the constituent assembly. The constituent assembly was by far more inclusionary than earlier national pacts since the 1958 pact, which divided rule among the two conservative political parties, to the exclusion of the left (Eisenstadt et al. 2017a). This inclusionary process, which accompanied active public participation, resulted in significant improvements in the democratic content of the Colombian constitution. The 2014 Constitution of Tunisia is a more recent example of a participatory and inclusive constitution-making process yielding significant democratic improvements. The constitutional renovation process in Tunisia started as an inclusive process where elected representatives, reflecting the public will and interests, were tasked with drafting a new constitution. However, political conflict and mistrust among different groups soon engulfed the process, and intervention by civil society organizations, most notably the National Dialogue Quartet, led to a more inclusive and participatory process, which yielded a constitution highly regarded as the most progressive constitution in the Arab world.

While participation led to more democratic constitutions in Colombia and Tunisia, it did not have a positive impact on the democratic content of the

Egyptian and Ecuadorian constitutions. The 2012 Constitution of Egypt was drafted through a mass participatory process but without political inclusiveness and fair and equal representation. More than 100,000 Egyptians enthusiastically participated in a process that was viewed as unfair, corrupt, and illegal by most non-Islamists. Public participation in Egypt did not result in a democratic outcome, mostly because public demands were not channelled through an inclusive constituent assembly. Although youth movements, unions, syndicates, and religious organizations were officially represented in the Constituent Assembly (CA), the Muslim Brotherhood (which had the majority of the seats in the CA) did not try to reach out to them during the constitutional bargain, and these societal groups were eventually forced to boycott the CA in a desperate effort to prevent the ratification of a unilateral constitution. The result of this noninclusive process was a constitution that was viewed as unfair and undemocratic by millions of Egyptians and aggravated a situation that led to a military coup and the revocation of the constitution only six months after its promulgation (Maboudi and Nadi 2016). Similar to Egypt, in Ecuador's constitutional reform process of 2008, public participation played only a "window-dressing" function. Although the constituent assembly was directly elected by citizens after a public referendum on the issue in 2007, President Rafael Correa managed the elections, and his PAIS (Proud and Sovereign Fatherland) Alliance won 74 of the 130 seats giving Correa the power to write his constitution. Although this participatory process resulted in a highly popular constitution at the time, it failed to improve the democratic outlook of the country.

As these cases demonstrate, not all participatory or inclusive processes result in successful democratic transitions or democratic constitutions. The cross-national analysis presented in this chapter shows a broad global trend that is generalizable to most but not all cases. It suggests that participatory and inclusive processes improve the democratic content of constitutions. The next chapter will take this analysis a step further in two ways. First, it will establish a direct link between participation and inclusion and the democratic content of constitutions through a content analysis of public deliberation input and content of draft constitutions in the case of Tunisia. Second, it will establish a causal link between the constitutional process and successful democratic transition in Tunisia by focusing on the role of a strong and independent civil society in steering constitutional debates, shaping the content of the constitution, and facilitating transitional negotiations.

3

Constitutional Negotiations and the Pathway to Democratic Transition

The Case of Tunisia

In January 2014, Tunisia ratified the most progressive constitution in the Arab world, receiving global praise including a Nobel Peace Prize. As John Kerry, the US Secretary of State, commented, the Tunisian constitution is a model for democratic political reforms in the Arab world (see Gordon 2014). The constitution itself was the result of months of negotiations and a remarkably inclusive process, which included several national dialogues with citizens, civil associations, and different political groups, as well as several constitutional workshops and conferences, and even online crowdsourcing for constitutional proposals.

The Tunisian path to democracy, however, was not without obstacles. Political cleavages, terrorist attacks by Islamists militias, and political assassinations posed serious threats to the democratic transition in the country. While political division and polarization were not as severe as it was in other countries such as Egypt, political standoffs during the transition period impeded negotiations several times. When Chokri Belaid, a left-wing opposition leader, was assassinated by militant Islamists in February 2013, the opposition blamed the moderate Islamist Ennahda party, the de facto ruling party during the transition. And when the NCA published the June 2013 draft constitution, which was not as progressive and inclusive as many had hoped, public pressure mounted with tens of thousands of people protesting against several constitutional articles and clauses for several months. The political turmoil reached its peak with the assassination of Mohamed Brahimi, an opposition political leader and founder of the left-wing People's Movement, on July 25 of that year. With the boycotts from several opposition members of the NCA in response to the draft constitution and the political assassinations and the temporary suspension of all legislative activities by Ben Jaâfar, the NCA's president, Tunisia's transition seemed to have faced a gridlock. The country, however, miraculously came out of this gridlock, standing out among all Arab "falls" and "winters" (Lesch 2011; Tétreault 2011; Davenport 2012; Prashad 2012; Wiarda 2012; Bernstein 2014) as the only country with a successful democratic transition (Allinson 2015; Szmolka 2015; Zoubir 2015). How could Tunisia manage its political turmoil and find a pathway to democratization in an exceptionally authoritarian region?[1]

Indeed, Ennahda and the secular liberals were long engaged in bargaining and negotiations. In fact, they had started dialogues to develop a mutual understanding eight years before the fall of Ben Ali (Stepan and Linz 2013, 23). Moreover, Ennahda's major constitutional concessions including withdrawing their pursuit of including Sharia as a source of legislation, accepting a semi-presidential system, and replacing a "complementary" role for women with "equality" had already been made before the mid-2013 crisis (Pickard 2012; Netterstrøm 2015). Nevertheless, ideological divisions and mistrust persisted among different political factions, leading to the mid-2013 political crisis. It was then that the National Dialogue Quartet stepped in and salvaged the transition. Tunisia weathered the political turmoil and successfully moved toward a relatively peaceful democratic transition because of the key role that the Quartet and other civil groups played in the constitutional negotiations.

This chapter seeks to explain Tunisia's successful pathway to constitution-making and democracy-building by examining the three theoretical propositions outlined in Chapter 1. More specifically, it explains (1) how an inclusive and participatory process led to a democratic constitution, (2) how a strong and independent civil society facilitated political compromises and constructive negotiations and created a public sphere for constitutional debates through a participatory and inclusive process, and (3) how the outcome of this process (i.e., the constitution) contributed to establishing democracy.

This chapter proceeds with an overview of the transitional and constitution-making process in Tunisia. Next, I discuss participation and inclusion in the Tunisian constitutional reform process. Recall from Chapter 2 that statistical analysis shows a significant relationship between participation and inclusion and the number of rights and freedoms in constitutions. This finding is examined against the case of Tunisia, and the empirical results show that as expected, public proposals related to rights and freedoms are more likely to be considered in the constitutional drafting process. The analysis in this chapter shows that 43 percent of Tunisian public proposals for the constitution were included in the adopted constitution, indicating that the process significantly improved the democratic content of the constitution. Next, I examine the

---

[1] See Bellin (2004) for authoritarian exceptionalism in the Middle East.

role of civil society in facilitating democratic negotiations. I also review the conditions that paved the way for civil associations to fulfill this crucial role. Finally, this chapter concludes with how the outcome of this process was a constitution that facilitated democratic transition in the country.

THE TUNISIAN TRANSITION

The fall of Ben Ali's regime happened very quickly, surprising the most domestic and international audience. Ten days after Mohamed Bouazizi set himself on fire on December 17, 2010, protests spread to the capital city of Tunis. Only then, President Ben Ali realized the severity of the problem and paid a visit to Bouazizi in the hospital. Bouazizi, however, died on January 4, 2011, and with his death, the protests heightened. On January 13, Rachid Ammar, the chief of staff of the Tunisian Armed Forces, refused to follow orders from Ben Ali to use lethal means to put down the protests by allegedly responding, "Agree to deploy the soldiers, to calm the situation, but the army does not shoot at the people" (Ghorbal 2016). The next day, Ben Ali and his family fled to Saudi Arabia, transferring the authority to his prime minister, Mohamed Ghannouchi.

Shortly after Ben Ali's departure, Mohamed Ghannouchi declared himself president. But a few hours later, the Constitutional Council, under Article 57 of the constitution, officially appointed Fouad Mebazaa, the head of the lower house of the parliament, as acting president. A presidential election was scheduled for sixty days later. The Tunisian public, however, staged two demonstrations on January 23, demanding the departure of Prime Minister Ghannouchi (who eventually resigned a month later), and on February 20, demanding the formation of a new constituent assembly. Demonstrations did not stop until all former allies of Ben Ali resigned and his ruling party, the Constitutional Democratic Rally, was dissolved on March 9 of that year (Kellner 2016, 49). A few days later, the High Council for the Realization of the Goals of the Revolution, Political Reforms, and Democratic Transition (the High Council) was formed. The High Council was created from the merger of the *Conseil de défense de la révolution* and the short-lived Higher Political Reform Commission and was presided by Yadh Ben Achour, a veteran lawyer. It had 155 members including representatives from 12 political parties, 18 CSOs, and public figures and acted as the transitional authority until its dissolution on October 13, 2011, a few days before the NCA elections (Ottaway 2011).

The NCA election was initially scheduled for July 24, 2011. Despite concerns about delaying the election, most parties ultimately agreed to

TABLE 3.1 *Major parties represented in the NCA, 2011 (total seats 217)*

Party Stream	NCA Seats (%)	Political Base
Ennahda Movement	41	Moderate Islamist
El Mottamar (CPR)	13.4	Center-left; secular
Aridha Shaabia	12.4	Populist
Ettakatol (FDTL)	9.2	Center-left; secular
PDP	7.4	Center-right; secular
PDM	2.3	A coalition of four centrist and leftist parties
Afek Tounes	1.8	Right; secular
El Moubadra	1.8	Centrist
Independent lists	3.7	–
Minor parties	6.9	–

postpone the election. Eventually, on October 23, 2011, the Tunisian public went to the polls (for the first and only time during the four-year transitional period) to vote for their constituent assembly representatives. With about 52 percent voter turnout, the moderate Islamist Ennahda won a plurality by securing eighty-nine seats (see Table 3.1). The NCA had 217 members, and it was responsible for building three major political institutions: First, the NCA was acting as an interim parliament entitled to all legislative power; it was also responsible for either installing a new government or extending the current one's term until the scheduled presidential elections in 2014; and finally, it was tasked with writing a new constitution. After the elections, a ruling coalition (known as Troika) was formed among Ennahda, El Mottamar (CPR), and Ettakatol, which formed a majority in all three bodies of the NCA. After the formation of the Troika, Hamadi Jebali (secretary-general of Ennahda) was named the Prime Minister, Moncef Marzouki (founder and leader of CPR) the President of the Republic, and Mustapha Ben Jaâfar (secretary-general of Ettakatol) the President of the NCA.

The NCA was initially given a deadline of one year to write a constitution, a process that, although required more time and concessions than what political parties anticipated, proved to be exceptional in the Arab world.

The Framework for the Constitution-Making Process

The Tunisian constitutional history is unique in a region, which is often described as "unconstitutional" (Brown 2002). The ancient Carthage constitution, which Aristotle describes in some detail in his *Politics*, dates back to as early as 400 BC (Aristotle 2013 (c. 350 BCE)).[2] Tunisia was also the first modern Arab state to have a written constitution. The *Qanun Al-Dawla Al-Tunisiyya* (Law of the Tunisian State) was adopted in 1861 and was in force for only three years when a rebellion against the constitution and tax increase forced Mohammed El-Sadik Bey, the governor of Tunisia, to suspend it in April 1864 (Brown 2002). Exactly one and half centuries after the suspension of the Arab world's first written constitution, the most progressive Arab constitution was adopted in Tunisia. Unlike the 1861 constitution, which was implemented by a decree, the 2014 Magna Carta was the cornerstone of a broader democratic transition process, which started with the first democratic elections in the country.

The first step in the constitution-making process, after the NCA election, was the drafting of an interim constitution on December 10, 2011, following which the NCA adopted the Rules of Procedure on January 20, 2012.[3] The Rules of Procedure, while emphasizing accountability and transparency, did not require direct citizen participation in the constitutional process. Rule 59 allowed constitutional committee members to "seek advice" from any person or organization that could help draft the constitution but not necessarily from the general public. Initially, most representatives – *à la* Jon Elster's (2012) "hourglass model" – shared the view that since they were directly elected by a popular vote, they did not need to include citizens to legitimize the constitution. The Rules of Procedure also required a two-thirds supermajority threshold for ratifying the constitution in the NCA. A public referendum was to be held only if the NCA approved the draft constitution with a simple majority and not a two-thirds majority. This representative model of constitution-making, however, evolved into a participatory and inclusive model as the conflict unfolded in the NCA.

A few days after the adoption of the Rules of Procedure, the NCA started the process of drafting the constitution by first electing 131 members assigned to draft the constitution (on February 1, 2012) and then appointing the elected members to six constitutional committees. The 131 constitution drafters did not assume any legislative power, thus separating the legislative and constitution-making tasks and preventing a potential conflict of "institutional" interests. However, all 217 representatives were able to vote on the final drafts prepared by the six constitutional committees. Each of the six committees consisted of twenty-two members, and each was responsible for drafting one or

---

[2] Modern Tunisia is built on the ruins of ancient Carthage.
[3] Also known as the Assembly's bylaws or *règlements*.

TABLE 3.2 *Constitutional committees of the NCA*

Committee Name	Committee Chair	Political Composition*
Preamble, General Principles, and Constitution Amendment	Sahbi Atiq (Ennahda)	Ennahda (9), Independent (5), Ettakatol (2), Democratic Transition (2), CPR (1), Democratic Bloc (1), Democratic Alliance (1), and Wafa Movement (1)
Rights and Liberties	Farida Abidi (Ennahda)	Ennahda (9), Independent (5), Democratic Transition (3), Democratic Bloc (3), and Wafa Movement (2)
Executive and Legislative	Omar Al-Shatwi (CPR)	Ennahda (9), Independent (5), CPR (3), Democratic Bloc (3), Democratic Transition (1), and Wafa Movement (1)
Judicial, Administrative, Financial, and Constitutional Justice	Mohamed Larbi Fadhel Moussa (Democratic Bloc)	Ennahda (9), Independent (6), Wafa Movement (3), Democratic Transition (1), Democratic Bloc (1), and Democratic Alliance (1)
Constitutional Bodies	Jamel Touir (Ettakatol)	Ennahda (9), Independent (6), Ettakatol (2), Democratic Bloc (2), CPR (1), Democratic Alliance (1), and Wafa Movement (1)
Public, Regional, and Local Institutions	Imad Al-Hammami (Ennahda)	Ennahda (9), Independent (3), Democratic Transition (3), Democratic Alliance (2), Ettakatol (2), CPR (1), Democratic Bloc (1), and Wafa Movement (1)

* Names of some major parties and blocs are different from Table 3.1 because several parties either changed names or joined alliances after the NCA was formed.

more chapters of the constitution.[4] These constitutional committees were also working closely with the Joint Committee for Coordinating and Drafting, which was formed by the president of the NCA and the chairs of the six committees and was responsible for putting the suggested articles in a comprehensive draft (Jamal and Kensincki 2016, 33).

[4] Only the Committee of Justice, Administrative, Financial, and Constitutional Judiciary had twenty-one members.

As Table 3.2 shows, Ennahda dominated the constitutional drafting process with 41 percent of the seats (54 out of 131), in addition to chairing half of the committees. This gave Ennahda a great advantage over controlling the agenda in the constitutional committees. It was also a major source of contention as opposition parties often protested Ennahda's unilateral decisions in adding, removing, or modifying important constitutional provisions.

Eventually, the NCA published the first constitution draft on August 14, 2012, which the opposition parties in the NCA contested fiercely. This was a very rough draft, with several provisions having multiple alternative versions to choose from. One month later, the NCA invited the representatives of CSOs for an open debate and brainstorming on this initial draft. Representatives of more than 300 civil associations participated in this debate, which took place on September 14–15. Taking the suggestions of CSOs into consideration, constitutional committees revised the first draft and published a second draft on December 14 of that year. Immediately after the second draft, the Ennahda-led majority in the NCA decided to expand Rule 59 of the NCA's bylaws and open the process to the general public, a decision which proved to be very consequential for the constitution and the broader democratization process in the country.

THE CONSTITUTIONAL NEGOTIATION PROCESS: PARTICIPATION, INCLUSION, AND COMPROMISE

Ennahda's decision to pursue public participation through a national dialogue with citizens was not sudden or random. It was a calculated move, albeit with some unintended consequences for the party. One of the outcomes of the deliberation sessions with civil associations in September 2012 was that several provisions proposed by Ennahda were changed in the December 2012 draft (Rabeh Khraifi [member of the Republican Party and the NCA], interview by author, January 15, 2015). Fearing that the majority of CSOs have liberal tendencies, Ennahda decided to counterbalance proposals by civil associations with the general public opinion, which they assumed would be more in line with their ideology. A prominent Ennahda member justified the move to open up the process by arguing that "civil society is not representative of all the people; therefore, for constitutional issues, general public engagement is necessary because the majority of people do not find themselves represented in associations and organizations" (Badreldin Abdelkafi [member of Ennahda and assistant to the president of the NCA], interview by author, January 22, 2015).

Initially, opposition parties were reluctant and skeptical about public inclusion in the writing of the constitution, even accusing Ennahda of populism (Badreldin Abdelkafi, interview by author, January 22, 2015). Lack of public outreach and insufficient communication and publicity about the national dialogue by political parties and CSOs resulted in a low public turnout in the first few sessions. Very soon, however, as the opposition parties became aware that the mobilization of the electorate and solicitation of public comments would directly impact the constitutional process, they began to encourage their supporters to attend these meetings (The Carter Center 2014, 70). This political mobilization yielded higher public participation from supporters of different groups in the later sessions. The opposition parties specifically recognized the merits of public participation for balancing the power of Ennahda, despite their initial skepticism. According to a prominent opposition leader, Ennahda wanted to impose its views on the constitution, but as they faced increasing opposition from citizens, they realized they were going to lose their electoral support; hence, they revised their position on several controversial issues (Samir Taïeb [secretary-general of Al-Masaar party and member of the NCA], interview by author, January 20, 2015).

The national dialogue with citizens consisted of forty-four meetings in Tunisia and abroad where people could meet with representatives from the six constitutional committees. There were no criteria for participation, but attendants were required to register in advance. Overall, about 5,000 people participated, providing more than 2,500 suggestions for the constitution. More than two-thirds of these suggestions were related to General Principles of the constitution and rights and freedoms and were submitted to the first two constitutional committees. Of the forty-four meetings where most of these proposals were submitted, twenty-six were held in Tunisia (including twenty-four meetings in twenty-four governorates and two regional symposia with students in Tunis and Sfax), and eighteen were held in different parts of Italy and France where three-fourths of all Tunisian diaspora live.

Although participants were representative of different political ideologies and interests in the society, women, and youth were particularly underrepresented (UNDP 2013b; The Carter Center 2014). For example, only 10–30 percent of the participants in different meetings were women (The Carter Center 2014, 70). Most participants were informed and concerned citizens, and the suggestions they provided reflected different political and ideological interests across the society. While members of different CSOs participated in these public fora (The Carter Center 2014, 72–74), they mostly tried to shape the constitutional discussion through a broader range of platforms including roundtables and conferences where they invited experts, NCA members, and citizens to debate issues in the constitution (Zied Boussen [member of Democracy Reporting International], interview by author, January 19, 2015).

During the national dialogue meetings, the majority of public suggestions were offered orally with the NCA staff members recording them, albeit on many occasions, participants delivered written proposals to the staff. The average number of citizens who participated in these meetings was 113, with some meetings hosting more than 300 citizens, while others had fewer than 15 citizens in attendance. Notwithstanding the low number of participants, the meetings helped inform the NCA of the public's concerns about the constitution.

Following the national dialogue meetings, the assistant to the president of the Assembly for Relations with Citizens and Civil Society drafted a report on the collected public suggestions. Next, the general rapporteur of the NCA's Constitution Drafting Committee (CDC) tasked the six constitutional committees with taking those comments and suggestions into consideration to write the third draft constitution (April 2013). Deputies of each constitutional committee only reviewed public suggestions related to their specific topic of interest through four separate documents. Three of these documents listed all the "raw" suggestions submitted in separate meetings with the Tunisian public, diaspora, and CSOs, and the fourth document reported the "most recurring" public suggestions related to that specific committee in all various meetings. The purpose of this last document was to ensure deputies would reasonably act on the popularity of public suggestions. In all four documents, the identity of individuals making suggestions was anonymous, and the documents did not specify from which meeting the proposal originated. Deputies, as such, could not act on subnational-level interests by weighting public proposals from their own strongholds.

In general, while Tunisians living in the country and abroad had a consensus over issues such as gender equality, role of religion, human rights, and liberties, there were several other issues that divided them. For example, while political asylum, rights of the Tunisian diaspora, global warming, and protection of national heritage were of primary concern for Tunisians in Italy and France, those living in Tunisia were more concerned about education, clean water, rights of the opposition, and other related issues (UNDP 2013a; Fliegelman 2016). These public proposals to some extent reflected the contentious political debates and divisions in the Tunisian society. Some of the most fiercely debated issues in the NCA including Sharia-based legislation, religion of the state, civility of the state, criminalization of blasphemy, and rejection of Zionism were also among the prominent issues raised in the public proposals. However, the issue of the parliamentary or presidential system, which was fiercely fought over by most political parties including Ennahda (Marks 2014, 26), was not a prominent subject for the participants, which further indicates that political parties did not systematically influence public suggestions.

All the evidence indicates that the participatory and inclusive process in Tunisia was genuine – unlike most other window-dressing processes across the region – and that the NCA had all the intentions to incorporate as much feedback they received from civil associations and the general public as they could without adversely affecting the political negotiations and agreements among different political factions. The question then becomes how much of the public input was reflected in the constitution, considering the inevitable political bargaining in the NCA.

Does the Process Matter for the Content of Constitutions?

Recall from the previous chapter that robust empirical evidence from across the world shows that participatory processes are more likely to yield democratic constitutions. The results from Chapter 2 particularly show that both participation and inclusion increase the number of constitutional provisions pertaining to political, individual, and collective rights and freedoms. The direct link between public feedback and the content of constitutions, however, is not clear. In other words, to what extent does public input affect the content of the constitution? Are particular public proposals more likely to be incorporated in the constitution than other proposals? Building on the previous chapter and the extant literature, I propose the following hypotheses:

H 3.1: *Public proposals with higher popularity are more likely to become constitutional provisions than those with lower popularity.*

H 3.2: *Public proposals related to General Principles are more likely to become constitutional provisions compared to other public suggestions.*

H 3.3: *Public proposals related to Rights and Liberties are more likely to become constitutional provisions compared to other public suggestions.*

The first hypothesis speaks to the median voter theorem (Downs 1957). More specifically, just as the median voter theorem predicts that radical candidates or parties rarely get elected, radical public proposals rarely get into the constitution. More often than not, policy preferences of office-seeking elites (here, NCA representatives) tend to reflect those of the majority in the society. Furthermore, when a large segment of society makes a constitutional demand in a transparent process, public pressure can positively affect the probability of its inclusion in the parchment. However, the popularity of citizen proposals alone does not determine whether they have a higher probability of inclusion in the constitution. The subject of proposals also matters for several reasons. As discussed previously, more than two-thirds of public proposals in Tunisia were related to the preamble, the General Principles, and Rights and Freedoms chapters. This is because the majority of people's concerns are related to the issues that affect their daily lives, such as those related to rights and freedoms and basic principles of the state covered in these chapters of the constitution. Additionally, these are the least technical chapters, compared to other chapters that are mostly related to the division of power, bureaucracy of state institutions, and other legal issues, which are not easily comprehensible for many people.

To test these hypotheses, I use a statistical analysis of public feedback during the national dialogue and the text of constitution drafts. The outcome of interest here is whether public suggestions were included as provisions in the constitution. Three draft constitutions were written following the national dialogue with citizens and CSOs, including the adopted constitution. The three dependent variables correspond to these three different versions of the constitution. Given that these three drafts are sequential in time, it is imperative to estimate the durability of public proposal admission into the constitution by measuring whether a proposal was incorporated into the third draft (April 2013) that immediately followed the national dialogue, continued into the fourth draft (June 2013), and eventually became a provision in the final draft (January 2014) of the constitution. As such, I created three dependent variables; each coded 0 if the suggestion is not included in that draft of the constitution and 1 if it is incorporated into the draft.

In total, Tunisian citizens provided over 2,500 suggestions for the constitution, of which 217 were collected online and 2,148 were provided in the 44 national dialogue meetings with the general public. Another 200 proposals were collected from representatives of CSOs in a 2-day open dialogue with civil society. From these public suggestions, I dropped 213 proposals as invalid for several reasons. As discussed above, the national dialogue meetings were held after the second draft of the constitution was published; however, some of the collected suggestions were related to the first draft, where citizens requested the addition of a provision that was already added in the second draft or deletion of a provision that was already dropped from the second draft. Other suggestions discarded as invalid included vague requests and questions, unclear suggestions, or nonconstitutional complaints. However, if a question or even a complaint had a clear implication, I included it in the data. For example, one suggestion reads, "This is a theocratic constitution aiming to create an Islamic state." While this is not precisely a suggestion, since its implication clearly is that the constitution should be more secular and that Islamic provisions in the constitution should be removed, I coded it as a valid proposal.

Next, I clustered all valid suggestions into 337 general categories, each of which is nested within one of the six constitutional topics. For example, one citizen proposed to "Change 'We the Representatives' to 'We the People' in the preamble." Another citizen wrote that "Ownership should return to the Tunisian people, and the Constitution should start with 'We the People'." Since we cannot identify the impact of each of these two proposals on the constitution independently, we should aggregate them under one category. To create these categories, I began with the reports on the "most recurring" public suggestions submitted to each of the six constitutional committees and listed each of these "most recurring" proposals as a general category. Then, I reviewed all the "raw" public suggestions to identify and create additional categories that were not listed in the "most recurring" report in order to account for all public proposals, even the least popular ones. Finally, I measured the popularity of each of the 337 general categories by counting the number of citizens who proposed them.

The main predictors are the popularity of each cluster of suggestions as well as the subject of suggestions based on their relevant constitutional committees. The *Popularity* variable measures how many people made a specific suggestion, and it ranges from 1 to 93. To reduce the effect of outliers, logged *Popularity* is used in the estimated model. I also created six binary variables for constitutional topics based on the six constitutional committees including "General Principles," "Rights and Liberties," "Executive and Legislative," "Judiciary and Independent Bodies," "Constitutional Bodies," and "Local Authority." I am specifically interested in examining whether public proposals related to General Principles (Hypothesis 3.2) and Rights and Liberties (Hypothesis 3.3) are more likely to be included in the constitution compared to proposals on other issues. As such, all other remaining topics are collectively taken as the base group. I also created binary variables to control for the origin of suggestions, that is, whether they were suggested by citizens living in *Tunisia*, *Abroad*, or both (base group in the estimated model). Since deputies reviewed two public feedback documents marked by their origin (from Tunisia or abroad), it is imperative to know if proposals suggested by only one of the two groups (compared to proposals suggested by both Tunisians and diaspora) have a higher likelihood of inclusion in constitutional drafts. The model also controls for whether the suggestion was made by the *general public*, *civil society*, or both (base group in the estimated model). Similar to the previous variable, deputies reviewed public feedback documents marked by whether they were submitted by a civil society group or the general public. Thus, I also estimate the probability of inclusion of proposals specifically suggested by one of these two groups compared to those demanded by both the general public and civil society.

One specific concern regarding the robustness of the findings is that proposals related to rights that made it into the constitution can be very generic constitutional features that are found in almost every constitution written today. In a study of the evolution of constitutional rights over six decades, Law and Versteeg (2011, 1164), for example, find a global trend of "generic rights constitutionalism," wherein an increasingly large number of constitutions possess a number of common rights. It can be argued that the "genericness" of these rights explains both why citizens proposed them and why they were included in the Tunisian constitution. To account for this, I created a control variable that counts the number of constitutions in the world that include the provision suggested by the Tunisian public. The *Generic Feature* variable is created using the CCP database, which records the characteristics of national constitutions since 1789 (Elkins et al. 2014a).[5] This variable ranges from 0 where no constitution in the world has the suggested proposal to 192 where all constitutions have that constitutional feature.

To examine the impact of public proposals on the content of the constitution, I use a logit model. Table 3.3 shows the results for the specified model. As the table shows, popular suggestions are more likely to be included in the third (April 2013) and final (January 2014) drafts of the constitution. The result for the *Popularity* variable, however, is not significant for the fourth draft (June 2013). We can see a similar trend for the *Rights and Liberties* variable, indicating that rights proposals are more likely to be included in the third and final drafts of the constitution but not in the June 2013 draft. In all models, however, the coefficient for *General Principles* is positive and significant, indicating that proposals related to this category are more likely to be included in all constitution drafts. While other coefficients are not statistically significant, it is important to note that almost all coefficients have positive signs in all three models, except for the *Abroad* variable, which has a negative sign and is statistically significant only for the June 2013 outcome. This indicates that proposals suggested only by the Tunisian diaspora are less likely to be included in the constitution. Also, the coefficient for *Civil Society* is positive overall and significant for the June 2013 draft indicating that if a proposal is suggested only by CSOs, it is more likely to be included in that constitutional draft. This can

---

[5] The *Generic Feature* variable has only 210 observations. The missing observations are mostly stylistic suggestions that could not be coded for their "genericness."

TABLE 3.3 *Probability of incorporation of public suggestions in the constitution*

VARIABLES	April 2013 Draft	June 2013 Draft	January 2014 Constitution
Popularity$_{ln}$	0.86***	0.27	0.49**
	(0.25)	(0.22)	(0.21)
General Principles	1.42***	1.22***	0.91***
	(0.43)	(0.36)	(0.35)
Rights and Liberties	1.22**	0.47	0.81**
	(0.49)	(0.44)	(0.41)
Tunisia	0.22	−0.31	0.19
	(0.46)	(0.43)	(0.42)
Abroad	−0.54	−2.21**	−0.81
	(0.88)	(1.11)	(0.75)
General Public	−0.06	0.67	0.05
	(0.50)	(0.47)	(0.44)
Civil Society	1.16	1.25*	0.49
	(0.73)	(0.66)	(0.61)
Generic Feature	−0.00	0.00	0.00
	(0.00)	(0.00)	(0.00)
Constant	−3.20***	−1.94***	−1.71**
	(0.84)	(0.74)	(0.69)
Observations	210	210	210

Standard errors are provided in parentheses. ***$p < 0.01$, **$p < 0.05$, and *$p < 0.1$

indicate that when assessing public input, the NCA weighted the proposals made by civil associations more than those suggested by the general public.

Overall, the results confirm all three hypotheses, indicating that suggestions related to General Principles and Rights and Liberties and those with higher popularity are more likely to be included in the constitution, compared to other suggestions. The magnitude of these correlations is also significant. Table 3.4 estimates the marginal effects at the means for the covariates in all three models. As this table shows, one unit increase in the popularity count of a public proposal increases the likelihood of inclusion in the final draft by 12 percent. The table also shows that if a proposal is related to *General Principles*, it has a 22 percent probability of inclusion in the final draft. Being in the *Rights and Liberties* category also increases the probability of public proposal inclusion by 20 percent. Most importantly, the data show that an impressive 43 percent of public proposals were included in the final draft of the constitution.

These results confirm the major findings of Chapter 2 that the process matters for the democratic content of constitutions. The results show that

TABLE 3.4 *Marginal effects of probability of incorporation of public suggestions in the constitution*

VARIABLES	April 2013 Draft	June 2013 Draft	January 2014 Constitution
Popularity$_{ln}$	0.17***	0.06	0.12**
	(0.05)	(0.05)	(0.05)
General Principles	0.28***	0.29***	0.22***
	(0.08)	(0.08)	(0.09)
Rights and Liberties	0.24**	0.11	0.20**
	(0.09)	(0.10)	(0.10)
Tunisia	0.04	-0.07	0.05
	(0.09)	(0.10)	(0.10)
Abroad	-0.09	-0.37***	-0.18
	(0.13)	(0.11)	(0.15)
General Public	-0.01	0.14	0.01
	(0.09)	(0.09)	(0.11)
Civil Society	0.26	0.28**	0.12
	(0.16)	(0.14)	(0.15)
Generic Feature	-0.00	0.00	0.00
	(0.00)	(0.00)	(0.00)
Observations	210	210	210

Standard errors are provided in parentheses. ***$p < 0.01$, **$p < 0.05$, and *$p < 0.1$.

participatory and inclusive processes can inject democracy into constitutions. However, as discussed in Chapter 2, several studies have warned against the dangers of direct public participation in constitutional processes. "Participatory distortion" can result in self-selected groups with extremist views dominating the public deliberation domain (Verba et al. 1995). Participation in constitutional reform processes can also run the danger of populism and manipulation of the people by interest groups and elites (Ghai 2012). Moreover, participation increases the number of veto players that can make reaching consensus more difficult (Tsebelis 2002). The Tunisian NCA avoided these problems to some extent by certain institutional choices it made, including using a "blank page" strategy and incorporating two anti-gridlock institutions.

The Blank Page

One of the first critical decisions any constitution-drafting body needs to make is where to start from. Most assemblies find the constitution they are replacing as a good starting point to begin the constitutional renovation. Others (mostly in postrevolutionary constitution-making processes) prefer a "blank page" strategy and start from scratch. There are indeed distinct benefits in each strategy. While the former allows for faster and more cost-efficient drafting, the latter allows for more constitutional innovations. In the Tunisian NCA, a similar debate took place early in the process. While some members wanted to revise and democratize the 1959 constitution, others insisted on a "blank page" strategy. As Ben Amor noted:

> Some of our colleagues suggested that we should start from the 1959 constitution, and we could change it and make it a democratic constitution. But we decided that we should start from a blank page. The 1959 constitution was written by another regime; it had its own constitution. This is another republic, and we should have our own constitution and not just copy and edit the previous one. So, we started from zero, gathered suggestions, wrote a draft, and then listened to groups and the public and came up with the final draft (Samir Ben Amor [a leader of CPR party and member of the NCA], interview by author, January 19, 2015).

In the end, the "blank page" strategy proved to be more effective in creating a democratic constitution than the "last draft" strategy that Egypt pursued in both its 2012 and 2014 draft constitutions, for two reasons. First, and as Ben Amor noted, it forced the NCA to open the process to different groups including civil society and the general public for soliciting feedback and input for the constitution. Second, starting from scratch pushed the NCA deputies to begin the drafting process by focusing on noncontroversial provisions that all groups agreed upon and keep the controversial issues for later. As Habib Khedher, the general rapporteur of the NCA's CDC, noted, "[t]o create an environment of cooperation, compromise, and mutual understanding in the Constituent Assembly, we decided to start working with issues that the Tunisian society agreed upon and not those that divide us" (Habib Khedher, interview by author, January 22, 2015). An unintended, but positive, consequence of this was the building of political trust among different political factions.

Anti-Gridlock Institutions
An inclusive and participatory process by definition increases the number of veto players that can make consensus-building exceedingly difficult, especially in a polarized transitional process. Participation and inclusion allow different ideologies to have a voice in the room, and sometimes, extreme voices become the dominant voices in the public deliberation sphere, which can increase polarization and decrease the prospect of reaching a consensus. Jon Elster's (2012) solution here is that public participation should be limited during the

debating stage of constitution-making that requires more secrecy to allow political elites to change their position without electoral consequences. A more democratic, but also difficult, alternative to Elster's "hourglass model" is to institutionalize some anti-gridlock mechanisms that facilitate consensus-building. These anti-gridlock mechanisms, while allowing all ideologies to be heard, can facilitate a dialogue between different blocs. Without such mechanisms, inclusive and participatory processes have a lower likelihood of succeeding in founding a consensual constitution. The Tunisian NCA used two such institutions: a supermajority vote requirement for approving the constitution, which prevented unilateral decisions by the majority group, and an ad hoc committee, which had the final vote on controversial provisions.

First, a supermajority approval requirement – compared to a simple majority and public referendum, which is more common – can facilitate consensus-building, especially in transitioning states where usually no single group or a coalition of parties can win a supermajority of the votes, and therefore, they need the vote of opposition parties to adopt the constitution. In Indonesia, for example, the initial two-thirds required vote for amending the constitution paved the way for reaching consensus (Horowitz 2013). In Egypt, however, the simple majority requirement for approving the constitution emboldened the Muslim Brotherhood (which had the majority in the Constituent Assembly) to unilaterally change several provisions and approve the constitution without reaching an agreement with the non-Islamist opposition (Parolin 2015).

Another anti-deadlock mechanism that the NCA employed later in the process (June 2013) was an ad hoc committee tasked with solving controversial issues in the constitution. One of the controversial issues in the Tunisian constitution, for example, was the role of religion in state and society. While the main Islamist party, Ennahda, wanted Islam to be the "religion of the state," secular parties including the Popular Front (*Aridha Shaabia*) opposed it. Another issue of discord concerned the institutional design of the new political system. Experiencing years of repression from Tunisia's former strongly presidential authoritarian system, Ennahda preferred a parliamentary system, but the secular and liberal opposition wanted to retain a presidential system. Facing these critical issues, the NCA created a special committee called "the Consensus Commission" (*Lajnet Tawafuqat*) within the NCA to which the six committees would refer the controversial issues. This committee was presided by the NCA President Ben Jaâfar, had twenty-two members representing the political parties in the NCA, and had the final vote on the controversial issues that were referred to it.

Together, the supermajority vote requirement and the ad hoc Consensus Commission facilitated constitutional negotiations and allowed the NCA deputies to reach agreements on some of the most divisive issues that polarized the Tunisian public for years. The outcome was a constitution that not only reflected 43 percent of public input but also was a "middle ground" the majority of parties could agree on. These two anti-gridlock institutions along with the "blank page" method mitigated, to some extent, the problem of increased veto players and "participatory distortion," which comes with inclusive and participatory processes. However, a more important factor that ensured the success of the participatory and inclusive process in fortifying democracy was the role that civil associations played in facilitating negotiation and steering the constitutional debate.

THE ROLE OF CIVIL SOCIETY IN TUNISIA

Compared to other countries in the region, Tunisia was endowed with certain features that not only contributed to a successful constitutional negotiation process but also facilitated its democratic transition. First and foremost, Tunisia stands out in the region for its history of a relatively independent and strong civil society. Indeed, without the involvement of UGTT, perhaps reaching national reconciliation would have been impossible (Chayes 2014). The UGTT, founded in 1946, with more than half a million members (5 percent of the Tunisia population) and branches in every province in Tunisia, is a politically strong organization that has played a significant political role since its foundation. Three other organizations that played a critical role during the transition include the UTICA, the Tunisian Bar Association (founded in 1887), and the Human Rights League (the first independent human rights association in the Arab world). These four organizations (the Quartet) owe their global reputation to the Nobel Peace Prize they jointly won in 2015 for their role in constitution-making, peacekeeping, and democracy-building in Tunisia.

Among other organizations that contributed to the democratic process in the country, a few stand up including Al Bawsala, Conscience Politique, Free Sight Association, I WATCH, the Ofyia Center, the Tunisian Association of Constitutional Law (Association Tunisienne de Droit Constitutionnel, or ATDC), the Association for Research on the Democratic Transition (Association de Recherché sur la Transition Démocratique, or ARTD), and the Center for the Study of Islam and Democracy (CSID). We should also consider the impact of more than 180 local associations that were engaged in activities around the constitution at the local level (The Carter Center 2014).

Together, these civil groups were among the most important democratic forces in the Tunisian society because of three major functions they fulfilled. First, they acted as a watchdog over the Constituent Assembly, ensuring the transparency and integrity of the constitutional process. Second, they steered the constitutional debate away from extremism by offering an important venue for all citizens to engage in the democratic process. Lastly, they facilitated national dialogue and negotiations between different political blocs, paving the way for building a national consensus on some of the most important constitutional matters. While the last role has received more scholarly and public attention, the first two functions were equally important for facilitating the democratic transition in the country.

Throughout the transitional process including the constitution-making process, civil groups closely monitored and informed the public about the NCA decisions. Al Bawsala was among the most active organizations in monitoring the NCA. It created a website, *marsad.tn*, which sought to inform the public about NCA decisions by giving them a digital access to the NCA, including every single vote casted, attendance rate of each deputy, and how they voted on each single issue. The website also gave citizens a platform to comment on constitutional provisions and amendments to those provisions throughout the constitution-making process. Another organization, Civil Constituent Assembly (CCA), was formed by a group of citizens including those who ran for the NCA election but did not win a seat. The CCA mirrored the NCA's constitutional commissions and sought to engage citizens in the constitution-making process, soliciting feedback, and offering suggestions to the NCA. Some of these recommendations, specifically on local democracy, were even considered by the NCA (The Carter Center 2014).

Another watchdog organization was I WATCH, a nonprofit organization advocating open democracy. The organization sent representatives to attend almost all NCA open meetings and provide public reports on NCA's decisions. It even sought to alter some of NCA's decisions. For example, when the NCA announced that the constitution would not be ratified via a public referendum, I WATCH developed an online platform for Tunisians to vote on the constitution.[6] More than 3,000 people participated by casting their votes on the constitution in the first few days of launching the website. I WATCH representatives then protested in the NCA's hallways holding banners that showed the results from their own public referendum on the constitution (Cummings 2014). Although it was unsuccessful in pushing for

---

[6] The online voting platform address is vot-it.org, and I WATCH official website is www.iwatch-organisation.org/

a national public referendum as the constitution adoption mechanism, the organization played an important role in raising public awareness about what was happening in the NCA.

These CSOs also attempted to provide a check on state behavior by occasionally organizing public protests and demonstrations around major constitutional issues. As discussed previously, for example, after the publication of a draft constitution that limited the role of women to "inside family" and assigned them a "complementary" role to men, several civil associations, including major women's rights advocacy groups, organized massive public protests. Similarly, during the article-by-article vote in January 2014, several lawyers, public prosecutors, judges, and civil groups went on strike protesting the amendments that they believed would weaken judicial independence. In both of these examples and several other cases, the public protests and strikes organized by CSOs were successful in reversing NCA's decisions (more precisely, Ennahda's decisions) and making the constitution more democratic.

The second important role that these civil groups played in facilitating the democratic transition was to provide a venue for public engagement. The Ofyia Center, for example, organized fora during which they invited citizens and NCA members to discuss constitutional matters. The ATDC and the ARTD often partnered together and organized conferences to offer critical analysis of constitutional provisions. The CSID also organized several conferences and workshops inviting both NCA members and experts to discuss the constitution and democratic transition both in Tunisia and across the region. Other groups like Sawty, a youth organization, launched several constitutional awareness campaigns ensuring the general public was informed about the content of constitutional drafts. At the local level, Association Citoyenneté de Gafsa, for example, collected public feedback and wrote a report on Gafsa women's expectations from the constitution.

Through these and numerous other conferences and workshops, civil associations provided an important opportunity for the people to meet with their NCA representatives, listen to experts, and express their opinions and concerns. These conferences and workshops played a key role in raising public awareness and engaging the Tunisian public (particularly those with moderate views who were not already mobilized) with constitutional negotiations. Several of these constitutional events (including those organized by CSID) drew a broad media coverage, which illustrates national interest in the events. This was, however, far from being perfect and came with two notable caveats. First, most of these workshops were concentrated in the capital city of Tunis, providing much less opportunity for the rest of the country to get involved.

And second, only few CSOs, mostly those strong groups that existed before the revolution, were engaged in direct lobbying with the NCA.

The most notable organizations that were directly involved in lobbying the NCA were the Quartet and in particular the UGTT, which played a key role in facilitating the national dialogue and negotiations among different political blocs specifically after the June 2013 draft constitution. In the wake of the breakdown of negotiations in the NCA in 2013 as a result of the publication of the controversial fourth draft constitution and the political assassinations of secular leaders, the UGTT called for a two-day general strike and was successful in mobilizing more than half of its members (Hartshorn 2017). Public protests outside the Bardo Palace and sit-ins inside the NCA further heightened the constitutional crisis. Fearing a civil conflict, the NCA President Mustapha Ben Jaâfar suspended all legislative activities on August 6. The UGTT-led National Dialogue Quartet invited twenty-four political parties to participate in the third national dialogue, which was convened on October 25, 2013.[7] In front of TV cameras, these parties signed a road map outlining the general goals of the convention, which included the formation of a new, nonpartisan government, establishment of a timeline for presidential and legislative elections, introduction of an impartial electoral commission, and the modification, completion, and approval of the constitution.

The role of UGTT, and the Quartet more broadly, was not however limited to the national dialogues. Throughout the process, they arranged meetings with political leadership across different ideological lines, threatened strikes, organized protests, and strikes and used their weight to pressure different political parties for particular ends. For example, under mounting pressures from the UGTT and opposition parties because of the assassination of Chokri Belaid in February 2013, Prime Minister Hamadi Jebali, a prominent Ennahda leader, disregarded the decision of his own party and resigned from the office. No other CSO was as powerful and influential during the Tunisian transitional process (and its aftermath) as was the UGTT.

In sum, whether through direct lobbying and pressures (as was the case for UGTT and the Quartet in general) or organizing conferences and workshops, civil groups played a key role in the Tunisian constitutional negotiation process, had a significant impact on the content of the constitution, and facilitated democratic transition in the country. Recall, however, from Chapter 1 that the role of civil society can be rendered ineffective under the

---

[7] The first two national dialogues were the National Dialogue with Civil Society (September 14–15, 2012) and National Dialogue with Citizens and Civil Society (December 16, 2012–February 24, 2013).

sway of unfavorable exogenous factors, such as domination of the process by one strong group, military intervention, or ethnoreligious and regional divisions. Tunisian CSOs, compared to other groups in the region, were able to fulfill their role partly because of the lack of such undemocratic forces.

Balance of Power

When a political group dominates the transitional process, the cost of breaching the bargain will be lower, and it can unilaterally decide the constitutional bargain without the need to involve groups from civil society as third-party arbiters. As O'Donnell and Schmitter (1986) argue, the balance of power between different factions within the opposition and incumbent camps has a significant impact on democratic transition. Conditions favorable to democratic transition occur when "[n]o social or political group is sufficiently dominant to impose its 'ideal project', and what typically emerges is a second-best solution which none of the actors wanted or identified with completely but which all of them can agree to and share in" (O'Donnell and Schmitter 1986, 43–44). This roughly equal balance of power is important for "institutionalizing uncertainty." As Przeworski (1986) argues, democratization is a process of institutionalizing uncertainty through which no one's interests can be guaranteed and all interests are subject to uncertainty. Without such balance of power and institutionalized uncertainty, collective actors each preferring a different institutional configuration cannot enter enduring compromises, and democratization will not advance (Rustow 1970). A diffusion of power and projected electoral uncertainties, by contrast, opens up a space for the civil society to function as a mediator when agreements cannot be struck.

A comparison between Egypt and Tunisia showcases the importance of balance of power for democratic transition (see Brownlee et al. 2015). In Egypt, the two major Islamist parties, Muslim Brotherhood's Freedom and Justice and the Salafist Noor Party, together won 70 percent of the seats in the parliamentary elections and dominated the Constituent Assembly (CA). Additionally, the NCA's bylaws that required only a simple majority vote for approving the constitution in the CA emboldened the Islamist parties that already had the votes in pushing for their "ideal project," which ultimately undermined their incentive for compromise. Faced with the uncompromising Islamists, the desperate non-Islamist parties had to resort to the military.

In Tunisia, by contrast, the Islamist Ennahda won only a plurality of the votes (40 percent), and the political power was more evenly balanced between different blocs. Furthermore, the NCA's bylaws required a two-thirds approval vote for the constitution in the assembly. Consequently, Ennahda knew from the onset of the process that it needed the other side of the isle for both effective governing and adopting the new constitution. As Eva Bellin notes, "[t]he fact that no party enjoyed a majority provided an incentive for coalition building and accommodation" (2013, 4). Furthermore, the balance of power in Tunisia and lack of it in Egypt played an important role in shaping the "non-Islamists' fear of the Islamists' ability to change state and society" in the two countries (Lust and Khatib 2014, 2). Indeed, the relative balance of power between Islamists and non-Islamists in Tunisia facilitated democratic transition through increased toleration. As Stepan (2000) argues, neither *laïcité* (states which disparage religious observance in public altogether, such as France) nor secularism (separation of religion and state but with the rights of all to observe in public) is empirically necessary for democracy to emerge. What is necessary for democracy to flourish is "a significant degree of institutional differentiation between religion and the state" or what can be called "twin toleration" (Stepan and Linz 2013, 17).

The balance of power in Tunisia was not, however, solely limited to the relatively equal relationship between Islamists and non-Islamists. There was also a balance between political elites and activists and CSOs in the constitution-making and the transition process. In particular, the labor union, UGTT, could establish a very strong alliance outside its structure and was able to shape legislation from the outside (Hartshorn 2017). Despite having leftist tendencies, UGTT was successful in becoming a major political mediator from the outside and used its power to shape the constitutional debate and democratic transition process. This balance of power between Islamists and non-Islamists, on the one hand, and the political parties and CSOs, on the other, created an "institutionalized uncertainty" that required all sides to compromise and work together to achieve their second-best choice.

A Professional Military

While military officials or experts are often consulted about provisions regarding the armed forces, militaries in general should be kept out of democratic transitional processes, including constitutional negotiations. The extent to which a military seeks to engage in or shape the transitional process depends on its economic and political power and independence from the civilian government, as well as ethnoreligious cleavages within the armed forces and across the country. When militaries are ethnically homogenous and are not economically or politically vested in an authoritarian regime, they are less likely to stand behind the regime (Barany 2011). This was clearly the case for Tunisia, where General Rachid Ammar, the chief of staff of the Tunisian

Armed Forces, refused to follow Ben Ali's orders to use lethal means to put down the protests.

Unlike most Arab countries, Tunisia has a professional, apolitical military, which has never been a key political actor. The Tunisian military did not win the country's independence, as was the case in Algeria. It did not have ethnoreligious ties to the authoritarian leader's ethnoreligious group, as was the case in Syria and Bahrain. It did not have strategic alliances with the autocrat, as was the case in Yemen and Libya. Neither did it control important sectors in the economy, as was the case in Egypt. As a result, the Tunisian military lacked any institutional interest for backing Ben Ali's regime or getting involved in the transitional process. The military as such could not disrupt the democratic transition by shifting the balance of power.

This professional military was the legacy of Habib Bourguiba, Tunisia's first President. Being aware of the obstacles that a strong military can pose to his civilian rule, Bourguiba intentionally kept the military small and did not involve military leaders in his ruling party or state administration. This legacy did not change under Ben Ali's regime, who, ironically, was a military man himself. Instead of relying on the military for coercion, Ben Ali built a strong security force through the Interior Ministry, making Tunisia a de facto security state rather than a military state (Barany 2011). And when he asked the military to use force to stop the revolution, they had no institutional incentive to do so. This professional and apolitical military was indeed an important factor that facilitated (or, rather, did not hinder) the democratic transition in the country.

Ethnoreligious and Regional Cleavages

Another exogenous factor that was favorable for Tunisia was the lack of ethnoreligious cleavages that derailed the democratic transitions in several other countries in the region from Bahrain and Syria to Yemen and Libya. Tunisia is one of the most homogenous countries in the region. More than 98 percent of the population are Arab-speaking Sunni Muslims. Imazighen are estimated to comprise about 1–5 percent of the population based on different reports.[8] The French colonial rule and urbanization eliminated tribal identity in the country decades before the 2011 revolution. While ethnoreligious cleavages were not a major issue during the transition process, one particular cleavage was important for the post–Ben Ali Tunisia.

---

[8] Amazigh (plural: Imazighen), which in the indigenous Tamazight language means "free people," are the indigenous North African tribes who populated the region before it was conquered by Arab Muslims from the Arabian Peninsula.

From the French colonial rule to Bourguiba's rule, the coastal regions in the north had become more economically affluent and politically influential than the inner regions. Since most elites were from the coastal areas (*Sahel*, in Arabic), during Bourguiba's regime, the *Sahel* region became synonymous with political power. During Ben Ali's regime, regional ties became a basis for clientelism and patronage networks. The two regions are separated not only by development and political power but also by political ideology. While the people in the coastal regions are more liberal and secular and have a more European lifestyle, the poorer inner regions are more conservative and Islamist-oriented.

These regional cleavages and economic grievances played an important role in spreading anti–Ben Ali protests. Even after Ben Ali's departure, the Islamist Ennahda enjoyed more popular support in the inner regions, while the secular Nidaa Tounes had more support in the coastal regions. Equal opportunities for regional development were also among the major demands of the people living in the inner regions, which were constitutionalized in Articles 136 and 141. Despite the tensions, regional cleavages in Tunisia (unlike those in Yemen or Libya, which are discussed in Chapter 6) were not a major factor that could negatively impact constitution-making or democratic transition process.

In sum, Tunisia had all it needed for a successful democratic transition. It is a homogenous country with no major ethnoreligious cleavages, and undemocratic forces, such as the military, were not strong enough and did not have any institutional interest to intervene in the process. Furthermore, a relative balance of power among different groups created an "institutional uncertainty" that required compromise by all sides. In this favorable environment, CSOs could not only rise as key players who functioned as a third-party arbiter of political and constitutional disputes but also steer constitutional debates to focus on the underlying political and social ills that had contributed to authoritarianism in the country for decades. Civil associations facilitated the democratic transition in Tunisia by emphasizing the need for constitutional remedies for those ills.

CONSTITUTIONAL REMEDIES FOR SOCIAL AND POLITICAL ILLS

As discussed in Chapter 1, to facilitate democratic transition and consolidation, constitutions should tend to the prevalent ills in a polity. That chapter reviewed two core issues that most Arab constitutions have failed to address. The first is a set of social and ideological issues that are at the center of public debate for every society. These mostly include issues that tend to polarize society. The second is a set of institutional issues, which may not be of public interest or at least may not be polarizing concerns, but matter significantly for democratic consolidation, balance of power, and constitutionalism. Major institutional designs, which are most often heatedly debated in constituent assemblies but not in the streets, fall in this category. The Tunisian constitution was the only document in the region that addressed both issues, partly because of the critical role CSOs played in steering the constitutional debate.

Ideological Cleavages

Constitutions can facilitate democratic transition if they address unresolved ideological cleavages in society. Although polarizing, if certain societal problems remain unresolved, they can pose serious threats to democratic stability. Several Arab constitutions had turned a blind eye to issues such as the role of religion in society or gender equality, but years and decades later, these issues resurfaced during the Arab Spring. While in some countries like Oman or Saudi Arabia, these issues were not debated, in most countries, there were robust societal debates surrounding these questions. The following pages discuss three ideological issues that were at the epicenter of public debate on the Tunisian constitution.

The Role of Religion and Sharia Law

From the outset of constitutional negotiations, the role of Islam and religion in the new constitution stirred the public, civil society, and political parties in Tunisia. Two issues emerged at the heart of this debate. The first issue was how to find a balance between the Arab-Muslim identity most Tunisians identify with and the secular nature of the state, which the majority desired. The second issue was how to guarantee equality for everyone regardless of their religion while recognizing Tunisia as a predominantly Muslim country.

Before the first draft of the constitution was written, political parties reached an agreement not to mention Sharia in the constitution, which made Tunisia a unique case in the Arab world in this regard. This, however, could not stop a debate from emerging among Ennahda members. This debate started in the spring of 2012 and created a major concern among the secularists who feared Tunisia would become "the next Iran." The secularists even accused Ennahda members of trying to push Sharia through the back window because in 2011, some party figures publicly promised that the party will not try to impose Sharia in the constitution. Even Rached Ghannouchi, the Ennahda leader, emphasized in an interview that "Islam is a philosophy, not rules" (Marks 2014, 20). Despite this initial position of Ennahda on the role of Sharia law in the constitution, a few conservative members of the party, including Sadok Chourou and Habib Ellouze, managed to persuade more party members to have a debate as a party on the role of Sharia. Eventually, the role of Sharia went on the agenda of Shura Council, a governing institution that determines all major party decisions via one-person, one-vote scheme, for the party debate (Marks 2014). After several days of discussion, Ennahda's Shura Council voted on not pursuing Sharia in the constitution.

A few opposition leaders, including Nidaa Tounes's Mohsen Marzouk, accused Ennahda of having the debate on Sharia, months after renouncing the idea, as a strategic move to gain time and leverage over the opposition parties (Marks 2014). This is because while the issue of Sharia was never really debated in the NCA, another debate emerged with the introduction of Article 148 of the second draft, which, instead of stating that certain provisions cannot be amended, listed a number of inviolable issues in the constitution including that of "Islam as the state religion." This was controversial because many secularists believed that it exceeded the *intentionally* vague language of Article 1, which states that "Tunisia is a free, independent, and sovereign state. Its religion is Islam." Eventually, the NCA's Consensus Commission reached an agreement to state clearly at the end of Article 1 that it cannot be amended. The adopted constitution similarly prohibits the amendment of Article 2, which states that "Tunisia is a civil state. . . ."[9] Many believe that the first two articles are contradictory because a state cannot be both civil and Islamic, and the inflexibility of the constitution in amending both can cause conflict in the future (The Carter Center 2014).

Another major issue related to the role of religion in the constitution that the NCA heatedly debated was freedom of religion and conscience. Freedom of conscience was not included in the first three drafts of the constitution, and its inclusion in the fourth draft was the result of months of debate and the national dialogue negotiations between different political parties. Following the national dialogue negotiations, the NCA eventually adopted Article 6, which states that "the state protects religion, guarantees freedom of belief and conscience and religious practices, protects the sacred, and ensures the impartiality of mosques and places of worship away from partisan instrumentalization." The article, however, changed in the final draft, after an incident outside the NCA. On January 7, 2014, only a few days before the approval of the final draft, Sadok Chourou, an Ennahda member known for his Salafist

---

[9] Besides these two articles, the constitution forbids the amendment of the constitution in a way that undermines the human rights and freedoms guaranteed (Article 49) and number and length of presidential terms (Article 79).

and extremist inclinations, accused Mongi Rahoui, from the Popular Front party, of being a *Kafir* (infidel). The following day, Rahoui reported that he received threatening phone calls, and the next day he gave a speech in the opening session of the NCA, urging the NCA to stop these accusations. That same day, the NCA amended Article 6 and added a new clause that criminalized any form of *takfir* (accusing individuals of being nonbeliever).

Since its initial implementation, Article 6 was a source of controversy. While some deputies believed that the state should be the protector of religion and the sacred, others believed that the constitution should leave people with freedom of choice. In the end, Article 6 of the adopted constitution tried to accommodate both views:

> The state is the guardian of religion. It guarantees freedom of conscience and belief, the free exercise of religious practices and the neutrality of mosques and places of worship from all partisan instrumentalization.
>
> The state undertakes to disseminate the values of moderation and tolerance and the protection of the sacred, and the prohibition of all violations thereof. It undertakes equally to prohibit and fight against calls for *takfir* and the incitement of violence and hatred.

Another related controversial issue that the NCA had to address was the issue of blasphemy. Ennahda members of the Rights and Freedoms Committee introduced a language that criminalized blasphemy in Article 3 of the first draft constitution, which stipulated that "the state guarantees freedom of religious belief and practice and criminalizes all attacks on that which is sacred. . .." Several Ennahda deputies strongly believed that any provocation against Abrahamic religions should be criminalized. Facing pressures from secularists and CSOs to international organizations and foreign governments, Ennahda had to make yet another difficult decision. Two provocative events put Ennahda members on a defensive stance regarding the issue of blasphemy. In 2011, a Tunisian TV channel aired Marjane Satrapi's film *Persepolis*, and in the summer 2012, an art gallery at Abdelliya held an exhibit by a group of secular artists. Both events were considered as direct insult to Islam by Ennahda, and the exhibit at Abdelliya caused days of riots and curfews in the city. Being on defense and under pressure from multiple CSOs, Ennahda's Shura Council took on the issue of criminalization of blasphemy for a party debate and vote. Eventually, many local leaders of Ennahda were convinced that the constitution should be about "positive, rights-affirming ideals rather than restrictive, prohibitory language" and decided to remove the language criminalizing blasphemy (Marks 2014, 26).

Additional religious elements that, unlike Sharia or criminalizing blasphemy, were included in the adopted constitution include the oaths of office sworn by elected officials, which has a religious language (Articles 58, 76, and 89) and the requirement of being Muslim for candidates running for presidency (Article 74), which was a legacy of the 1959 constitution.

The Tunisian Constitution, as such, engaged with the public debate over the role of religion and attempted to resolve the question of religion by accommodating the opposing views in the society. For instance, the constitution establishes Islam as the religion of the state but does not establish Sharia as a source of law. It guarantees freedom of religion yet, at the same time, condemns *takfir*. Language criminalizing blasphemy was removed from the final draft, but the constitution requires that the President of Tunisia be Muslim. This constitutional "middle ground" solution for the divisive provisions pertaining to religion stemmed further polarization in the Tunisian society and created a constitution, which is highly regarded by citizens with different ideological inclinations.

This constitutional solution to polarizing issues evolved over time as a solution to keep most groups invested in the constitution. Tunisia's approach to addressing ideological issues, thus, comes closest in the Arab world to Lerner's "incrementalist approach" to constitution-making. For Lerner (2011), when society is deeply divided across ideological lines and competing definitions of state and society's identity, constitutions should avoid a clear language about those polarizing issues. Instead, by formulating vague, ambiguous, and contradictory provisions on these divisive issues, constitutions should defer decisions on controversial choices to the future. This "incrementalist" strategy will inevitably transfer these decisions from the constitutional sphere to the political sphere and hence will lower societal tensions. The Tunisian constitution-makers avoided a winner-takes-all approach and instead deferred to an "incrementalist approach" by formulating contradictory and vague provisions on controversial issues such as the role of religion and Islamic Sharia, which had polarized other Arab nations such as Egypt.

Gender Equality and the Role of Women

Similar to the role of religion, the issue of gender parity was heatedly debated in the Tunisian NCA, nation-wide conferences, and workshops and on the streets. The Ennahda-drafted Article 28 of the first draft constitution (August 2012) stipulated a "complementary role" for women in the society by mentioning "the complementary role of men and women inside the family."[10] Limiting the role of women to "inside the family" and not mentioning equality between men and women yielded a public outcry against Ennahda. Even prominent female representatives from Ennahda, including Souad Abderrahim, opposed the clause. The NCA removed the "complementary role" clause in the second draft (December 2012) and subsequently wrote more moderate articles on gender issues. The second draft constitution considered women independent from the family.

After criticisms of the June 2013 draft mounted, the now-empowered opposition parties proposed stronger language for gender equality, arguing that per the fifty-year-old Personal Status Code and popular demand, equal rights for women should be guaranteed in the constitution. Ennahda, on the other hand, argued that a "total equality between men and women" in the constitution would contradict the well-accepted Personal Status Code because the latter, for example, has adopted Sharia-based inheritance and property-ownership laws, which are gender discriminatory. In response to the deadlock over gender equality, opposition parties and civil associations mobilized tens of thousands of women and men to protests against Ennahda's stance on gender equality. These protests were organized by the same opposition parties and civil groups that were previously successful in raising public awareness on gender inequality in the first draft of the constitution (Samir Taïeb, interview by author, January 20, 2015). Due to public pressure on the streets, Ennahda soon acceded to the proposed changes (Mahjoub 2016).

The issue of gender parity, once again, became a contentious issue during the final vote on the constitution. A pressure group, mostly from women representing different blocs, was formed that tried to push for a stronger language on women's rights in the constitution. The Consensus Commission addressed the issue and, despite divisions in the Commission, proposed to amend Article 45 of the fourth draft (Article 46 in the adopted constitution), which now stipulates, "[t]he state commits to protect women's accrued rights and work to strengthen and develop those rights. The state guarantees the equality of opportunities between women and men to have access to all levels of responsibility in all domains. The state works to attain parity between women and men in elected Assemblies. The state shall take all necessary measures in order to eradicate violence against women." This language by no means had universal support in the NCA, and in the first few days of voting, it was not even clear if the amendment would pass in the

[10]   The idea that women *complement* men in society (rather than being equal to them) has long been articulated in modern Islamic discourse (see, e.g., Stowasser 1993; Haddad 1998; Mir-Hosseini 1999, 2003).

assembly. Eventually and after days of negotiations and lobbying, Article 46 was adopted with 116 votes in favor, 32 abstentions, and 40 against.

The new constitution also adopted gender-sensitive wording regarding some rights including the right to work (Article 40) and the right to standing for elections (Articles 34 and 46). Most importantly, for the first time in the Tunisian history, Article 74 of the adopted constitution guaranteed women the right to stand for election for the position of president of the republic. This is a notable progress in the advancement of women's rights in Tunisia and more broadly in the Arab world.

The Issue of Palestine

Since the creation of the state of Israel in 1948, *Qadhiyat Filastin*, or "the issue of Palestine," has dominated the public debate in the region. However, being a political issue rather than a social concern, like the role of religion or gender equality, the issue of Palestine was never a major constitutional issue in the Arab world. Therefore, the incorporation of this issue in the constitutional debate in Tunisia was an unsettling matter, which could have important consequences for constitutional debates across the region.

The "criminalization of normalization of relations with Israel" (*tajrim al-tadbi'*) for the first time appeared in the first draft constitution under Article 27. The introduction of this article was perhaps one of Ennahda's most politically sensitive and controversial moves. The general feeling in Tunisia, just like in most parts of the Arab world, was anti-Israeli, and the article garnered popular support. All other Islamist parties as well as the leftist Arab nationalist parties and even the UGTT supported the provision (Petrucci and Fois 2016, 400–401). The opposition parties, thus, accused Ennahda of populism, arguing that since the general feeling in the country was against Israel, Ennahda proposed this article to attract more popular support (Badreldin Abdelkafi, interview by author, January 22, 2015). After consulting constitutional experts from Germany, the United States, and Morocco, the Ennahda representatives were convinced that legalizing or illegalizing the normalization of relations with any foreign country is a legislative issue and not a constitutional matter and as such agreed to remove this article in the second draft. International constitutional experts as well as CSOs were in general successful in influencing NCA deputies that constitutions should not "criminalize" issues (such blasphemy) or policies (such as relationship with Israel).

After removing the provision from the second draft constitution, many people from the Islamist and leftist camps demanded bringing this article back to the constitution (Samir Taïeb, interview by author, January 20, 2015). In one of the national dialogue meetings with citizens, for example, a public petition was signed by seventy-four attendees requesting a constitutional provision on the criminalization of normalization of relations with Israel. Backed by popular demand to reintroduce this provision, Ennahda included the same provision in the third draft (April 2013) as part of the preamble and not as an article. Faced with another round of opposition in the NCA, Ennahda insisted to keep this "popular demand" in the constitution. An NCA member who spoke to me on the condition of anonymity mentioned that even the Ambassador of Palestine to Tunisia was against mentioning the name of Israel in the Tunisian Constitution since it could have a negative impact on the Palestinian negotiations for statehood. Eventually and under pressure from some opposition blocs, CSOs and even foreign governments including the United States, Ennahda was forced to drop this provision from the adopted constitution.

Although the issue of Israel and Palestine has always been a political challenge for Arab states, debating the issue in the NCA and engaging the Tunisian people in the debate were inevitable. While the adopted constitution left out the language criminalizing relationships with Israel, it reflected public support for Palestine in the preamble, "supporting all just liberation movements, at the forefront of which is the movement for the liberation of Palestine. . . ." It is, however, unclear whether this support should be binding or not. On the one hand, the language of this clause in the preamble is vague. On the other hand, Article 145 states that "[t]his constitution's preamble is an integral part of the constitution," which should make the preamble and its clauses binding.

In sum, as the three ideological and social issues reviewed previously demonstrate, the adopted constitution took the "middle ground" on issues of religion and Palestine, by trying to appease different opinions in the society as much as possible. Only on the issue of gender equality, the constitution took a more progressive stance and included several provisions to empower Tunisian women. Regardless, on all three issues, CSOs played a crucial role in making the language of the adopted constitution more moderate and progressive than the four draft constitutions.

Constitutionalizing Democratic Institutions

Unlike debates regarding ideological issues that equally engaged the general public, civil associations, and political parties, constitutional negotiations regarding institutional design choices were mostly confined to the NCA and civil groups, as the general Tunisian public did not show as much interest in those debates. Review of the 2,500 public proposals for the constitution also shows that the majority of Tunisians were more interested in issues pertaining to the General Principles and Rights and Liberties. Despite the public's relative indifference, issues of institutional design were major sources of contention in the NCA. For example, while Ennahda was readily willing to compromise on issues such as Sharia or gender equality, the party was much more adamant on its position regarding several institutional design choices including a parliamentary political system and the role of judiciary. With the absence of public interest in these issues, the role of CSOs in creating public interest and awareness as well as ensuring that constitutional negotiations yield democratic institutions that fortify constitutionalism and rule of law was of utmost importance for democratic transition in Tunisia.

Structure of the Political System

The choice of political system was among the most contentiously debated constitutional issues in the NCA. Given Ennahda's history of being suppressed under a presidential regime, this was the single issue the party was most resistant to compromise about (Marks 2014). After a few days of within-party debate, Ennahda's Shura Council decided to back a parliamentary system. Ennahda argued that because of a long history of presidential authoritarianism in the country, a parliamentary system is the best solution for a democratic Tunisia. Several Ennahda members, including Rached Ghannouchi, who were in exile in the United Kingdom for years, often brought up the UK's parliamentary system as an example of how a parliament can prevent a single person from taking over the country. Ennahda, thus, was committed to ensure the history of strong men would not repeat itself in Tunisia.

The opposition parties, by contrast, were not ready to relinquish the old presidential system. Their reasoning rested on two arguments. First, they believed that a parliamentary system would prevent charismatic leaders with national popularity, like Essebsi, founder of the main opposition party, Nidaa Tounes, from taking power. Major opposition parties genuinely believed that they could win the presidential election with their popular candidates from Moncef Marzouki and Abdelraouf Ayadi to Beji Caid Essebsi and Ahmed Nejib Chebbi. Second, they believed that Ennahda sought a parliamentary system because it was the most powerful, organized, and coherent party in Tunisia, which could easily win parliamentary elections. To their credit, Ennahda was in fact the only party during the transition period, which did not lose a single member due to shifting alliances and party switches. Ennahda also openly accused small, unorganized, opposition parties of pushing for a presidential system because they were hopeless in winning legislative elections (Marks 2014).

Under mounting pressure from the opposition parties and CSOs and in particular the UGTT, Ennahda eventually agreed to a semi-presidential system with a strong parliament. Given Ennahda's strong stance on a parliamentary system, the party eventually ceded a great deal of ground by agreeing to a semi-presidential system (Marks 2014). While it seemed that political blocs settled on the structure of political system, constitutional debates were far from over. In the following months, two new debates emerged that revolved around the issues of balance of power between the legislature and the executive, on the one hand, and between the president and prime minister as the two heads of the executive, on the other. While the third draft constitution granted considerable power to the parliament, the fourth draft tried to create more balance between the two branches. It also attempted to clarify the role of the two heads of the executive and create a balance between the two. The fourth draft also introduced a new provision stating that both the president and prime minister hold executive power (Article 70 in the fourth draft; Article 71 in the adopted constitution).

Several NCA members criticized these modifications as being insufficient. In the end, the adopted constitution clarified major roles and responsibilities of the head of state and head of government. Several areas, however, have remained unclear in the constitution. For example, Articles 77, 78, 80, and 106 stipulate that the president shall make certain decisions "after consultation with the Head of Government." Yet, it is not clear what will happen if there is disagreement between the two heads of the executive. Neither is there any punishment mechanism if the president fails to do so. Only Article 101 foresees that in case of dispute between the two heads of executive, the matter can be referred to the Constitutional Court for a ruling within a week. The problem remains, however, that as of 2020, the Constitutional Court as the ultimate arbiter of constitutional disputes has not been established yet. Regardless of these gray areas of separation of power, the adopted political system established a semi-presidential political system with strong presidency, *à la* French model, which is far from what Ennahda initially hoped for.

Role of the Judiciary

Unlike the structure of the political system, the role of the judiciary was not a polarizing issue in the NCA. Moreover, the general Tunisian public showed the least interest regarding this issue. As Rabeh Kraifi noted, the Tunisian public was not concerned or enthusiastic about judicial issues even when they participated in national dialogue meetings about the judicial review:

> During the meetings [with the public] some citizens were not concerned with the judicial issues in the constitution at all. They were constantly

accusing us of stealing money and doing nothing. As such, I spent most of my time defending myself rather than discussing the constitution (Rabeh Khraifi, interview by author, January 15, 2015).

The reason for this lack of public engagement or divisiveness across the NCA with regard to the role of judiciary can be that major parties and groups agreed on its main feature: Everyone wanted a strong and independent judiciary. During Ben Ali's regime, the judiciary lacked any independence and was subservient to the executive. Under this historical context, all parties wanted an independent judiciary because a judiciary that is not vulnerable to the executive power can function as an insurance policy for the losing party (Ginsburg 2003). Despite this universal understanding, NCA deputies fiercely debated different provisions (mostly at technical rather than political level) in their quest to establish an effective and independent judiciary.

Article 102 of the adopted constitution guarantees that "the judiciary is an independent authority," and Article 109 prohibits "all kinds of interference in the functioning of the judicial system." The final constitution draft also strengthened the immunity of judges. In the fourth draft (and the previous iterations), a judge's immunity could be removed if he or she was caught *in flagrante delicto*. The adopted constitution, however, allows lifting judges's immunity if they are caught red-handed committing *a crime* (Article 104). The debates in the NCA also led to improved constitutional text regarding the High Judicial Council, which is tasked with the appointment, promotion, dismissal, and career progression of judges. Before the final draft, only half of the members of the High Judicial Council were to be judges. The adopted constitution increases the number of judges to two-thirds.

The final draft also changed the appointment mechanism of the Constitutional Court members. In the fourth draft constitution, the twelve Constitutional Court members would be elected by the constituent assembly from a list of candidates proposed by the president of the republic, the head of government, the president of the assembly, and the president of the High Judicial Council. In the final draft, this "cooperative" appointment mechanism was changed to a "representative" appointment mechanism, where the appointment responsibility is divided among different branches.[11] Article 118 of the adopted constitution stipulates that "the President of the Republic, the NCA of the Representatives of the People, and the Supreme Judicial Council shall each appoint four members, three quarters of whom must be legal

[11]   See Ginsburg (2003) for a review of different appointment mechanisms.

specialists." The constitution also adopted a single nine-year term for the Constitutional Court members.

It is important to note that the first and second draft constitution mandated that all members of the Constitutional Court be legal specialists with at least twenty years of professional experience. The Ennahda-dominated drafting committee lowered that bar to a majority of legal specialists with a minimum of ten years of experience. This was strongly opposed by the opposition parties, CSOs, and members of the Judicial, Administrative, Financial, and Constitutional Justice Commission in the NCA, which drafted the original provision. Ennahda's changes to Article 118 were part of a broader scheme to unilaterally change several constitutional provisions by the Drafting Committee that led to yet another turmoil in the constitutional negotiation process. As discussed earlier, the Joint Drafting Committee was responsible for compiling the constitution and coordinating the content of different chapters. The turmoil, however, started when the committee went beyond its mandate and introduced substantial changes to the proposals that the six constitutional committees had submitted to it (including Article 118) and published a new constitutional draft on June 1, 2013. These unilateral changes that were made in complete secrecy by the Ennahda-dominated Joint Committee were specifically related to the preamble, rights and freedoms, the form of the political regime, judicial powers, the transitional provisions, and an article on education (Samir Taïeb, interview by author, January 20, 2015). The Joint Committee never communicated with the other constitutional committees, and the minutes of its meetings were never made public (Mahjoub 2016). This move led to a backlash against Ennahda; civil associations organized demonstrations, and in protest to these unilateral changes, Fadhel Moussa, the only member of the Democratic Bloc in the Joint Committee withdrew from the NCA. A compromise was later reached through the Consensus Commission, and NCA members agreed to increase the number of legal specialists in the Constitutional Court to three-quarters (nine members) and bring back the initial requirement of twenty years of professional experience.

In sum, unlike the ideological issues, constitutional matters relating to democratic institutions were rarely discussed among the general public. While the general public was not readily mobilized and engaged in these debates, civil society played an undeniably important role in creating public interest and awareness to some extent. Most importantly, however, in the absence of public enthusiasm and engagement, civil society played a crucial role as the representative of public's interests in those constitutional negotiations. In particular, the role of civil associations, including the UGTT and the Tunisian Bar Association as well as local and international NGOs such as the Carter Center, Human Rights Watch, Al Bawsala, and Amnesty International, in ensuring the inclusion of important provisions in the constitution was significant. These organizations were particularly influential in drafting constitutional provisions related to a strong and independent judiciary, in addition to individual and group rights (including the minority and opposition rights) or limiting constitutional restrictions on these rights.

CONCLUSION: DEMOCRATIC TRANSITION AT THE INTERSECTION
OF PROCESS, DESIGN, AND INTRACTABLE DIFFERENCES

We can draw three major conclusions from the success of Tunisia's constitution in establishing democracy. First, in order for constitutional negotiations to facilitate democratic transitions, both participation and inclusion in the process are necessary. Genuine and meaningful participation not only legitimized the process but also created a sense of ownership of the constitution among citizens, an important step toward building constitutionalism and rule of law in democratizing societies. And the inclusive constitution-making process transformed interpersonal relationships between the Islamists and non-Islamists, enhanced intergroup trusts, and strengthened cross-partisan ties, which ultimately facilitated constitutional negotiations (Jermanová 2020). A potential caveat of increased participation and inclusion, however, is that increased number of voices makes reaching agreement more difficult. Hence, institutionalizing anti-gridlock mechanisms becomes vital in inclusive and participatory processes. The Tunisian NCA adopted two such institutions. First, a two-thirds vote threshold for approving the constitution forced major political blocs to compromise as they needed the votes of other parties. The second anti-gridlock institution was the Consensus Commission, an ad hoc committee comprising different political parties that had the final vote on divisive issues that were referred to it. When the process is inclusive and participatory and agreement-facilitating mechanisms are incorporated, public participation in the process becomes more meaningful. More than 43 percent of citizen proposals were included in the adopted constitution that makes the Tunisian Constitution a true enshrinement of people's will.

The second conclusion we can draw from the Tunisian experience is that through this inclusive and participatory constitutional process, civil associations managed to play an important role in facilitating the democratic transition. CSOs fulfilled three core functions. They acted as a third-party arbiter of constitutional and political disputes among different groups. Different CSOs also acted as watchdogs, ensuring the integrity and transparency of the process. Lastly, they created a public sphere for constitutional debates by offering an inclusive venue for citizens to engage in constitutional negotiations. Civil groups can be successful in fulfilling their role if they are strong and independent and if a favorable environment exists. This favorable environment depends on a balance of power between different groups, which leads to "institutionalized uncertainty" and facilitates compromise and democratic transition. Next, a professional, apolitical military is important because if the armed forces have institutional interests and the capacity to intervene, authoritarian backsliding might be inevitable. Lastly, ethnoreligious and regional cleavages that can derail the democratic constitutional bargaining should be minimal.

Finally, as inclusive and participatory processes inevitably broaden constitutional debates across the society, steering these debates becomes crucial for democratic transition. More specifically, democratization is likely to be on the horizon when constitutional debates and negotiations encompass both political institutions and social and ideological issues. In the Tunisian constitutional negotiation process, two types of contentious debates emerged. On the one hand, ideological and religious provisions of the constitution (from role of religion and Sharia to gender equality to the Israeli–Palestinian issue) were heatedly debated among the general public, civil groups, and political parties. To avoid societal polarization, the constitution adopted a middle-ground solution to address these issues. The NCA achieved this through an "incrementalist" approach to constitution-writing that involved avoiding clear-cut provisions on polarizing issues and instead using ambiguous legal language and inserting contradictory provisions on polarizing ideological issues (see Lerner 2011). On the other hand, contentious debates on designing political institutions emerged mostly in the NCA, without much public engagement. In the absence of public enthusiasm, civil society played a crucial role in keeping people informed and ensuring that constitutional negotiations yield democratic institutions that fortify constitutionalism and rule of law.

In sum, Tunisia's unique experience was due to several factors working in conjunction. An inclusive and participatory constitution-making process facilitated cross-societal negotiations. An independent and organized civil society, working in a relatively friendly political environment, played an active role in steering those constitutional debates. And these constitutional debates led to a democratic and consensual constitution accepted by most people and groups in the country, paving the way for a successful democratic transition. The next three chapters expand on these three factors by examining the failed pathways of constitutional negotiations in facilitating democratic transition in the region.

4

Pathways of Failure

The Importance of the Process

On January 15, 2015, Yemen's CDC, a panel of seventeen independent experts, published a draft constitution based on 1,800 recommendations drafted by the National Dialogue Conference (NDC) after several months of negotiations and public outreach. That same day, the Shia Houthis expressed their dissatisfaction with the draft constitution by kidnapping the president's chief of staff on his way to deliver the draft constitution to President Hadi. A week later, the Houthis surrounded and bombed the presidential palace forcing President Hadi to sign his resignation letter and pushing Yemen into a civil war, which has so far claimed more than 100,000 lives. The 2015 draft constitution was the most democratic one in Yemen's history: it created a federalist system with semi-independence for different northern and southern regions; it envisioned a balance of power between the executive and legislative branches; and it was not short on guarantees on various human rights. This raises the question, why did such a democratic constitution instigate a civil war? The answer, this chapter argues, lies in how the constitution was crafted. In countries struggling with historically rooted ethnic cleavages and experiencing a security vacuum, noninclusive constitution-making processes raise the risk of prolonged ethnic conflict, as was the case in Yemen and Libya.

The previous chapters offered empirical evidence, from across the world, the Middle East, and Tunisia, that the most ideal procedure of constitution-making is an inclusive and participatory process. The inclusion of major political blocs, ethnic groups, civil society associations, and societal interests in the constitution-making process legitimizes the constitution and increases its democratic quality. By far, only Tunisia's constitutional process included these aspects. All other constitutional reforms in the aftermath of the Arab Spring failed to adopt democratic and inclusive processes. What emerged, instead, were four different pathways of constitutional reform processes, all of which were incapable of ushering in democracy in Arab countries.

The first or "populist" pathway, best exemplified in the case of Egypt in 2012, is through constitutional processes where the general public is mobilized to participate in the constitutional debate for populist purposes, but the process does not ensure the inclusion of public input because representatives of major societal interests are excluded (Maboudi and Nadi 2016).[1] The second failed pathway of constitution-making involves "window-dressing" constitutions. These processes emerged in either poor monarchies, where a minimal degree of political and civic participation existed (Jordan 2011 and Morocco 2011), or in Arab republics that were under immense pressure to democratize (Egypt 2014 and Algeria 2016). The third failed pathway is through the "closed" constitutional reform process, which emerged in three specific contexts. The first context is the rule by an ethnic minority, where an authoritarian ruler is from an ethnic minority and governs by exploiting ethnic divisions. In this case, power-sharing through an inclusive process was not an option for the ruler and his ethnic group (Bahrain 2012 and Syria 2012). The second context for these authoritarian governments involves oil-rich, stable monarchies with no history of constitutionalism where the monarch did not feel the pressure or necessity for an inclusive process (Oman 2011 and Saudi Arabia 2013). The third context is marked by democratic backsliding, where constitutional reform is a crucial step to strengthen the incumbent's grip over power (Egypt 2019). The last failed pathway of constitution-making includes "conflict" constitutions (see Johnson 2017). Yemen and Libya are the prime examples of conflict constitutions that involve a noninclusive process in ethnically or regionally divided nations, and where the process of crafting the constitution only exacerbates the existing conflict. Before explaining each of these four failed pathways of constitution-making in the aftermath of the Arab Spring, this chapter first offers an overview of some of the key dimensions of constitution-making processes, which have been explored in the extant literature.

DOES THE PROCESS MATTER?

In the last few decades, a growing body of literature has emerged that contends that the process of constitution-making has serious implications for various constitutional outcomes including democracy and political stability (Widner 2008; Eisenstadt et al. 2015). Normatively, procedural features of constitutional negotiations determine whether a country can establish a stable democratic government. Empirically, however, it is difficult to assess the effectiveness of

---

[1]   See Table 7.1 for the summary of different types of constitution-making processes.

the process in specific cases. Recent scholarship shows that several procedural factors have a unique impact on constitutional outcomes, including the duration of the process, the size of the constitution drafting assemblies, the procedural rules of constitutional adoption, and, perhaps most importantly, who is involved in the process and to what degree.

The first dimension of the process is the duration of constitution-making. In a study of 148 constitutional cases, Ginsburg et al. (2009, 209) find that the average length of constitutional processes is sixteen months with a standard deviation of twenty-two months. They find that both very short and very long processes occur in nondemocracies and prescribe average-length processes because "speedy processes do not allow sufficient time for mobilization of the public and civil society, whereas extended processes are unlikely to hold public attention for the duration" (Ginsburg et al. 2009, 209–210). The Arab Spring constitutional reform processes confirm this observation. The process in Tunisia lasted for about two years from February 1, 2012, when the 132 constitution drafters held their first meeting, to January 26, 2014, when the NCA adopted the constitution. By contrast, undemocratic processes were either too long or too short. For example, the constitutional reform process in Algeria lasted almost five years (2011–2016). By contrast, the process of the first Egyptian constitutional change lasted about six months (from June 2012 to December 2012), and in Syria (from November 2011 to February 2012) and Morocco (from March 2011 to July 2011), the process took only about four months.

Another important aspect of the process is the size of CDCs. Evidence from recent constitution-making experiences seems to support medium-sized committees. On the one hand, very small committees are often unrepresentative, as was evident in the cases of Morocco and Yemen, for example, where the CDCs had fewer than twenty members. Very large committees, on the other hand, can make reaching agreement more difficult or result in incoherent Magna Carta (Bannon 2007). A general rule of thumb is that constitutional committees should be large enough to represent different political spectrums, ethnoreligious groups, and regions but not too large to hinder negotiations.

The procedural rules of constitutional adoption are a third aspect of the process. Since the Third Wave of democracy, there has been an emphasis on constitutional referenda as a democratic means for fostering accountability. In one of the most comprehensive studies of the content of constitutions, Elkins et al. (2009) evaluate the content of 806 constitutions since 1789 and find that constitutions that require a referendum for ratifying any future modifications have more human rights provisions than those without the referendum requirement. However, appeal to a referendum is not necessarily the best adoption mechanism for constitutions. In a study of 132 national constitutions between 1974 and 2011, Eisenstadt et al. (2015) show that the emphasis on referenda is wrongly placed, and what really matters for the democratic outcome of constitutions is more inclusion in the early stages of the process than in the later stage of ratification. Indeed, while most of the nondemocratic processes during the Arab Spring wave employed public referenda for ratifying the constitution, the only democratic process (i.e., Tunisia) did not utilize this mechanism for adopting the constitution.

The last, and most important, aspect of the process involves the actors engaged in constitution-making. Actors bring along a wide range of institutional, collective, or personal interests in constitutional negotiations. As Elster (1997, 130) argues, for a democratic constitution, the self-interest of the drafters is less important than the interests of their constituents. However, drafters always have a certain degree of self-interest that they take into consideration when drafting the constitution. In the Tunisian National Dialogue with Citizens, for example, a large number of citizens demanded that the NCA representatives should not be allowed to switch political parties while in office, out of respect for their constituencies. The Constituent Assembly deputies, however, did not consider this suggestion simply because a large number of them had already switched parties or did not want to bind themselves to such a restrictive rule. The question remains whether these individual, collective, or institutional interests have any impact on the content of the constitution. Elkins et al. (2009) examine one aspect of the drafters' institutional interest: whether legislatures produce constitutions that give more power to the parliament than the executive. They found no statistical support for this hypothesis, concluding that legislature-centered processes do not necessarily produce constitutions with more parliamentary power than special constituent assemblies (Elkins et al. 2009, 213).

The military is another actor often striving to secure its institutional interests. Eisenstadt et al. (2017a) argue that "top-down" processes by executive or military decree produce less democratic constitutional outcomes than "bottom-up" processes. A number of case studies show how the exclusion or inclusion of the armed forces affected the democratic content of constitutions. For example, the exclusion of the Colombian armed forces from the constitution-making process eventually led to the prohibition on prosecutions of civilians in military courts (Marulanda 2004, 24). In Guatemala, by contrast, the military *junta* leading the political transition (1982–1985) dictated the content of constitutional reforms concerning military institutions, even though the military was not directly involved in the National Constituent Assembly (Brett and Delgado 2005, 10). Constitutional processes under military rule are not, however, always undemocratic. Ginsburg et al. (2009) find that the modal design process for both military and civilian dictatorship regimes is the referendum-executive model with forty-seven out of ninety-two constitutions promulgated under military rule holding public referenda for constitution ratification.

More recently, the general public's engagement in the process has stirred a debate on participatory constitution-making. This literature posits that citizen participation and the inclusion of different societal groups can positively affect the democratic outcome of constitutions (Bannon 2007). For example, Hart (2003, 10) finds that women's active engagement in Uganda's 1996 constitution-making process ensured substantial gains for women's rights. Several other case studies suggest that participatory processes resulted in the inclusion of several provisions on social and economic justice and corruption in Kenya (Cottrell and Ghai 2007), civil rights such as the right of the disabled people in Colombia (Brett and Delgado 2005), and rights of indigenous people in Guatemala (Marulanda 2004). In a case study of twelve constitutional processes, Samuels (2006) shows that in general, more participatory processes tend to generate constitutions with a more democratic content. Ginsburg et al. (2009) also show that processes involving referenda generally produce constitutions that are more likely to have various rights provisions.

The cross-national statistical analysis in Chapter 2 also shows that more inclusive and participatory processes are likely to generate more constitutional rights. Building on deliberative and participatory theories of democracy, Chapters 2 and 3 suggest that the inclusion of different societal groups and the general public in the process has significant implications for the democratic content of constitutions. This chapter shifts the focus to nonparticipatory and noninclusive processes and their implications for democratic outcomes by examining four distinct failed pathways of constitution-making and democratization in the aftermath of the Arab Spring, including populist, window-dressing, closed, and conflict constitutions.

THE ARAB SPRING CONSTITUTIONAL REFORM PROCESSES

Since the 2010–2011 uprisings, six Arab nations wrote new constitutions: five new constitutions were adopted in Morocco (2011), Syria (2012), Egypt (2012 and 2014), and Tunisia (2014), and two other constitutional reforms failed to adopt a permanent constitution in Yemen (2015) and Libya (2017). Furthermore, six nations amended their constitutions: Jordan (2011, 2014, and 2016), Oman (2011), Bahrain (2012 and 2017), Saudi Arabia (2013), Algeria (2016), and Egypt (2019).

Five of these constitutional events followed a regime breakdown or fall of a leader in Egypt (2012 and 2014), Tunisia, Libya, and Yemen. Yet, all of these cases took very different paths to write the new constitution. As the previous chapter showed, Tunisia was the only country to embark on an inclusive and participatory process. In Egypt, the first constitutional reform process started out with widespread public participation and was relatively inclusive but gradually became less inclusive and lost its public legitimacy. And the inclusion of a select number of groups (along with limited participatory platforms) in the second constitutional process in the country fulfilled a window-dressing function. Lastly, in Libya and Yemen, ethnoreligious or regional cleavages overwhelmed the process, leading to a failure in adopting the new constitution.

Where an authoritarian regime initiated the constitutional reform process, as was the case in the remaining eleven constitutional events, a trend started to emerge. Window-dressing constitutional processes emerged in most contested regimes that were under immense popular pressure for liberalization. By contrast, closed constitutions with completely top-down processes emerged in stable regimes or those with minority rule where power-sharing was not even an option for the challenged incumbents. The remainder of this chapter examines each of these pathways in detail.

Populist Constitution-Making: Participation without Inclusion

As the previous chapter shows, genuine (as opposed to window-dressing) participatory processes mobilize large segments of the society. This public mobilization carries certain risks. In Tunisia, increased public mobilization pressured Ennahda, the incumbent party, to modify its position on several constitutional issues. Previous studies show that public engagement in the process is likely to lead to increased public knowledge about the constitution (Moehler 2008; Elkins et al. 2009). Increased constitutional knowledge leads to more expectations, and if these expectations are not met, they can lead to widespread frustration. The Tunisian Ennahda party compromised on several ideological matters to meet these public expectations and stem public frustration. As discussed in the previous chapter, Ennahda showed flexibility in part because it did not hold the two-thirds majority required for approving the constitution. However, a group in a constituent assembly that has the required threshold for adopting the constitution will have fewer incentives to compromise, in which case opposition groups are most likely to boycott the process. And if the opposition boycotts the process, the in-power bloc might mobilize widespread public participation to legitimize its constitution. In short, the main function of public participation in this context is for populistic purposes.

While populist constitution-making indeed utilizes populist rhetoric – which can also be seen in window-dressing processes – it is not merely defined by rhetoric. The populist pathway of constitution-making, similar to populist governments or movements, is an extreme form of majoritarianism, which stands in tension with the democratic values of pluralism (see Mudde 2013; Weyland 2013). Populist constitution-making involves massive public mobilization to impose the will of the majority. By excluding whoever opposes the majority's will, the populist pathway is best defined as a noninclusive process. The massive public mobilization that excludes opposition voices from constitutional debates, however, increases the danger of rising public frustration, which can even lead to rebellion. If a process with massive public engagement and mobilization fails to incorporate dissenting public opinion, the opposition will have a loaded weapon ready in hand: the already mobilized and frustrated citizens. In other words, populist participation without inclusion can backfire, as was the case in Egypt's 2012 constitutional reform process.

From Participation to Rebellion: Egypt 2012

Scholars commonly contrast the post-revolution constitutional outcomes in Tunisia and Egypt to explain the trajectories of success and failure in democratic transitions in the Arab world (see, e.g., Johnson 2015; Parolin 2015; Cross and Sorens 2016; Jamal and Kensicki 2016; Hartshorn 2017; Genauer 2020). Indeed, the Egyptian constitutional reform in 2012 was the closest in the region to the modal process in Tunisia. Although the two processes had important differences that eventually led to very different outcomes, they were both extensively participatory. The Egyptian constitutional reform, similar to that of Tunisia, was the result of regime breakdown. On February 11, 2011, Hosni Mubarak, Egypt's president of thirty years, stepped down after eighteen days of demonstrations during the 2011 uprising in Cairo and other major cities and transferred authority to the Supreme Council of the Armed Forces (SCAF). Mubarak was the second Arab leader to step down after Tunisia's Ben Ali was forced to flee to Saudi Arabia on January 14, 2011. Unlike in Tunisia, the military was a key player in the transitional process and emerged as the ultimate winner by eliminating Mubarak as well as non-Islamist and Islamist oppositions (Brown 2013, 47).

The military's success in sidelining both the Islamists and non-Islamists was mostly because of the division, polarization, and mistrust between the two groups. From the onset of the revolution, Egyptian opposition groups were divided over several critical issues, unable to agree on a unitary plan for the transitional period. When they agreed, it was usually because of the military's threat. At the start of the transition, for instance, the question of whether elections or constitution-writing should come first divided these groups. Most young non-Islamists who stirred the protests argued that the constitution should precede elections, reasoning that the Muslim Brotherhood was so strong (and fundamentally undemocratic) that if there were any elections, they would dominate the post-election constitution-making process (The Carnegie Endowment 2011). The Muslim Brotherhood (along with SCAF), by contrast, supported holding elections prior to constitution-making (Stepan and Linz 2013, 21–22).

Ultimately, it was decided that parliamentary and presidential elections would be held prior to writing a new constitution. However, the SCAF and opposition groups failed to specify the powers of the parliament. As a result, when Islamists won the January 2012 election of the House of Representatives (HOR), they came to realize that this electoral victory gave them no real power to change the status quo and discharge their duties, including the selection of the 100-member Constituent Assembly (Brown 2013, 48–49). The 100 seats of the first Constituent Assembly (CA) were allocated to different political parties by the HOR based on the results of the election. The CA as such enjoyed some democratic legitimacy (Brown 2012). However, Egypt's Supreme Administrative Court dissolved the CA on April 10, 2012, only one month into its life, due to lawsuits and complaints from liberal and non-Islamist groups who claimed that the Constituent Assembly did not represent the diversity of the Egyptian society (Knell 2012). After a short while, the SCAF threatened all opposition groups that it would impose its own assembly if all political parties involved did not reach an agreement on the allocation of seats to different groups. Under the military threat to take over the constitution-making process, representatives of twenty-two political parties and the military reached an agreement on June 7 to start the constitution-making process (Bell 2012).

The structure of the second Constituent Assembly was, as such, hammered out only after a military ultimatum. The agreement on the composition of the second Constituent Assembly came only seven days prior to the dissolution of the democratically elected HOR, which was dissolved by the SCAF after a court ruling decided that the parliamentary elections were unconstitutional (BBC News Middle East 2012). Another blow to the Constituent Assembly came after the military added a new provision (Article 60B) to the provisional constitution on June 17, giving itself the power to dissolve the Constituent Assembly if it "encounters obstacles that prevent it from completing its work" (Rashwan 2012).

It was under these circumstances that on June 26, the first session of the Constituent Assembly convened to begin the drafting process by choosing the subcommittees. In the new Constituent Assembly, thirty-nine members were elected from the sitting HOR dominated by the Muslim Brotherhood's Freedom and Justice Party and the Salafist Noor Party. Six seats were allocated to judges; nine seats were given to law experts; and one seat each was given to the armed forces, police, and justice ministry. Additionally, thirteen seats were given to unions, five to Al-Azhar University, and four to the Coptic Orthodox Church of Egypt, and the remaining twenty-one seats were allocated to public figures (Bell 2012). This composition gave the Islamists more than a simple majority, which was required to approve the constitution. Soon after the establishment of this second Constituent Assembly, the non-Islamists again complained that the composition of the CA was nonrepresentative and that they only agreed to it under the military's threat to take over the process. Despite these complaints, the non-Islamists agreed to start the constitution-making process by creating the constitutional committees of the Constituent Assembly.

The Constituent Assembly was made up of five committees, including the Drafting and Research Committee, which was assigned the task of receiving suggestions from the general public and experts. Believing that the majority of people support them, the Islamists speculated that extensive public outreach would only strengthen their position in the constitutional bargain; therefore, they vehemently advocated for a participatory process. According to Justice Hossam Ghariani, chairman of the Constituent Assembly, the various committees toured different governorates in the country and solicited people's suggestions. These consultations consisted of 160 sessions in all provinces (Ikhwan Web 2012). By December 4, the CA had received 35,000 proposals from the public consisting of one or several articles or even full constitutions. Furthermore, beginning on August 11, the proposed constitutional drafts were put online, and people were able to comment on the drafts or show their support or disapproval by voting on each article. All the meetings of the Assembly including all the 408 committee sessions, which amounted to 1,622 hours, were broadcast through media outlets (Ikhwan Web 2012).

After the publication of the first draft constitution on October 10, the Constituent Assembly launched the "Know Your Constitution" campaign to encourage community dialogue and to provide a channel for citizens to familiarize themselves with it (Egypt Independent 2012b). Joining the campaign were television and radio programs explaining the content of the constitution. Furthermore, public consultation meetings were held with substantial public attendance to receive suggestions on the first draft (Ahram Online 2012a). Also, ninety-five information centers were established nationwide in order to provide information to citizens (Egypt Independent 2012a). Among other activities of the Campaign were special panels held for public discussion. One panel, for example, discussed "the articles that caused a dispute among civil powers" (El-Behairy 2012).

These public outreach platforms utilized different innovative means to solicit public feedback. As mentioned previously, one of the means that the Constituent Assembly used for engaging citizens was crowdsourcing. Following Iceland, Egypt was only the second country in the world to use social media and internet resources to promote public participation and receive citizen feedback on each proposed draft of each article. Egyptian citizens were able to sign in to the official website of the Constituent Assembly using their Facebook, Twitter, Gmail, or Yahoo Mail accounts, to comment on the drafts and express their preferences by voting "yes" or "no." The name of this webpage was *Sharek* (Participate) and its logo read "The Nation Writes Its Own Constitution." That the Assembly refused to consider most of the public's input after the boycott by the opposition demonstrates that this slogan was nothing but populist rhetoric (Maboudi and Nadi 2016).

Overall, 68,130 citizens made 653,718 online contributions to the draft constitution. Of this number, 75,626 (12 percent) were comments on various drafts, and 578,092 (88 percent) were feedback in the form of "likes" and "dislikes." Similar to the participatory process in Tunisia, the majority of both online and on-site comments were related to general principles as well as rights and freedoms, demonstrating the concerns of participants. The most controversial article (with the largest number of both online public approval and disapproval) was Article 2, which stated that Islamic Sharia is the main source of legislation. Article 2 was also the most discussed provision and received 15,761 comments from participants who discussed the proposed draft and provided their opinions on the subject.[2]

Despite the extensive citizen participation, the 2012 constitution-making process was not inclusive because most non-Islamist Assembly members withdrew from it, due to the increased polarization between Islamists and non-Islamists, making the Muslim Brotherhood the sole author of the constitution. The Islamist and non-Islamist fronts in the Constituent Assembly failed to agree on the broader future they envisioned for Egypt, and their discord derailed the process. Even several months after Mubarak's ouster, these two major opposition groups had not held a single joint meeting to discuss a road map for democratic transition (Stepan and Linz 2013, 23). And when the SCAF handed over power to the civilian president on June 30, 2012, the division between the two major opposition groups (Islamists and non-Islamists) became deeper. Chairs of all constitutional

---

[2]   See Maboudi and Nadi (2016) for more on the online crowdsourcing process in Egypt.

committees were selected from the Muslim Brotherhood's Freedom and Justice Party in the first round of meetings in mid-July, prompting six members of the Constituent Assembly from the Egyptian Bloc to resign. They cited their concern over the Islamist monopolization and the lack of representation for women, young people, and Coptic Christians (Ahram Online 2012c). The wave of withdrawals by non-Islamist members of the Assembly continued with the highly publicized resignation of Manal El-Teiby. El-Teiby, a Nubian rights activist and advocate for freedom of religion, cited a smear campaign by the Islamist members of the Assembly as the main reason for her resignation (Enein 2012). Several other waves of withdrawal and boycotts by non-Islamists took place from late September to November 2012, mainly as a strategy to try to stop the Islamists from writing the constitution by stripping the Constituent Assembly of legitimacy.

Withdrawal from the Constituent Assembly, however, was only one of the strategies the non-Islamists used to force the Islamists to compromise. Another attempt was to file a lawsuit against the constitutionality of the Assembly. The process of drafting the constitution nevertheless continued, with the Administrative Court postponing its verdict on the constitutionality of the Assembly several times. On October 23, the Administrative Court finally gave its verdict and referred the lawsuit against the Constituent Assembly to the Supreme Constitutional Court (SCC). This decision came as a relief to the Islamists since it gave them time to finish the drafting process. The SCC was to examine the case in forty-five days that gave ample time for the Assembly to finalize and put the draft to a referendum and consequently avoid the threat of dissolution by the SCC (Ibrahim 2012). This decision by the Administrative Court prompted criticism by non-Islamist groups. Ahmad Said, the head of the liberal Free Egyptians Party, accused the Muslim Brotherhood of using the situation "to confuse the political scene in order to earn more time until it can pass a constitution that doesn't represent the Egyptian people" (Ibrahim 2012).

Despite the growing number of withdrawals from non-Islamist members of the Constituent Assembly, the Assembly accelerated the pace of reviewing and voting on the constitution's articles in order to finish drafting before the SCC's sessions. The Assembly held its last meeting on November 29, and after a nineteen-hour marathon session, the draft constitution was approved with only eighty-five members present and the complete absence of non-Islamist members (Russia Today 2012).[3] After the Assembly approved the constitution, it was put to a referendum on December 15.

---

[3] The CA had 150 members, 100 of which were the main members and 50 were reserve members. Of these 150 members, only 85 remained and voted on the proposed constitutions.

To ensure victory in the referendum, the Muslim Brotherhood's Freedom and Justice Party launched a campaign called "With the Constitution the Wheel of Production Will Spin," to encourage people to participate in the referendum. As part of this campaign, a website was launched to encourage discussion, questions, and suggestions about the new constitution (El-Behairy 2012). The Muslim Brotherhood's extensive campaign for public participation, while it refused to compromise on key issues or share power with other opposition groups, raised more suspicion among the non-Islamist opposition that the Muslim Brotherhood was using public participation as a populistic tool to legitimize the constitution without much input from other groups (Ahmed Maher [co-founder of April 6 Youth Movement], interview by author, May 7, 2013). As a result, the opposition and non-Islamist groups protesting the constitution initiated their own awareness campaigns educating people about the content of the constitution and the reasons why they should reject it. For example, the April 6 Youth Movement launched the "Protect Your Constitution" campaign explaining the issues of disagreement in the constitution, why the April 6 Youth Movement rejected it, and accusing the Muslim Brotherhood of attempting to deceive the public by spreading misinformation regarding certain articles (El-Behairy 2012). Other groups, such as former members of the defunct National Democratic Party, launched a similar campaign informing people about the "dangerous" articles of the constitution and urging them to reject it (Ahram Online 2012b).

Despite these campaigns, the constitution was eventually approved with a 64 percent vote. However, the referendum turnout was low with only 31 percent of eligible voters participating. In Cairo, about 57 percent of the voters rejected the constitution, indicating the public's discontent with the constitution in the largest city in the Arab world (Stamboliyska 2012). Immediately after the referendum, the opposition mobilized protests and demanded comprehensive amendments to the constitution while the SCC postponed all elections until reforms were made to electoral laws (Ahram Online 2013).

While public demonstrations against the Muslim Brotherhood government and its constitution were growing every day, the Muslim Brotherhood's intransigence in rejecting inclusive dialogues pushed the opposition to their last resort, military intervention. The opposition had already organized a rebellion campaign, called *Tamarod*, against the Muslim Brotherhood and its constitution before some opposition figures turned to the military. When the opposition to the Muslim Brotherhood grew more violent in the summer of 2013, the military took the opportunity to intervene and regain its control of the state. Capitalizing on the popular discontent with the Muslim

Brotherhood's government and constitution, the military staged a coup, removed President Morsi, and suspended the constitution.

The broad public engagement in constitution-making, which early in the process included all major groups, raised expectations about a successful democratic transition in Egypt. The Muslim Brotherhood, however, used the participatory process to serve a populistic purpose. In spite of its emphasis on extensive public participation, the Muslim Brotherhood excluded the opposition from constitutional negotiations, leading the opposition to conclude that the participatory process was not genuine but rather a populistic strategy to legitimize the Muslim Brotherhood's constitution. The wave of boycotts and withdrawals that followed rendered public input ineffective because representatives were no longer in the room to advocate for their constituencies' demands (Maboudi and Nadi 2016). Major factors that contributed to the failure of constitutional negotiations include a rushed process that took less than six months, the absence of a strong independent civil society as the arbiter of disputes between different groups, and a powerful military that overshadowed the whole process. Nevertheless, the populist constitutional reform process that led to public frustration and a rebellion was a major contributor to the failure of democratic transition. In sum, despite unprecedented public participation in the history of constitution-making in the Arab world, a noninclusive process paved the way for the first democratic backsliding following the Arab Spring.

Window-Dressing Constitution-Making

In the wake of regime breakdowns in Tunisia and Egypt, which were once the strongholds of authoritarianism in the region, Arab leaders began to feel vulnerable. When they encountered masses of people protesting against social, economic, and political problems in their countries, these leaders attempted to tame their demands by promising a wide range of concessions and reforms, including constitutional reforms that were set up to be participatory and inclusive. However, it soon became clear that Arab leaders initiated these seemingly inclusive constitutional reforms only as a superficial expression of support for democratic governance. Although a few of these countries allowed, for the first time in their constitution-making histories, the opposition parties to be part of the constitutional debate, this inclusion was limited to nonradical groups that did not have regime change on their agenda. These window-dressing constitutional reform processes emerged in two particular settings. The first were constitutional reforms in Morocco and Jordan, poor monarchies that resorted to inclusive processes to co-opt the opposition because they did not possess the material resources for economic co-optation. The second group of window-dressing constitutions took place in two troubled Arab republics (post-2013 Egypt and Algeria) that were under immense and unprecedented public pressure to liberalize. In both countries, the de facto leaders (General El-Sisi in Egypt and President Bouteflika in Algeria) had to incorporate some degree of inclusion in order to legitimize the process and stabilize their countries. That is, in contrast to the populist pathway that excludes representatives of minority groups, the window-dressing pathway includes representatives of a select group of "insiders" including some minorities. Furthermore, unlike the populist pathway that emphasizes mass public participation, the window-dressing pathway seeks to demobilize the general public as much as possible.

Inclusion as Co-Optation: Morocco and Jordan

Demonstrations in Morocco were much smaller in size compared to Egypt or Tunisia, but the country was the first to respond to the uprisings by adopting a new constitution on July 1, 2011 (Molina 2011). Following in the footsteps of other Arab citizens, a group of Moroccan youths (later came to be known as the February 20 Youth Movement) organized mass protests in Rabat, Casablanca, and other cities on February 20, 2011 (Benchemsi 2012). Demonstrators called for a new constitution to institutionalize political reforms. The February 20 Youth Movement had three major demands. First, they wanted a new constitution to be written by an elected constituent assembly (Mohammed El-Hachemi, interview by author, November 23, 2014). The other two major political demands for the constitution were an independent judicial system and, most importantly, a constitutional monarchy in which the king only holds a ceremonial role (Molina 2011). They also demanded economic and social reforms to address corruption, poverty, and unemployment (Maddy-Weitzman 2012). In response to the protests, King Mohammed VI gave a rare, televised speech known as the "March 9 speech" promising (without mentioning the February 20 Youth Movement) a "comprehensive constitutional change" featuring "the rule of law," an "independent judiciary," and an "elected government that reflects the will of the people, through the ballot box" (Banani 2012, 11–15). The king declared that he had prepared a plan and agenda to draft a new constitution and that he would assign an Advisory Committee to review and reform it in less than four months and submit the proposed constitutional reforms to a referendum by the first of July that year (El-Madani et al. 2012).

The process of reforming the constitution consisted of the creation of two constitution-making bodies, including an expert, independent drafting commission and a political consulting commission. The king appointed nineteen independent constitutional experts to an ad hoc Consultative Commission for the Reform of the Constitution (CCRC).[4] The president of the CCRC was Abdellatif El-Manouni, one of the king's former professors and a renowned law expert at the University of Rabat. The CCRC members were then divided into five subcommittees: the Basic Rights, Government, Parliament, Judiciary and Decentralization, and Civil Society and Opposition Rights committees. Each of the subcommittees was responsible to study and revise certain sections and chapters of the constitution.

The CCRC's work was to be supervised and complemented by the Political Mechanism for the Monitoring of the Constitutional Reform (PMMCR), a political consulting commission composed of leaders of political parties, trade unions, and CSOs (Molina 2011). Seven political parties representing different ideologies participated in the PMMCR, with the right-wing parties having a slight majority. The king appointed Mohammed Moâtassim, a royal advisor and confidant, as the head of the PMMCR. Moâtassim was responsible for inviting political parties, CSOs, and activists to the PMMCR to listen to their arguments and demands and give a report to the CCRC for consideration (El-Madani et al. 2012). All recognized social and political groups were also invited to directly submit their proposals to the CCRC. A few groups, including the February 20 Youth Movement, minority left-wing parties, and three human rights associations boycotted the process (Molina 2011), arguing that their most important demand, that is, an elected constituent assembly to write the constitution, had not been met (Mohammed El-Hachemi, interview by author, November 23, 2014).

When the CCRC started its work, four members, including Edris El-Yazmi, argued that the process should be open to the general public and that the commission should solicit public feedback. The majority disagreed, however, arguing that the king's March 9 speech was clear and that they should follow the guidelines he set forth in that speech, rather than following public suggestions. Eventually, Moâtassim, who was considered the architect of the constitution-writing process, weighed in and opened up the process for public consultation (anonymous member of the CCRC, interview by author, January 30, 2019). However, the CCRC did not receive public feedback directly from citizens. Under Moâtassim's guidelines, the PMMCR dedicated a phone number and an email address for the Moroccan people to submit their suggestions. After collecting public suggestions, the PMMCR sent

---

[4] None of the CCRC members had any official affiliation with any political party, but all were loyal to the king.

a separate report to each of the CCRC's subcommittees listing the relevant suggestions they solicited. Overall, the PMMCR forwarded about 1,000 public suggestions almost equally divided among the five subcommittees (anonymous member of the CCRC, interview by author, January 30, 2019). Due to the lack of transparency in the process, however, it is not known how many people participated, how many citizen proposals were really received, or what were the content of those citizen proposals. The fact that the Judiciary subcommittee received roughly the same number of public proposals as the Basic Rights subcommittee did, for example, raises suspicions on its own.[5] Moreover, it is unclear how much of the input from the general public or different societal and political groups was included in the final constitution. Such information has never been reported or publicized (Ma'ati Monjib, interview by author, November 19, 2014). The nineteen members of the CCRC rarely gave public interviews and did not formally document the public input that they received from the PMMCR.[6] The CCRC only issued extract memos from its own meetings with political parties and civil groups. This was because the majority of the CCRC members did not bind themselves to public suggestions as they were mainly following the king's guidelines in his March 9 speech (anonymous member of the CCRC, interview by author, January 30, 2019).

Despite this secrecy, most legal political groups and CSOs participated in the process by voicing their opinions to the appointed commission. A boycott would likely have cost them their status as "insiders," excluding them from future political decision-making. As Table 4.1 shows, overall 461 individuals representing 101 institutions and organizations participated by providing their views about the constitution.[7] The CCRC held less than 100 hours of hearings with all these organizations and institutions. In other words, each institution or organization had on average less than one hour to express its views.[8] At the end of these hearings, 185 memos were created. The participating organizations were not given another opportunity for consultation or debate on potential provisions.

The CCRC eventually submitted its draft constitution to King Mohammed VI who approved it in mid-June. The king gave a televised speech on June 17,

---

[5]   In most participatory processes including those in Tunisia and Egypt, the majority of citizens were more interested in issues related to rights and freedoms and offered a significantly larger number of inputs on these topics compared to state institutions, for example (see Maboudi and Nadi 2016).

[6]   A CCRC member who spoke to me on the condition of anonymity said that they just took note of the input they received from the general public in their personal notebooks.

[7]   About 18 percent of participants (eighty-three individuals) were women.

[8]   On average, each individual had only thirteen minutes to speak.

TABLE 4.1 *Participation of institutions, organizations, and individuals in Morocco*

Institutions and Organizations	No. of Institutions	No. of Individuals	Hearing Hours	Memos
Political Parties	32	142	48	32
Unions	5	33	7.5	10
Human Rights Associations	10	26	4	12
Women Rights Associations	11	32	4	17
Judicial Reform Associations	5	13	4	5
The Moralization of Public Life	5	17	4	1
Amazigh Associations	4	13	4	4
General Confederation of Moroccan Enterprise	1	5	2	7
Experts	4	4	2	7
Media Organizations	2	8	2	2
Development Associations	8	16	4	4
Art and Culture	1	18	2	1
Sport Clubs	1	20	1	1
Youth Associations	12	38	5	6
Individual Youths	–	76	5	21
Various Volunteer Bodies	–	–	–	55
Total	101	461	98.5	185

Source: Banani (2012)

outlining the draft constitution and inviting the public to vote "yes" for the constitution in a referendum on July 1. The February 20 Youth Movement and Al-Adl Wal-Ihsan (Justice and Benevolence) – a strong Islamist association, which is banned but reluctantly tolerated by the state – boycotted the constitutional referendum (Maddy-Weitzman 2012). The king, however, ordered all mosque preachers around the country to preach for a "yes" vote. The constitutional referendum was the very first since Mohammed VI's reign started in 1999 and as such was seen as a test for the king's popularity (Rached Touhtouh, interview by author, November 20, 2014). With a strong state-sponsored campaign for the constitution, the draft constitution was approved with a 98.5 percent "yes" vote and a turnout of about 73 percent of eligible voters (Benchemsi 2012, 57).

The constitution-making process was criticized for its short timeframe and the secrecy that shrouded the proceedings (Molina 2011).[9] There was also no deliberation between the CCRC and political parties; rather, the whole

---

[9] The writing of the constitution took less than three months, and the whole process from the formation of the two commissions to the public referendum lasted about four months.

process was a one-way communication with political parties submitting their proposals to the CCRC (Rached Touhtouh, interview by author, November 20, 2014). The CCRC wrote the constitution and submitted it to the king without further interaction or consultation with the participating groups. The parties received a written copy of the draft the night before the king officially announced the constitution on June 17 and called for a constitutional referendum, which took place two weeks later (Molina 2011). The invited political parties (excluding those that did not participate) were only verbally briefed about the outline and the main content of the draft a week earlier (Molina 2011). Moreover, the constitution was modified three times after the political parties were briefed about its content. First, Moâtassim introduced some modifications to the draft only three hours before the king announced the constitution on June 17.[10] Then, only one day before the constitutional referendum, three articles relating to the judiciary were modified. And finally, a week after the referendum, the palace modified another article about judicial independence (Ma'ati Monjib, interview by author, November 19, 2014). A few members of the CCRC, most notably Mohamed El-Touzi and Amina Bouayach, were adamant that the constitution could not be changed after their submission, but the majority remained silent and preferred not to challenge the king's decision (anonymous member of the CCRC, interview by author, January 30, 2019).

The opposition, however, protested to these changes, arguing that altering the constitution after it was approved by the public rendered it illegitimate. The opacity of the process along with unilateral changes to the draft constitution raised serious doubts about the whole process, as some opposition figures and activists suggested that there was a "third commission" (beside the CCRC and PMMCR) chaired by the king himself and a group of his close advisors and confidants including Mohammed Moâtassim who wrote and revised the constitution (Ma'ati Monjib, interview by author, November 19, 2014).

Regardless of the existence of a "third" secret commission, one thing is certain: the whole process was neither participatory nor inclusive. It was an autocratic process ordered and orchestrated by the king's decree, designed to give the impression of being inclusive and participatory. For instance, one of the PMMCR's tasks was to invite the public to submit their suggestions via mail or email, but this campaign was never widely publicized as the palace only wanted to brand the process as a "participatory approach" (Mohammed El-Hachemi, interview by author, November 23, 2014). In contrast to the

---

[10]   These modifications came after Moâtassim appointed a small committee to translate the new constitution into Arabic, as the CCRC's draft was written in French.

populistic process in Egypt (2012) that involved extensive public mobilization, public feedback was very limited during the process of constitution-making in Morocco, and citizens were only able to vote on the constitution through a referendum. The process was also noninclusive because the major opposition groups (the February 20 Youth Movement and Al-Adl Wal-Ihsan) were excluded. These groups protested against the constitution and the process by which it was drafted for months, even after the constitution was adopted. They claimed that their three main demands (an elected constituent assembly to draft the constitution, a constitutional monarchy, and an independent judiciary), which were the only guarantees of democracy, were ignored by the monarchy (Ma'ati Monjib, interview by author, November 19, 2014). Eventually, these protests faded away, as the February 20 Youth Movement failed to achieve what it hoped to gain.

In sum, the Moroccan process of constitutional reform was one of the least inclusive among the post–Arab Spring reform processes. The constitutional reform was initiated by the king, under pressure from the February 20 Youth Movement. Public participation and the inclusion of legal parties and civil associations fulfilled a window-dressing function. Because of the secrecy of the process, there is no information on the magnitude of public participation. And each participating political party and civil group had on average only about one hour to express their opinions in a one-shot, one-way communication format. Not surprisingly, the monarchy agreed to implement limited social rights but did not accede to any public demands that targeted the political system.

In Jordan, another relatively poor monarchy, demonstrations started on January 14, 2011, when a few thousand people poured into the streets of the capital city, Amman, and other major cities protesting against mounting food prices, unemployment, and corruption. Similar to Morocco but unlike Egypt, Tunisia, and other countries, protesters did not demand the fall of the ruling regime. However, they demanded the resignation of Prime Minister Samir Rifai, an appointee of King Abdullah II. Since the onset of the uprisings, the Islamic Action Front (IAF), the political arm of the Jordanian Muslim Brotherhood and the largest opposition party, took the lead in mobilizing protesters. A few weeks into the demonstrations, the IAF added calls for political reforms to its demands of economic reforms. Under mounting pressure from protesters, Rifai resigned, and the king appointed Marouf Al-Bakhit as the new prime minister on February 1, 2011. However, the IAF immediately rejected the king's selection, accusing Al-Bakhit of corruption and electoral fraud during his previous tenure as the prime minister between 2005 and 2007.

Continued protests and popular frustration forced the government to take more serious steps. On March 14, Al-Bakhit's cabinet commissioned an independent National Dialogue Committee (NDC) to review the popular demands for reform. The NDC was composed of fifty-two members representing different political groups. The king appointed Taher Al-Masri, the president of the Senate and a former prime minister, to chair the NDC. The IAF refused, however, to join the NDC because it was not mandated to discuss constitutional changes that would potentially curb the king's powers. They also believed that the appointment of Al-Masri, a loyalist, signaled that the king did not want to implement serious reforms. Although this was the very first and most inclusive process in the history of constitution-making in Jordan, the NDC lacked representativeness. Major groups that organized the protests and called for reform, including the Al-Hirak Youth Movement, were excluded. The Workers' Union and important activists such as Laith Shbailat and Toujan Al Faisal, both well-known opposition figures, were not invited either. Only four members represented women, and the youth, which comprise 75 percent of the Jordanian population, did not have any representation. Furthermore, handpicked appointments and lack of transparency added to the lack of legitimacy of the process.

Jordan's NDC functioned at two interrelated levels. First, the general assembly of the NDC included all fifty-two members who debated and voted on the proposed changes. Second, the general assembly established three working groups, which were tasked with drafting an electoral law, drafting a political party law, and formulating general recommendations for legislation. The general assembly met every other week to discuss the proposals presented by the three working groups. The last draft was voted on during the last meeting of the general assembly. During its second meeting, the three working groups were tasked to consult with various segments of the Jordanian society. The working groups visited all governorates, met with people, listened to their views, and presented to them their ideas regarding the new electoral and political parties' law. The public input collected from the governorates were then presented to the general assembly of the NDC.

Several events interrupted the work of the NDC. For example, major deadlocks in the debates, especially related to the electoral system, slowed down negotiations.[11] But the most important interruption to the work of the NDC took place very early on in the process. In late March 2011, less than two weeks after the NDC was formed, sixteen members resigned in protest against

---

[11] Eventually, the UNDP organized a meeting with some international experts on different electoral systems to facilitate the negotiations.

two days of violent clashes between the demonstrators and government loyalists. They denounced the violence and argued that the work of the committee was to manipulate the Jordanian public because, by its violent behavior, the government revealed that it had no intention to make real reforms. The committee members also demanded to meet with the king in person. Following the meeting with the king, who promised to implement the committee's recommendations for reform, all sixteen members revoked their resignation.

Taking the public suggestions and experts' views into account, the NDC developed several recommendations, including the need to amend the constitution together with political reforms regarding electoral laws, partisan pluralism, and the formation of parliamentary governments (Bani Salameh and Ananzah 2015). Based on the recommendation of the NDC, King Abdullah II decided to form a royal committee to review the constitution and draft a proposal for reforming it. On April 26, the king tasked Ahmad Lawzi, a former prime minister, to head the Royal Committee on Constitutional Review (RCCR). The RCCR had ten members, all of whom were conservative politicians and loyal to the king. Ironically, none of the members of the RCCR previously favored constitutional reform as the state's response to the protests (Bani Salameh and Ananzah 2015, 145). Excluded from constitutional negotiations were constitutional experts, civil society representatives, political activists, and major opposition groups. The composition of the RCCR itself led to skepticism regarding the seriousness of the reforms (Seeley 2011).

The RCCR presented its proposal to amend forty-two articles (about one-third of the constitution) on August 14. The king welcomed the proposals, which included the requirement to hold the election within four months (instead of two years) of the dissolution of the lower house by the king, the establishment of a Constitutional Court, and lowering the minimum age of parliamentary election candidates from thirty-five to twenty-five years. On September 30, King Abdullah II issued a decree to approve these constitutional amendments. The IAF and other opposition groups believed, however, that the amendments did not live up to their expectations for democratic reforms. Focusing on Articles 34–36, which address the powers of the king, the IAF argued that these reforms did not make the constitution democratic. The king retained the authority to appoint and dismiss the prime minister and the cabinet members, appoint all members of the upper house of the parliament and judges, issue decree and laws, suspend the parliament, and postpone elections. The only amendment to limit the king's power was that he no longer could postpone elections *indefinitely* (Muasher 2011). The palace, by contrast, framed the constitutional reform process as inclusive and the reforms as democratic, arguing that the IAF itself decided not to be part of the constitutional negotiations and could not, therefore, make any claim about whether the reforms were democratic or not.

Unlike in Morocco, where the monarch managed the opposition to the new constitution very quickly, the constitutional amendments in Jordan did not appease the protesters. And under pressure from the parliament, the king had to sack Prime Minister Al-Bakhit for his failure to implement the promised reforms and appoint Awn Khaswaneh to form a new government. The pressure to reform and protests in Amman and other major cities continued for several more months, often becoming violent. The king subsequently implemented more reforms including his announcement to give lawmakers a say in appointing the cabinet on October 26, 2011, and several electoral reforms in early 2012.

The 2011 constitution was merely window-dressing. That the king appointed four prime ministers in just fourteen months and implemented several legal reforms just weeks and months after accepting the new constitution demonstrates that his intention was never to bring about genuine democratic change.[12] As Chapter 2 shows, constitutional reforms lead to more democratic constitutions only if the process is inclusive and participatory. The Jordanian constitutional reform was neither genuinely inclusive nor participatory. CSOs, political activists, and major opposition groups including the Muslim Brotherhood were all excluded from the constitutional debates. When constitutions are revised only for window-dressing purposes without considering the opinion of major groups in society, the outcome will not be democratic, and the underlying social and political problems that instigated the reforms remain unresolved.

Although participation and inclusion were limited and accepted only for window-dressing purposes, the inclusion of some opposition parties in the. constitutional reform process was unprecedented in the history of Jordan and Morocco. We should note that the majority of protesters in both countries did not seek a regime change and were merely protesting against lack of freedom, corruption, unemployment, and rising cost of living. The two countries are the poorest monarchies in the Arab world.[13] Despite having a large base of supporters among their general public, the two monarchs struggled to appease the protesters unhappy with years of imposed structural adjustment programs,

---

[12]   Prime Minister Khaswaneh resigned on April 26, 2012, due to criticisms of his draft electoral laws. He was replaced by Fayez Al-Tarawneh.

[13]   In 2011, Jordan had a GDP per capita of approximately 3,800 USD, while Morocco ranked the poorest Arab monarchy with a GDP per capita of around 3,000 USD.

which cut public spending. And unlike their oil-rich counterparts in the Gulf region, they had little financial means to meet people's demands. Thus, limited power-sharing through an inclusive process that promised more than it delivered seemed to be their only option to co-opt the angry protesters. The window-dressing processes enabled the monarchs in these two countries to curb the situation without losing power. These constitutional reforms failed to democratize Jordan and Morocco because the inclusion of different opposition groups in the process was merely a strategy by the monarchy to appear inclusive.

Inclusion in Challenged Republics: Egypt (2014) and Algeria (2016)
Two other constitutional reform processes that were relatively inclusive and participatory but failed to democratize were the 2014 Constitution of Egypt and the 2016 Constitution of Algeria. Rulers in both of these Arab republics faced grave challenges that needed decisive actions with a semblance of democracy. In Egypt, General El-Sisi was in desperate need to justify and legitimize his coup against the first and only democratically elected president, and he initiated a seemingly inclusive constitutional reform as a way to quiet his critics. In Algeria, President Bouteflika, called on by protesters to resign, pledged to implement serious democratic reforms, including an inclusive constitution, to accomplish a similar end.

The 2014 Constitution of Egypt was intended to remedy some of the problems with the 2012 constitution. As discussed above, the Muslim Brotherhood's noninclusive government and the constitution it adopted in 2012 instigated massive public protests and boycotts by different political and social groups. The wave of protests and demonstrations continued and increased after the promulgation of the constitution. Demonstrators and political leaders demanded drastic amendments to the constitution to reflect the diversity of the society. According to Magdi Sherif, the head of the centrist Guardians of the Revolution Party, "the amendment of the new constitution is one of the primary demands of the people and parties taking part in anniversary rallies" (Morrow and Al-Omrani 2012). The civilian protests reached their peak in June 2013 when the *Tamarod* (Rebel) campaign circulated a mass petition, allegedly signed by more than 22 million Egyptians, to remove President Mohamed Morsi and amend the constitution. The military meanwhile saw public dissatisfaction with the Muslim Brotherhood's government as an opportunity to crack down on both opposition groups, one after another, and return the old order. On July 3, 2013, General Abdel Fattah El-Sisi removed President Morsi from power and suspended the constitution. Immediately after the coup, the military started a huge and unprecedented crackdown on its opposition. Within six months after the coup, the military arrested more than 21,000 people including 2,590 leading Muslim Brotherhood figures (Spencer 2014).

The process of writing a new constitution started under the heavy fist of the military. This time around, the constitutional process was completely top-down with no citizen engagement. It also lacked transparency and was not inclusive since the Muslim Brotherhood, the April 6 Youth Movement, and any political figure who opposed the military's rule were excluded from the process. Nevertheless, the military tried to brand the process as democratic and inclusive. Shortly after the suspension of the 2012 constitution in July 2013, the interim president of Egypt, Adly Mansour, appointed a "committee of legal experts" (also known as the Committee of Ten), consisting of six senior judges and four constitutional law professors, to review and amend the sus-pended constitution.[14] The committee worked for one month and submitted its review of the suspended constitution in August 2013. The committee retained 74 out of the 236 original articles from the 2012 constitution without any changes, removed 38 articles, and amended 124 articles. One of the criticisms of the work of the expert committee was its secrecy and lack of transparency. No official details were ever published regarding its meetings, discussions, or voting process.

The interim president then appointed fifty new members of the Constituent Assembly to discuss and vote on the amendments suggested by the Committee of Ten.[15] Members of the new Constituent Assembly represented different political and social groups, but they were all allies of the military in its coup against President Morsi. The Assembly was chaired by Amr Moussa, a veteran diplomat from Hosni Mubarak's government. The Committee of Fifty was given sixty business days to finish its work. Unlike the Committee of Ten, which basically amended the Muslim Brotherhood's constitution, the Committee of Fifty wrote a whole new constitution, creating multiple incon-sistencies between the drafts of the two committees. The Assembly approved the new constitution and submitted it to the interim president on December 2, 2013 (Brown and Dunne 2013). The constitution was approved by a 98 percent vote in a public referendum in mid-January 2014, with only 37 percent voter turnout (Spencer 2014). The April 6 Youth Movement and the Muslim Brotherhood officially boycotted the referendum, and the Muslim

---

[14] Adly Mahmoud Mansour was the president of the SCC before he was appointed by the military as the interim president and swore in on July 4, 2013.

[15] The Constituent Assembly was also known as the Committee of Fifty.

Brotherhood-backed "Anti-Coup Alliance" claimed that the true turnout was less than 10 percent (Spencer 2014).

In sum, the process of the 2014 constitution, similar to the 2012 constitution, was noninclusive because major social and political groups were excluded.[16] These two processes differ significantly, however, in terms of public engagement. While the process of the 2012 constitution was indeed participatory with citizen engagement in all stages of constitution-making, the process of the 2014 constitution was not participatory at all. Except for the ratification phase in which citizens were involved by voting in the referendum, both the origination and deliberation phases were nonparticipatory. Although the 2014 process was nonparticipatory and no citizen proposals were formally solicited, the Constituent Assembly tried to mimic the 2012 process by launching an online platform for public feedback. However, the second constitution was put online for public feedback only two weeks before the constitutional referendum and ironically was still available for public proposals two years after the constitution was promulgated. Drafting the constitution by an independent Assembly comprising different groups, rather than the direct involvement of the military, was meant to create the impression of inclusiveness. This inclusion was window-dressing and only intended to legitimize the military regime that was slowly trying to restore the old political order, albeit with a different face. Although the outcome was a constitution that was to some extent more liberal than the Muslim Brotherhood's constitution, those liberal reforms were meaningless so long as the military was in power.

Algeria was another Arab republic that, under immense public pressure for democratization, initiated a seemingly inclusive process of constitutional reform. Unlike the swift action in Egypt, which took about six months, Algeria's President Bouteflika used a very slow and lengthy process spanning over five years. This very lengthy time period was one of the main reasons that the Algerian public lost interest in the constitution, despite their initial enthusiasm about the reforms. Soon after the fall of Ben Ali in neighboring Tunisia, Abdelaziz Bouteflika, Algeria's president since 1999, promised multi-level reforms including changes to the constitution in order to calm the angry young protesters. Constitutional reforms were accomplished in four phases. The initial phases, marked by political instability and uncertainty because of the uprisings throughout the Arab world, were much more inclusive and participatory. By the time of the last phases of the process, however, the winds of the Arab Spring had calmed down, and authoritarian leaders

---

[16] In the cross-national data presented in Chapter 2, the process of Egypt's 2012 constitution is coded "mixed," and the process of Egypt's 2014 constitution is coded "non-inclusive."

regained their grip on power. Consequently, Algerian constitutional reform became more and more autocratic, noninclusive, and nonparticipatory.

The first phase of the constitutional process started in May 2011 and included two parallel dialogues with citizens, civil society, constitutional experts, and political groups. The first national dialogue was conducted by the Social and Economic Council (CNES in French) and lasted about six months. The CNES created an assembly of civil society representatives, which was called the General Convention of Civil Society (or EGSC, French abbreviation for *États Généraux de la Société Civile*). The dialogue with these representatives was inclusive and transparent and documented in a dedicated website for the general public to view.[17] When the final report of the CNES was released later that year, participants in the EGSC were surprised to learn that the report only focused on local development and did not reflect many recommendations regarding democratic governance, elections, fundamental rights, and the role of the youth (Benyettou 2015). The second national dialogue, which took place around the same time as the EGSC, was a purely political dialogue with political leaders and took longer to conclude. President Bouteflika created a special commission of advisors headed by Abdelkader Ben Saleh, president of the Council of the Nation, the upper house of the Algerian parliament. The commission invited more than 250 political leaders to participate in the national dialogue. This dialogue was innovative and unprecedented in the history of Algeria. The commission reached out to even remote areas, consulted people, and listened to their concerns. The debates within the commission, however, were kept secret. The commission sent its final report based on the feedback it received from the general public and political leaders to the president. The report was never made public, but many of the recommendations are known to concern the adoption of a different system of government, limiting the powers of the president, and enhancing judicial independence (Benyettou 2015).

After a brief hiatus, the second phase started in April 2013 when a small Committee of Experts was commissioned to prepare constitutional revisions based on the results of the two dialogues. The committee comprised five constitutional experts[18] whose mandate was unrestricted except for the obligation to observe the "fundamental principles of the Algerian society."[19] The Committee of Experts worked for a year and submitted the draft revisions to

---

[17] CNES's dedicated website for civil society dialogues could be accessed at www.cnes-forum-civil.dz/.

[18] The five experts were professors Kerdoun, Benbadis, Lazhari, Mekamcha, and Zouina.

[19] According to Article 178 of the Algerian Constitution, the "fundamental principles of the Algerian society" include provisions related to republicanism, democracy, Islamic religion,

the government in May 2014. The constitutional reform process was shortly interrupted after President Bouteflika suffered a stroke and was hospitalized for four months in the spring and summer of 2013. Nonetheless, he ran again for office and was elected for the fourth time in April 2014.

The third phase of the process started a month after Bouteflika was reelected and included another round of national dialogue with political groups. This time, Bouteflika appointed his chief of staff, Ahmed Ouyahia, to fulfill the long-awaited promise of constitutional reforms. Ouyahia invited 150 stakeholders including leaders of 64 political parties, 36 national figures, 12 academics, as well as representatives from several CSOs to the third national dialogue. However, the majority of opposition groups, including the Algerian Muslim Brotherhood, Al-Islah, Ennahda, and the Socialist Force Front, refused to participate, questioning the credibility and transparency of the process. These groups had earlier boycotted the 2014 presidential election, calling on Bouteflika to resign and arguing that any constitutional reform under the current presidency lacked legitimacy. Additionally, the invitation of the former chief of the Islamic Salvation Army (AIS) to participate in the national dialogue increased the criticisms of the new commission (Benyettou 2015).[20] Not only did most opposition parties refuse to participate, by the time of the third national dialogue, but also the Algerian public had lost interest in the promised constitutional reforms.

The final phase of the constitutional reform process, which included the finalization and adoption of the amendments, started in late 2015. On November 1, 2015, Bouteflika announced that the constitutional reform package was ready, and it included a constitutional review mechanism in addition to the amendments proposed by the Committee of Experts. At that point, no one knew what that reform package included as opposition parties were kept in the dark. Eventually, Ouyahia unveiled the draft constitution in a press conference on January 5, 2016. The constitutional reform package included sevety-four amendments and thirty-eight new inclusions. The most important change was made to Article 74. In 2008, this article was amended to lift the two-term limit on the presidency, which allowed Bouteflika to run for third and fourth terms. Article 74 was changed once again in the 2016 constitution to

---

Arabic language, human rights, the unity of the state, the national anthem, and the flag. These provisions are not amendable.

[20] The AIS was the largest armed group involved in the Algerian civil war, which caused 200,000 deaths from 1992 to 2000 until the group decided a unilateral ceasefire in 1997. Under the Charter for Peace and National Reconciliation, which was voted by referendum in 2005, the AIS should have been banned from any political activity.

reinstate the presidential term limit, but it allowed Bouteflika to finish his fourth term in 2019 and run for a fifth term (Maboudi 2019).

The draft amendments were approved by the Council of Ministers on January 11 and validated by the Constitutional Council on January 28. The amendments were promulgated after a parliamentary vote on February 3, 2016, during which 499 out of the 517 present lawmakers voted in favor, with 16 abstaining. Since the National Liberation Front (FLN); the government's main party, along with the Democratic National Rally (led by Ouyahia); and other pro-government parties had the absolute majority of the seats in both chambers, this outcome did not come as a surprise to opposition parties that boycotted the vote (Markey and Ahmed 2016). After five years, three national dialogues, and an initially promising inclusive and participatory process, the constitutional amendment did not meet the expectations for democratic reforms. The lengthy process and lack of transparency created a sense of participatory fatigue, which led to the lack of interest in the constitutional debate among the general public. This strategy was not intentionally designed by President Bouteflika from the start. Rather, it evolved over time in response to events in other Arab countries. Nonetheless, the inclusive process was a window-dressing effort by the government to calm the angry youth protesters in the country, rather than a true democratic effort to resolve its political ills.

Algeria's constitution of 2016 was written in a very different context than those in Egypt, Morocco, and Jordan, but it served the same function: to legitimize a challenged state. The constitutional outcomes in all four cases were indeed more liberal than their predecessors, but those reforms were not strong enough to democratize the state (in Algeria, Jordan, and Morocco) or prevent democratic backsliding (in Egypt). The main reason was that the major political and social groups were not present at constitutional negotiation tables despite the state's efforts to brand these processes as inclusive and democratic.

Closed Constitution-Making Processes

Unlike the aforementioned constitutional reforms, which tried to brand the process as inclusive and participatory, several regimes changed their constitutions with no inclusion or participation. As discussed in Chapter 1, autocratic constitution-making processes are the historic norm in the region. Yet, in the wake of the Arab Spring, only a handful of Arab leaders chose that route for revising their constitutions. The vast majority were initiated and completely controlled by authoritarian incumbents and emerged in three particular settings. First, closed constitutional reforms took place in Syria and Bahrain, both governed by an authoritarian president or king from an ethnic minority group. And as ethnic majorities in these countries suffer institutionalized discrimination, the risk of including opposition groups in the constitutional negotiations was too high for the state to consider. Second, closed constitutions were crafted in the oil-rich monarchies of Saudi Arabia and Oman that, unlike the poor monarchies of Jordan and Morocco, had sufficient resources to co-opt the protesters and did not see the need to engage the opposition in the constitutional negotiation. Democratic backsliding is the third context for closed constitutional reforms in the aftermath of the Arab Spring, which happened in Egypt. The third constitutional change in Egypt since the 2011 uprisings marked the full restitution of authoritarianism in the most populous Arab nation. Unlike the 2014 window-dressing process, which appeared semi-inclusive, the 2019 process was completely closed since opposition groups, different social stakeholders, and the general public were barred from the constitutional debate.

Where Power-Sharing Is Not an Option: Constitutional Change in Syria and Bahrain

Syria and Bahrain are the only countries in the Middle East governed by an ethnic minority. When the waves of uprisings reached these two countries, it was hardly surprising that the rulers refused to surrender power. In both cases, the regime played the sectarian card to mobilize their ethnic communities in the face of the protests. In Syria, the regime's message to the president's Shia Alawi community was that if "we die, you will die with us" (Reese 2013, 13–14). Bashar Al-Assad came to power in 2000 after the death of his father, President Hafez Al-Assad. For almost three decades, Hafez Al-Assad ruled Syria by capitalizing on the country's sectarian divisions. He created certain social and economic inequalities as part of his divide and rule strategy. At the same time, he promoted pan-Arabism and socialism through his Ba'ath Party to mobilize supporters across different sects. As a result, Hafez Al-Assad had the support of Sunni peasants and poor workers who make up over 60 percent of the population. He also created a strong alliance with small minorities including Christians (about 10 percent), Druze (about 3 percent), and, indeed, his own Shia Alawi community (about 10 percent). Excluded from his coalition were the Kurds (12–15 percent) and the Sunni elites (Phillips 2012).

When Bashar Al-Assad came to power, he initiated vast economic reforms. Syria's GDP increased as a result, but subsidies were slashed and public sector employment decreased, which hurt the working class. These economic reforms alienated the poor Arab Sunnis from Al-Assad's regime (Phillips 2012). Additionally, a major drought from 2007 to 2010 led to increased urban migration of mostly poor Arab Sunni peasants to the cities, causing more unemployment (Phillips 2012). Under these circumstances, when the Arab Spring uprisings eventually reached Syria in March 2011, the regime found itself without domestic allies besides the Shia Alawites and other small groups. Not surprisingly, the protests started in conservative and poorer Sunni-majority towns such as Daraa, Jisr Al-Shughour, Homs, Idleb, Douma, and Hama. Protests were peaceful; protesters did not initially demand the resignation of Al-Assad and only called for economic and political reforms. Al-Assad responded, however, with a violent crackdown of protesters while simultaneously promising liberal reforms. The cornerstone of his promised reforms was a new constitution.

In his third speech since the protests began, on May 21, 2011, President Al-Assad promised to rewrite the 1973 constitution to address the constitutional demands of the protesters. In November 2011, Al-Assad appointed a twenty-nine-member Constitutional Committee to write a new constitution. Ironically, the Constitutional Committee was presided over by Mazhar Al-Anbari, a lawyer who chaired the drafting committee of the 1973 constitution. The Constitutional Committee included a group of independent lawyers and experts as well as members of the Ba'ath Party and the National Progressive Front, which is a coalition of pro-government parties. Al-Assad tried to include some prominent opposition figures in the CDC, in order to create the illusion that the process was inclusive, but he was not successful. All opposition groups boycotted the constitution drafting, citing the illegitimacy of the process. The Constitutional Committee convened in several sessions, drafted a new constitution based on the 1973 document, and presented their draft to Al-Assad on February 15, 2012 (Hafez 2019).

The most important changes in the new constitution included the removal of Article 8 of the 1973 constitution, which designated the Ba'ath Party as the "leader of state and society," the introduction of multicandidate elections, and the inclusion of new provisions on human rights (Fares 2014). The opposition viewed these changes as insufficient in bringing any meaningful change to Syria. For example, while the constitution subjected the presidency to two seven-year term limits, it put this change into effect only after 2014, which would allow Al-Assad to potentially stay in power until 2028 (Attasi 2012). Thus, when the constitution was put to a public referendum on February 26, all opposition groups boycotted it. They cited the government's brutal violence against protesters as a testimony to its unwillingness to make real changes.[21]

---

[21]   Based on some estimates, the government killed over 7,600 civilians in just 11 months from the start of the protests to the day of the constitutional referendum (Al-Jazeera 2012).

Despite the ongoing violence and instability throughout the country and organized boycotts, the government claimed that 89.4 percent of the Syrian voters approved the constitution in the referendum (Norberg 2018).

The process of drafting the new Syrian constitution was strikingly similar to that in Bahrain, as constitutional negotiations in both countries were undermined by authoritarianism and ethnic divisions. The ethnic divisions in Bahrain are more complex than in Syria. The small, oil-rich island has only 1.2 million people, half of which are not Bahraini nationals. Bahraini nationals are divided into two groups: Shia and Sunni. The Shia, comprising about 70 percent of the population, are divided into Ajam (Persian Shia) and Baharna (Arab Shia) who are believed to be the original, pre-Islamic inhabitants of the island. The Sunnis, comprising the other 30 percent of the Bahraini nationals, are also divided into several groups. The first major Sunni group is Najdi, which are originally from the Arabian Peninsula. The second major group are those Arab Sunni tribes that migrated from Kuwait, including the ruling Al-Khalifa family. Lastly, Huwala are the Persian Sunnis who moved to the island in the nineteenth century (Mecham 2014).[22]

In addition to ethnicity and sect, family affiliation is another important identity-maker that can determine citizens' future. Since Bahrain's independence in 1971, Al-Khalifa's regime has discriminated against Shia, especially the Persians. In the social hierarchy, the Persian Shias are the most marginalized group. Arab Sunnis occupy all the senior bureaucracy positions, finance and trade sectors, and military high ranks. Shias, both Arabs and Persians, by contrast, are excluded from holding major governmental positions. This institutionalized discrimination is systematic and encompasses all social, economic, and political opportunities. For example, while subsidized housing is easily offered to international workers, it is more difficult for Shia citizens to receive them. Additionally, in order to balance Shia's demographic advantage, the government readily grants citizenship to foreign Sunni laborers. When Sheikh Hamad acceded to the throne in 1999, after the death of his father, Sheikh 'Isa, this sectarian social structure had been well-established in the society. Sheikh Hamad departed from his father's rule, making several reforms to integrate the Shia into the society by granting them more economic and political opportunities. Those reforms could not, however, eliminate the institutionalized discrimination, and grievances among the Shia did not abate (Mecham 2014).[23]

---

[22] This complex ethnic division, in addition to Iran's historic claim over the island, puts the Arabian Peninsula states and Iran at the center of Bahrain's domestic issues.

[23] Among these reforms was a constitutional change in 2002 that changed the state from an Emirate to a Kingdom, in addition to creating an upper chamber in the parliament with all

When the Shia youths in Bahrain witnessed the unfolding news in Tunisia and Egypt, they called for their own "Day of Rage" demonstrations on February 14, 2011. The February 14 Youth Movement managed to organize widespread protests in the capital city of Manama and other parts of the country. The government responded by a mix of crackdowns and concessions. During the peaceful protests in February, the opposition started an open dialogue with Crown Prince Salman Ben Hamad. However, in March, the king imposed an emergency law, inviting Saudi Arabia and the United Arab Emirates to send troops and tanks to clear the streets of protesters (Stevenson and Solomon 2011). Consequently, the talks between the opposition and the Crown Prince broke down. Two months later, the king announced new constitutional reforms to meet the demands of the protesters, a move that was immediately rejected by Al-Wefaq, the main opposition Shia party. The king commissioned the national dialogue by inviting 300 stakeholders representing different groups. Three opposition parties, which together won 55 percent of the seats in the 2010 parliamentary election, including Al-Wefaq, were given only five seats each. In total, opposition groups were given only 35 seats in the national dialogue, with the remaining 265 seats divided among the pro-government groups. About 37 percent of the seats in the Bahraini National Dialogue (BND) were reserved for political groups, 36 percent for CSOs, 21 percent for prominent figures and activists, and 6 percent for representatives of the media. The major group that did not receive the invitation was the February 20 Youth Movement.

The BND was chaired by Khalifa Ben Ahmed Al Dhahrani, speaker of the parliament, and was mandated to discuss four subjects including political, social, economic, and human rights issues. Before the BND started its work, King Hamad pledged that "all options were on the table" for negotiation (Stevenson and Solomon 2011). The national dialogue started on July 2, 2011, and lasted three weeks. Just a day before the BND was to start its work, the Al-Wefaq party decided to join the BND. This was harshly criticized by the February 14 Youth Movement, which had more radical demands, accusing Al-Wefaq of betrayal and working with the regime. Two weeks into the constitutional debates, Al-Wefaq decided to boycott the BND and withdrew its representatives from the process, arguing that the state was not committed to reforms and that its proposed changes were merely cosmetic. Nonetheless, Al-Wefaq's initial participation and enthusiasm about the reforms gave the king the legitimacy he sought. Based on the work of the BND, the parliament

members being appointed by the king. These constitutional changes were criticized by the Shia opposition as a move by the king to further his control over the parliament.

prepared and voted on amendments to twenty articles of the 2002 constitution. Following the approval by both chambers, King Hamad ratified these amendments on May 3, 2012.

The amendments in Bahrain, similar to the new constitution in Syria, were modest at best. In both countries, major opposition groups were excluded from constitutional negotiations, despite the regime's attempt to bring them in for cosmetic purposes. The general public was not engaged in the process either, mostly because the governments did not intend to mobilize them. Considering the ethnic composition of these two countries, the political cost of an inclusive and participatory process was extremely high for the regime to even consider. Suffering from decades of oppression and discrimination by the state, opposition groups demanded real reforms. Fearing the risks associated with inclusive reform processes, the two regimes opted for a controlled, autocratic process instead, which did not appease protesters. Lingering grievances led to a devastating civil conflict in Syria and remained unresolved under an oppressive minority rule in Bahrain.

Unchallenged Oil-Rich Monarchies: Saudi Arabia and Oman

With the exception of Bahrain, the oil-rich monarchies in the Gulf region were the countries least affected by the 2010–2011 uprisings. These countries saw the lowest number of protests and proved to be the most stable Arab states. The oil-rich monarchies spent billions of dollars to quash or prevent uprisings in their countries. For instance, Saudi Arabia's King Abdullah promised over 100 billion USD in domestic spending in the early months of 2011 to blunt popular discontent and co-opt existing client groups (Gause 2013, 25). Saudi Arabia also committed to some reforms including a constitutional amendment in 2013. Oman was another oil-rich monarchy that committed to a constitutional reform in 2011. In both cases, the process of amending the constitution was completely closed and managed by the monarch.

Protests in Saudi Arabia started on January 23, 2011, when a man in his sixties set himself on fire in the city of Samitah in the southwest of the country. This self-immolation was similar to many other incidents across the region, which mimicked Bouazizi's self-immolation in Tunisia. Five days later, a group of protesters gathered in the streets of Jeddah after the Friday prayer to express their frustration with the poor infrastructure after deadly floods swept the streets of Saudi Arabia's second-largest city. Major protests began a few weeks later and centered on the kingdom's systematic discrimination against Shia minorities. Protests started in February and early March and were mostly concentrated in the cities of Qatif, Hofuf, and Al-Awamiyah, all of which have sizeable Shia populations (Laessing 2011). When social media users organized the "Day of Rage" demonstration on March 11, the government tried to stop the protests and killed one of the organizers a few days before they were scheduled. Nonetheless, several hundred people protested on the "Day of Rage." The government's brutal response provoked more protests targeting human rights concerns. These events were followed by another wave of protests in April in Riyadh, Ta'if, and Tabuk, which focused on unemployment and economic grievances in the wealthy kingdom. The months of May through July witnessed different protests against a wide range of issues from political prisoners to women's rights. They continued, albeit on a smaller scale, through 2012.

Most of these protests were relatively small in size, lacked focus, and were spread over time, which made them easier for the government to quash. Nonetheless, King Abdullah made several concessions including economic and political reforms. These gradual political reforms were eventually institutionalized by amendments to the Basic Law, the de facto constitution of Saudi Arabia, in 2013.[24] The process of amending the constitution was completely closed and shrouded in secrecy. Consequently, the amendments did not change the status quo. The king and senior members of the Al-Saud family retained their hold on the reins of power. The Consultative Council, Saudi Arabia's parliament, has only a consultative role, and all its members are appointed by the king. The king is also the supreme judicial authority, appointing all judges while also acting as the final authority for judicial appeals and pardons. Still, in a conservative country where the Quran is considered the official constitution and in which women are second-class citizens, the king's appointment of a few women to the Consultative Council was regarded by some observers as revolutionary (Hakala 2013).

In Oman, the southeast neighbor of Saudi Arabia, protests were even more modest in size. They started on January 17, 2011, a few days after Ben Ali fled to Saudi Arabia, with about 200 people protesting low wages. Protests escalated in February and became violent in cities with high unemployment rates such as Sohar (Worrall 2012). Just like in Saudi Arabia, the regime was stable, and protesters never focused on overthrowing the regime. Unlike Saudi Arabia, however, the protests were more focused, as the majority of protesters demanded higher wages and lower costs of living. Sultan Qaboos responded with a package of economic reforms including higher minimum wage rates across the sultanate. He also made a swift move to reform the country's constitution. Similar to the Saudi case, the process was completely autocratic, controlled by the sultan. While the constitutional amendments were a step

---

[24]   According to the Basic Law of Saudi Arabia, Quran is the official constitution of the kingdom.

forward in the country, the sultan remains the ultimate power. Oman's sultan enjoys even more powers than the Saudi King, who shares some powers with the Al-Saud family members. The sultan of Oman still holds the positions of prime minister, foreign minister, minister of defense, and finance. Additionally, he acts as the head of the central bank (Gause 2013).

Saudi Arabia and Oman represent the most autocratic and closed form of constitution-making. In both countries, the king or the sultan and their advisors wrote the new amendments, without even appointing an expert committee (like in Jordan or Morocco). The constitutions that came out of these extremely closed processes were the least ambitious, compared to most other constitutional reforms in the region. This outcome was in part the result of the absence of strong challenges to the rule of the two oil-rich monarchies during the Arab Spring, which enabled them to appease pro-testers by enacting economic reforms instead. The lack of a history of constitutionalism in these countries can also explain the autocratic nature of the reforms. Despite being among the oldest and most stable monarchies in the Arab world, Saudi Arabia and Oman have a very limited constitutional history. Three Royal Decrees established Saudi Arabia's Basic Law as its de facto constitution in 1992 (Ahmed and Gouda 2014). And the Basic Statute of the State of Oman (also referred to as Basic Law) was issued in 1996, which makes the sultanate the last Arab country to adopt a constitution. Oil wealth and the absence of a history of constitutionalism and strong democratic movements created a situation where the monarchs did not feel the pressure to amend their constitutions through inclusive processes, even for window-dressing purposes.

Democratic Backsliding: Egypt 2019

The third context in which a closed constitutional reform process was enacted marks Egypt's full circle back to authoritarianism in the aftermath of the Arab Spring. The 2019 constitutional amendments were first introduced by the Coalition in Support of Egypt, a pro-government parliamentary bloc, on February 3, 2019. The proposal was then referred to the General Committee of the HOR, which approved it two days later. Next, the HOR conducted an initial vote on the proposed amendments on February 14, and the proposed amendments were agreed upon in principle by a 485–16 vote in the parliament. Upon the preliminary approval of the initiative, Ali Abdel-Aal, speaker of the parliament, announced that the parliament's Constitutional and Legislative Affairs Committee would receive remarks and suggestions about the amendments within thirty days. Following that, two weeks of Societal Dialogue sessions were held.

The process of the Societal Dialogue was criticized by the opposition as all participants were handpicked by the government and there was no dissenting voice. The Constitutional and Legislative Affairs Committee prepared a list of 720 figures to attend the sessions: 116 of the participants were known to be staunch government supporters, and the remaining 604 participants were selected by government officials and independent bodies (Mostafa 2019). As Table 4.2 shows, participants in the Societal Dialogue, distributed across six sessions, represented almost every segment in society from banks, media, police, judges, ministers, and political parties to artists, sports figures, academics, NGOs, and religious institutions. No participant fundamentally opposed the amendments in any of these sessions. Rather than a space for societal dialogue, these sessions were merely a stage for the participants to pledge allegiance to President El-Sisi.

TABLE 4.2 *Participants in the 2019 societal dialogue of Egypt*

Date of Session	No. of Participants	Affiliation of Participants
March 20	120	Heads of universities, teaching boards, and student unions (60); the National Media Organization, national press organizations, radio and television channels (30); Al-Azhar University and the Coptic Church (30)
March 21	120	Representatives of cabinet ministries and provincial governorates (80); the National Council for Women, the National Council for Childhood and Motherhood, the National Council for Human Rights, the National Council for the Disabled, the National Bank of Egypt, the Public Authority for Financial Control, the Central Auditing Agency, and the Administrative Control Authority (40)
March 23	120	The minister of justice and representatives of judicial authorities, the Armed Forces, and the higher council for the police
March 24	120	Representatives of professional syndicates (80); representatives of private sector companies, leading banking officials, and the Federation of Egyptian Industries and Chambers of Commerce (40)
March 25	120	Representatives of political parties
March 28	120	Constitutional law professor and public figures (40); intellectuals, sports figures, members of Egyptian diaspora, representatives of NGOs, and other civil society organizations (80)

Following the Societal Dialogue, a report was prepared, and the amendments were returned to parliament for a second vote. On April 16, 531 members of the parliament voted in favor of the revised constitutional amendments, while 22 members rejected the amendments and 1 member abstained (Ahram Online 2019). Finally, the amendments were voted on in a public referendum that took place on April 19–22 for Egyptians abroad and on April 20–22 domestically. The state reported that 88.9 percent of the voters approved the constitutional changes with a 44.3 percent voter turnout (Kennedy 2019).

The most controversial change to the constitution was the length of presidential terms, which increased from four to six years with a two-term limit. This change would allow the incumbent President Abdel Fattah El-Sisi to potentially remain in office until 2030, without lifting the term limit. Despite the official reports, many Egyptians opposed this change as it marked the return to the military's authoritarian rule. Throughout the constitutional amendment process, the government used all tools at its disposal to suppress the opposition movements and prevent public mobilization against the constitutional changes. In the three months from the introduction of the amendments to the referendum, security forces conducted an organized crackdown against individuals expressing dissatisfaction with the performance of the government. There are several reports of dissidents disappearing, being arrested, or being ordered into detention (Tahrir Institute 2019). Courts also moved to ban or order cancellation of protest events during this process. For example, when the Civil Democratic Movement, a movement of opposition political figures, tried to organize a protest against the proposed amendments outside of the parliament, a judge in the Cairo Court for Urgent Matters ordered its cancellation for national security reasons (Tahrir Institute 2019).

As some opposition leaders noted, the 2019 constitutional amendments took Egypt back to "absolute dictatorship" (Al-Jazeera 2019). This democratic backsliding happened gradually over several years starting with the military's coup against the controversial, but nonetheless democratically elected, President Morsi in July 2013. The constitutional process through which this "absolute dictatorship" was recreated might seem democratic as it was initiated and executed by an elected parliament. This top-down process, however, was the latest step of a broader trend whereby the Egyptian parliament merely rubber-stamped President El-Sisi's agenda.

The constitutions of Egypt, Syria, Bahrain, Oman, and Saudi Arabia, although enacted in very different circumstances, share a key characteristic: they were all closed and top-down, as these constitutional changes were all initiated and carefully executed by the incumbent/ruler whether through an elected parliament, and appointed committee, or directly by the monarch. The main purpose of these constitutional changes was either to retain power or further empower the authoritarian incumbent. When a constitution is crafted for authoritarian purposes, the process is always noninclusive and nonparticipatory.

Conflict Constitution-Making Processes

The last pathway in constitutional reform processes that failed to democratize Arab nations emerged in countries where constitutional negotiations became entangled in the web of conflict negotiations. The process of crafting these "conflict constitutions" in Libya and Yemen was overwhelmed by the ongoing conflict and failed to yield permanent constitutions (see Johnson 2017). Political transitions propelled by the Arab Spring devolved into civil wars that have resulted in tens of thousands of deaths in the two countries (Johnson 2017). Although constitutional reforms were supposed to usher transitions in these two nations, armed rebel groups utilized the existing political tensions, including those related to constitution writing, to draw out conflict. As Johnson (2017, 297) suggests, such "conflict constitutions" tend to prolong rather than remedy sources of conflict. Unless key groups such as relevant political parties, blocs, movements, civil society, and ethnic or religious groups are included in the reform process, particularly in ethnically or regionally divided societies with weak political institutions, any efforts are most likely to fail to result in a constitution that can remedy the sources of conflict.

One State, Two Governments, No Constitution: Conflict Constitution in Libya

The Arab Spring in Libya started in mid-February 2011 when a group of protesters gathered in Benghazi, Libya's second-largest city, to protest the arrest of human rights lawyer, Fethi Tarbel. Muammar Qaddafi, Libya's dictator for over four decades, responded to the increasing protests by ordering his militia and security forces to open fire on civilian protesters. A few days later, the NTC, comprised a coalition of rebels, opposition activists, and expatriates, was created in Benghazi. Soon, the NTC was recognized by several states as the legitimate transitional government of Libya. On March 19, the United Nation's Security Council adopted Resolution 1973, paving the way for international military action against Qaddafi's government. Two months before Qaddafi was killed by the rebels, the NTC adopted an interim constitution (Constitutional Declaration) on August 3, 2011

(Geha and Volpi 2016). Article 30 of this constitution called for the election of a national legislative body, the GNC, in less than a year. The to-be-elected GNC was tasked with appointing a committee to draft a permanent constitution in sixty days and submit the draft for approval in the GNC, with subsequent ratification coming through a public referendum. This timeline proved, however, to be too much optimistic. The death of Qaddafi and the lack of strong political institutions throughout his reign since 1969 led to a political and security vacuum, creating a fertile ground for civil conflict (Vandewalle 2014).

The roots of Libya's conflict can be traced back to before its independence. Libya has historically been a federal state, comprised three main regions: Cyrenaica, Tripolitania, and Fezzan. Each of these three regions was administered independently by the Italian colonial rule before one governor administered them all beginning in 1929. After Italy's defeat in World War II, British forces occupied Cyrenaica and Tripolitania, and the French took control of Fezzan. In 1951, Libya gained its independence and adopted a constitution that established a monarchy with a federal system. General Muammar Qaddafi led a military coup in 1969, overthrew the monarchy, and abolished the 1951 constitution. Qaddafi ruled for forty-two years without a parliament, political parties, proper judicial institutions, or a constitution. Instead, he used the historical tribal and regional divisions and lack of state institutions to stay in power. Following Qaddafi's death, these muted tribal and regional cleavages gradually became a major source of conflict and contestation during the transitional and constitution-making process (Johnson 2017).

The transitional process began relatively smoothly and peacefully. The Interim Constitution defined the NTC and interim government's powers during the transition process, slated to end with the election of a new president and legislature (Johnson 2017). The election of a transitional legislature, the GNC, was scheduled for July 2012. The GNC would be then tasked to select sixty members of the Constitutional Drafting Assembly (CDA). Still, various groups opposed the NTC's plan for constitutional reforms as Libyans from less populated regions, women, and other minority groups protested against not having equal representation in the CDA (Johnson 2017). Some tribes and citizens from the less populated regions of Cyrenaica and Fezzan threatened to boycott the GNC elections.[25] Just before the scheduled GNC Election Day, the NTC amended the Interim Constitution to address these concerns. The amended Interim Constitution determined that the sixty members of the CDA

---

[25] Almost 30% of the Libyan population lives in Cyrenaica, 60% in Tripolitania, and 10% in Fezzan.

would be directly elected by a popular vote rather than appointed by the GNC. It also equally distributed the CDA seats among the three regions: Tripolitania, Cyrenaica, and Fezzan.

Another source of conflict surrounding the formation of the CDA was the underrepresentation of minority groups and women. The three main Libyan minority groups, Amazigh, Touareg, and Tebu, expressed concerns regarding their underrepresentation. Under Qaddafi's brand of Arab nationalism, these groups suffered the most and consequently were among the early opponents of Qaddafi's regime. They demanded equal representation in order to protect their historically suppressed cultural and linguistic rights. The GNC enacted a law in 2013 that reserved six seats (or 10 percent) for women and two seats each for the Amazigh, Touareg, and Tebu minority groups. The Imazighen, which comprise more than 10 percent of the Libyan population, were not happy with the arrangement and boycotted the CDA election. While the Imazighen remained out of the constitution-making process, the Touareg and Tebu groups used boycotts as a strategy and on several occasions withdrew and returned to the negotiation table.

Despite disruptions by ongoing violence in some areas, the CDA election was held in February 2014. The CDA started its work with fifty-six members as the Amazigh's seats were not fulfilled and representatives of Derna could not attend the meetings due to the conflict. The CDA held public meetings that included town halls with about 400 people to explain the constitution-drafting process to the Libyan public. Despite attempting to reach out to women, the CDA was criticized for including only male tribal leaders in meetings and neglecting marginalized populations (International Commission of Jurists 2015). In general, the constitutional review was not inclusive and left out key groups from the debate. A controversy over time constraints also hindered the inclusion of marginalized populations. The failure to draft a constitution was exacerbated in 2014 and 2015 with the escalation of tensions and conflict between armed groups in the two rival parliaments competing for control over the country (International Commission of Jurists 2015).

As early as 2012, Benghazi, the largest city in the eastern region of Cyrenaica, became the center of conflict between the Islamist militia and the transitional government. In May 2014, General Khalifah Haftar, commander of the Libyan National Army, embarked on a military campaign, called Operation Dignity, against the Shura Council of Benghazi Revolutionaries, a coalition of Benghazi Islamist militia groups. Meanwhile, Haftar was accused of plotting a failed coup through his Operation Dignity. The election for a permanent HOR to replace the GNC, held in the midst of conflict in 2014, saw the electoral defeat of Islamist politicians. Shortly after the election, a violent clash erupted between a coalition of Islamist militia, called Libya Dawn, and General Haftar's Operation Dignity government forces. The Libya Dawn coalition then staged a coup in the capital city of Tripoli in support of the Islamist parties that lost the HOR election. The elected HOR, Prime Minister Abdullah Al-Thinni, and all his cabinet members fled to the eastern cities of Tobruk and Beidi where they were backed by General Haftar's Operation Dignity forces. Meanwhile, the Libya Dawn coalition took complete control of Tripoli and reinstated the GNC as its legislature. Since then, two governments, in Tripoli and Tobruk, govern Libya, with the latter being officially recognized by most of the international community including EU nations and the USA.

In December 2015, representatives from the two separate Libyan governments signed an UN-brokered peace deal, the Skhirat Agreement, which included a vision for a unity government and agreements for rival governments to end hostilities (Abdessadok 2017; Johnson 2017). The agreement sought to end the conflict and included discussions of disarmament and a new constitution (Abdessadok 2017). The agreement also created the Government of National Accord led by a majoritarian Presidency Council, which would be charged with executive power in Libya and assume responsibility for Libya's next phase of political transition (Abdessadok 2017; Johnson 2017). By signing this power-sharing agreement, both Libyan governments were agreeing to cede authority to the Government of National Accord (Johnson 2017). But the peace accord failed as the legitimacy of the NTC waned among the public due to a noninclusionary approach and lack of power-sharing.

The conflict among Libyan tribes, regions, and groups was reflected in the CDA's constitutional process. As Johnson argues, "extreme conflicts between drafters mirrored tensions between the Libyan-Dawn backed Islamist government in Tripoli and the Operation-Dignity backed nationalist government in Tobruk over local representation and central authority, and the Amazigh, Touareg and Tebu minority groups boycotted the assembly and rejected nonconsensus constituent assembly solutions regarding minority rights" (2017, 319).

The CDA published its first constitutional proposal in December 2014, while peace negotiations just started but the violent conflict was still ongoing. Two months before the UN-brokered peace deal, the CDA published its first draft constitution, which was revised in February 2016. A year later, on July 29, 2017, the CDA achieved the impossible and was voted by a two-thirds majority in favor of the final draft constitution (Al-Ali 2017). The CDA then sent the constitution to the HOR for its endorsement in February 2018. Earlier that month, the Supreme Court overturned a legal appeal from a lower court against the validity of the draft constitution, paving the way for the adoption of the constitution through a public referendum. However, the Tobruk-based HOR rejected the CDA's constitution and the Supreme Court's ruling, calling instead for forming an expert committee to draft the constitution (Mahmoud 2018). The HOR's decision has practically halted Libya's constitution-making for the time being. Almost a decade after the removal of Qaddafi, Libya is still vying to write a constitution. The constitutional process in Libya has failed to create a consensual constitution due to its noninclusive nature, power and security vacuum, and nonexisting state institutions. These lacunae entangled with ethnic and regional conflict have led to a cycle of violence, which has undermined state-building in the country.

A Constitutional Recipe for Civil War: Conflict Constitution in Yemen

Similar to Libya, the constitutional reform in Yemen unfolded against the backdrop of an ongoing civil conflict. Constitution drafters in Yemen were under immense pressure from different ethnic and regional groups with competing interests and were therefore unable to write a consensual Magna Carta. And just like in Libya, the regional cleavages in Yemen date back to the formation of Yemen's modern state (Johnson 2017). In 1904, under an agreement between the Ottoman Empire and Great Britain, modern Yemen was divided into two separate territories of Ottoman north and British south. North Yemen became an independent state after the fall of the Ottoman Empire in 1918. The Mutawakkilite Kingdom of Yemen, established by Imam Yahya Muhammad, a Shia Zeidi Imam, ruled North Yemen until 1962 when Arab Nationalists, backed by Egypt, toppled the Imam and established the Yemen Arab Republic. Shortly after its creation, the Yemen Arab Republic fell into a decade-long civil war between the new government and loyalist forces of the kingdom backed by Saudi Arabia. Meanwhile, South Yemen remained a British protectorate until 1967 when armed rebels forced out the British and established a Marxist state, the People's Democratic Republic of Yemen (PDRY), with support from the Soviet Union, in 1970. It took another twenty years for the two Yemeni states to unite and create the Republic of Yemen in 1990. Ali Abdullah Saleh, President of North Yemen since 1978, became the President of the Republic of Yemen, and Ali Salem Al-Beidh, the head of South Yemen, became the Vice President (Tharoor 2010). Despite this apparent unification, North and South Yemen maintained their distinct identities and rivalries. In 1994, leaders from the south, dissatisfied with the power-sharing arrangements and the unresolved regional grievances, attempted to declare independence. Saleh quashed the rebellion and continued to build his political power through an expansive patronage network. Despite a resistance movement against Saleh by southern tribes, Houthis, and a Zaydi revivalist movement, he was able to hold onto power until the Arab Spring uprisings awakened the neglected grievances (Williams et al. 2017).

The Yemeni Revolution of Dignity started on January 27, 2011, when thousands of angry protesters gathered in the capital city of Sanaa to protest against unemployment, economic conditions, and corruption. However, very soon protesters started to demand the departure of President Saleh. On February 2, Saleh announced that he would not run for reelection in 2013 or transfer the presidency to his son. But protests escalated very quickly and spread to the south and its major city, Aden, by February 3. Saleh announced a referendum on a new constitution on March 10, a proposal, which was immediately rejected by the opposition. Starting in April 2011, the GCC mediated peace talks between the government and the opposition. While Saleh agreed to the deal, he backed down from signing it three times. On May 23, only one day after Saleh refused to sign the treaty for the third time, Sheikh Sadiq Al-Ahmar, the head of the Hashid tribal federation, the largest and most powerful tribal confederacy in Yemen, joined the armed rebellion against the government. Saleh was injured and nearly escaped death after a bombing at the presidential compound on June 3. Eventually, fear of assassination, government defections, armed violence, and widespread protests forced Saleh to accept a peace deal brokered by the GCC in November 2011. Saleh formally ceded power to his deputy, Abdrabbuh Mansur Hadi, on February 27, 2012.

After Saleh's resignation, Yemen seemed to be on track for a democratic transition. The transitional government included the former opposition bloc, the Joint Meeting Parties, a five-party alliance that included the leading Islamist party, Al-Islah, as well as the Yemeni Socialist Party, the Nasirist Popular Unity party, and two small Zeidi parties (Alley 2013). However, violent conflict soon overshadowed the transitional process (Mujais 2017). After violence broke out in 2013, the United Nations sponsored a NDC. The NDC commenced its work on March 13, 2013, chaired by President Hadi, with 564 delegates, 50 percent of whom were from the south. Overall, women comprised 30 percent of the delegates in the NDC, and youths had 20 percent of the seats (Alley 2013; Mujais 2017). The NDC crafted an interim constitution and held several public debates to discuss the underlying causes of conflict. After much debate during the NDC, it was concluded that a federal system best suited Yemen. The NDC made approximately 1,800 recommendations and commissioned a CDC to transform these recommendations into a federalist constitution (Williams et al. 2017). On March 18, 2014, President

Hadi appointed the seventeen members of the CDC from lawyers, diplomats, and other professionals (Mujais 2017). However, several groups including southern secessionists, the Socialist Party, and youth groups objected to the lack of representation in the CDC, in addition to the lack of experience among the CDC members (Johnson 2017).

The CDC finalized the draft constitution and publicized it on January 15, 2015, but the Shia Houthis and several parties in the south immediately opposed the draft constitution. That same day, Ahmed Awad Bin Mubarak, the chief of staff, was kidnaped by the Houthis on his way to a meeting with President Hadi to discuss the constitution (Mujais 2017). The Houthi rebels took over the capital city of Sanaa and surrounded the presidential palace, forcing President Hadi to resign on January 22, 2015. Once Hadi and his cabinet members moved to the southern city of Aden, he rescinded his resignation. In response, Saudi Arabia and the GCC led a military coalition against the Houthis. The Southern Hirak movement also allied with President Hadi and played a critical role in pushing back the Houthi forces from Aden. In the north, former President Saleh, who was secretly behind the Houthi's takeover of Sanaa, joined a formal alliance with the Houthis in July 2016. These alliances, however, were as fragile as the constitution itself. In 2019, Hirak engaged in a battle with Hadi forces, and on December 4, 2017, the Houthis assassinated former President Saleh.

It is estimated that the Yemeni civil war has claimed more than 100,000 lives since 2015 (Beaumont 2019). Although the civil war in Yemen started in response to the 2015 draft constitution, its causes were deep-rooted. The CDC focused heavily on constitutional requirements to form a federalist system without emphasizing an inclusive decision-making process. Although the constitution was intended to create six federal regions in Yemen, that division was not satisfactory to the Houthis in the north and secessionist parties in the south. Accordingly, the national dialogue ended without a new constitution, and the idea of federalism only exacerbated conflict (Schmitz 2014; Mujais 2017). In the end, the absence of key groups, particularly representatives from the south, in major negotiations during the writing of the constitution, and the emphasis on federalism, instigated the Houthi's coup and takeover of the country (Mujais 2017).

When a constitutional process leaves out key groups from the negotiation table, the outcome will be a nonconsensual constitution, which runs the risk of exacerbating the conflict (Johnson 2017, 328). Indeed, the emergence of conflict constitutions depends on whether a conflict-prone environment exists. In both Yemen and Libya, such an environment was created by a lack of strong state institutions, historically rooted ethnic, tribal, and regional cleavages, and a security vacuum, which followed the fall of an authoritarian regime. The experiences of Libya and Yemen show that when regional and ethnic cleavages accompany a noninclusive constitution-making process, they create a perfect recipe for prolonged conflict and constitutional failure.

CONCLUSION: WHEN THE CONSTITUTION-MAKING PROCESS HINDERS DEMOCRACY

As discussed in the previous chapters, recently developed theories in participatory and deliberative democracy as well as a new generation of empirical studies in comparative constitutionalism contend that participatory and inclusive constitution-making has significant implications for constitutional outcomes. Chapters 2 and 3 provided empirical evidence from statistical analyses in support of this thesis. Particularly, the case of Tunisia discussed in Chapter 3 lays out a causal mechanism for the relationship between the process and democratic outcomes. Indeed, "success" cases such as Tunisia draw more scholarly attention than "failure" cases as they can help us study the conditions under which the causal mechanism works. As a result, we do not have sufficient knowledge about the conditions under which nonparticipatory and noninclusive processes hinder democracy and democratic transitions. This chapter reviewed four such failed pathways.

The first failed pathway of constitution-making that emerged in Egypt under the Muslim Brotherhood's government is the populist constitutional process. The 2012 Egyptian constitutional reform process was indeed participatory, albeit with two major caveats. First, the noninclusiveness of the constitutional bargain on the one hand and societal polarization on the other led to a very hasty and tortuous process that essentially nullified any democratic gains of public participation. Second, and perhaps more importantly, the participatory process was motivated by the Muslim Brotherhood's populist rhetoric rather than nonpartisan societal involvement. As a result, the participatory process did not yield a more democratic constitution. In effect, when participatory processes merely serve populistic purposes, they are more likely to yield undemocratic outcomes by partly or thoroughly limiting minority rights. As Weyland (2013, 20) notes, "populism ... inherently stands in tension with democracy and the value that it places upon pluralism ...." In that sense, populism is an extreme form of majoritarianism that frames democracy not as an inclusive bargain but as a battle between majority's will and whoever opposes it (Mudde 2013). And "given that constitutionalism limits both popular sovereignty and majority rule, populism is fundamentally opposed to constitutionalism" (Mudde 2013, 6).

The second pathway of constitution-making that failed to yield democratic outcomes is the window-dressing process, which contrary to the populist pathway involves public demobilization and limited inclusion of co-opted groups including some minorities. The window-dressing pathway emerged in some troubled republics (Egypt 2014 and Algeria 2016) and resource-poor monarchies (Jordan 2011 and Morocco 2011). In all of these cases, the authoritarian states were under immense pressure to democratize. Unwilling to relinquish power, however, these states opted to reform their constitutions through seemingly participatory and inclusive processes. The state adroitly managed the process by including some moderate societal and political stakeholders while excluding major extremist groups from the constitutional negotiations. These inclusive- and participatory-branded processes mostly served window-dressing purposes for the troubled states. Rather than yielding democratic outcomes, window-dressing constitutional processes release popular pressure on the state and thus stabilize the nondemocratic status quo. Constitutions that emerge from these processes might seem more democratic than their predecessor by encompassing political liberalization and guaranteeing more rights. Yet even the promises in such window-dressing constitutions are mere talk and pure fiction (Ginsburg and Simpser 2014, 7). Indeed, the limited inclusion of opposition groups in the constitutional dialogue yielded some democratic gains, but these gains fell short of democratizing the constitution or the state.

The third failed pathway of constitution-making reviewed in this chapter is the closed constitutional process. Both normatively and empirically, closed constitution-making does not lead to democratic outcomes. Closed constitution-making should be distinguished, however, from other forms of autocratic, elite-based constitutional reform processes, which are inclusive. In closed constitutional processes, the incumbent writes or rewrites the constitutional bargain unilaterally with no input from any societal or political groups. In such cases, the content of the constitutional change has already been decided, even if the incumbent brings some opposition figures and representatives of societal groups to the negotiation table for cosmetic purposes. As Przeworski (2014) argues, these authoritarian constitution-making processes are often secretive, making it difficult to evaluate the drafters' intentions. While indeed the autocrats in Bahrain, Syria, Oman, Saudi Arabia, and Egypt (2019) had different motivations for revising their constitutional orders, the outcomes were very similar as they all hindered the prospect of democratization in their countries.

The last failed pathway of constitution-making that hindered democratic transition in Libya and Yemen was the conflict constitutional process. Unlike "consensus constitutions," which tend to remedy sources of conflict by bridging different societal interests, "conflict constitutions" are often themselves the source of prolonged violence and civil conflict (Johnson 2017). Noninclusive constitutional bargains usually increase the political tensions in deeply divided societies (Lerner 2011). In states transitioning away from authoritarianism, severe ethnic divisions, lack of political institutions, and security vacuum provide groups deploying violence with an opportunity to utilize these political tensions to draw out conflict. Conflict constitutions, as such, hinder democratic transition mostly because of their noninclusive processes and nonconsensual designs.

Conflict constitutions pose as much of a serious threat to democracy and democratic reforms as populist, window-dressing, and closed constitutions do. Together, these four failed pathways of constitution-making shed some light on the conditions under which nonparticipatory and noninclusive processes hinder democracy and democratic transitions by either empowering and enabling authoritarianism or exacerbating the political and societal divisions. As such, these processes either yield undemocratic constitutions or – in the case of conflict constitutional processes – fail to produce a permanent constitution.

With thousands of civilians killed during years of conflict, Yemen and Libya exemplify the worst possible outcome stemming from noninclusive constitutional reform processes. The same grievances that instigated massive uprisings in Yemen, Libya, and other Arab countries exacerbated the failure of constitutional processes in these countries. Systematic ethnic discrimination, political and economic corruption, regional and group-based grievances, unemployment and poor economic conditions, and the government's recurring violations of basic human rights are all among these grievances. During the Arab Spring uprisings, protesters demanded constitutional remedies for the various social and political grievances rampant in their societies. However, all but Tunisia failed in democratizing their nations. This chapter distinguished among four failed pathways of constitution-making processes. These pathways had different degrees of inclusion and public participation, but they had one shared feature: they all failed to include major societal interests including independent civil associations in constitutional negotiations. The next chapter explores this in detail and evaluates another common feature among all these failed constitutions, which is the lack of a strong and independent civil society.

5

Pathways of Failure

The Importance of Civil Society

At the height of the 2011 uprisings in the region, Tawakkol Karman, a Yemeni human rights activist, became the co-recipient of the Nobel Peace Prize for her role in advocating for women's rights both before and after the Arab Spring. The first Arab woman to win the Nobel Peace Prize, Karman was the president of Women Journalists Without Chains, an NGO she co-founded. She organized peaceful protests advocating for a free press, women's rights, and human rights, and her activism culminated during the Arab Spring, garnering her the nickname "Mother of the Revolution." Four years later, the Tunisian National Dialogue Quartet, a group of four CSOs, received another Nobel Peace Prize for ushering in democracy in the country. While Tunisian civil society, led by the Tunisian National Dialogue Quartet, played a major role in the country's constitutional negotiations and its path toward democracy, the Yemeni civil society was unable to play such a role. Why did the Yemeni civil society fall short of facilitating constitutional negotiations and democratization?

The answer to this question partially lies in the characteristics of constitution-making in Yemen. As discussed in the previous chapter, the noninclusive nature of "conflict" constitution-making processes (as was the case in Yemen and Libya) had a negative impact on the works of civil society during the constitutional bargain. Similar to "conflict" constitution-making, all other noninclusive forms of constitutional processes, including "populist," "window-dressing," and "closed," weaken the role of civil society in the constitutional bargain.

In "populist" processes, characterized by majority or incumbent rule without minority rights, CSOs, which usually advocate for minority rights and counter-majoritarian views, are silenced during the process. In "window-dressing" constitution-making, only select groups of co-opted CSOs are consulted – for superficial purposes – and in a "closed" process, CSOs are systematically excluded from the negotiation table. Subsequently, in all of these noninclusive processes, civil society is not a real partner in the constitutional negotiations. By contrast, the inclusive and participatory process of constitution-making in Tunisia empowered CSOs and enabled them to play a more significant role in the constitutional negotiations. Indeed, when the constitutional negotiation process is inclusive and participatory, civil society can play a more consequential role in the constitutional bargain. Inclusion and participation, however, are necessary but not sufficient conditions for the success of civil society. Besides constitution-making features, several other factors may create hurdles for civil society.

This chapter examines a few of these endogenous and exogenous factors that had important implications for the outcomes of the Arab Spring uprisings. At the onset of the Arab Spring, most CSOs faced two major endogenous challenges, which undermined their work. On the one hand, most youth, women, and diaspora movements suffered from a lack of organizational capacity and essential political skills and training. On the other hand, many of the established unions and NGOs that had organizational capacity were struggling with a lack of public legitimacy due to either state co-optation or foreign donors' influence. I also examine two exogenous challenges including societal divisions and military intervention that create an unfavorable environment for civil society. First, most CSOs had to operate in challenging political environments rife with ethnic, religious, regional, and ideological polarization. Rarely can civil society rise up against all these hostile conditions and make a difference in the constitutional bargain or the broader democratization process. Second, foreign and domestic military interventions pose another grave challenge for civil society. The interference of these undemocratic forces usually constrains the civic space, muting CSOs and preventing them from playing a more consequential role in the democratic transition. When civil society operates in a hostile sociopolitical environment, it is likely to fail in its democratizing role.

Each of these endogenous and exogenous issues posed a serious challenge for civil society even before the Arab Spring. Together with the noninclusive nature of constitutional processes in the region, they explain why the Arab civil society could not play a more prominent role in constitution-making and democracy-building during the Arab Spring. Only when civil society is able to overcome these internal and external hurdles, it becomes the critical link between constitutional bargains and democratization. Before explaining each of these contributing factors, I briefly explain why civil society matters for democratization and how it has evolved in the Middle East and North Africa in the past century.

DOES CIVIL SOCIETY REALLY MATTER?

Since the early 1990s, civil society has become integral to the discussion of liberalization and democratization across the world (Altan-Olcay and Icduygu 2012). The civil society thesis boldly contends that "no civil society, no democratization" (see Yom 2005, 15). As discussed in Chapter 1, while the theoretical foundations of the civil society thesis go back to Tocqueville (1969), the thesis has been reinvigorated since the Third Wave of democracy and particularly as a result of democratic transitions from military regimes in Latin America in the 1970s and 1980s and popular mobilizations in Eastern Europe in the 1980s. In both series of events, observers attributed the peaceful transformation of authoritarian regimes to civil society associations (Altan-Olcay and Icduygu 2012). With the popular upheavals of the so-called colored revolutions in countries such as Georgia, Ukraine, and Kyrgyzstan in the 2000s, the role of CSOs in liberalization and democratization has received even more scholarly attention.

Not surprisingly, Western observers, particularly after September 11, 2011, embraced civil society as a solution for the democratic deficit in the Middle East and North Africa (Yom 2005). Despite skepticism about the mechanisms through which participation in CSOs is said to foster tolerance and produce democratic-minded citizens (see Levi 1996), Western donors poured hefty sums of funds into establishing and promoting CSOs in the region. For these international donors, CSOs are considered the sine qua non for democratic development. Subsequently, the primary test of civil society's effectiveness becomes its success in enabling democratic transitions (Carapico 2019, 100).

In examining the role of civil society in democracy-building, Arato (1996, 2000) emphasizes the importance of civil society's institutionalization, arguing that when civil society is weakly institutionalized, it interferes with the emergence of workable political parties, which are crucial for new democracies.[1] CSOs, as such, facilitate democratic constitutions only if they are institutionalized, particularly during moments of transition. This institutionalization, in turn, facilitates democratic consolidation (Linz and Stepan 1996). The institutionalization of civil society associations is achieved through the establishment of several formal institutions and practices, including constitutional guarantees of fundamental rights of association, assembly, speech, and press; the separation of powers, especially independent courts; recognition of the operation of national

---

[1]   See also Cohen and Arato (1992).

and international human rights watchdogs; political and economic decen-tralization; the financing of CSOs; and the constitutionalization of demo-cratic role for CSOs (Arato 2000, 71–72). Without these institutions and practices, civil society cannot play a prominent role in democracy-building. By these criteria, civil society was at best weakly institutionalized in most parts of the region when the Arab Spring uprisings erupted.

At the onset of the Arab Spring uprisings, civil society, and in particular youth and women movements, led the peaceful protests against their authoritarian regimes. From Jordan's Hirak Shababi (or Youth Movement) to Egypt's April 6 and Morocco's February 20 Youth Movements successfully mobilized millions of people in their countries. However, these movements ultimately failed to bring liberal reforms or facilitate democratic transitions, and soon they lost their momentum and popular support. Civil society's failure in transforming uprisings into liberal democracy provided evidence for many critics that civil society in most of the Middle East was impotent (see Carapico 2019). Some take this a step further arguing that an independ-ent civil society (from state pressure and manipulation) does not exist in most of the Arab world (Wiktorowicz 2000; Yom 2005). However, in evalu-ating the role of civil society, the focus should not be on whether a "real" civil society exists in the Arab world. As will be discussed in the following pages, civic associational networks have been active for decades and have been able to weather and adapt to all sorts of state manipulations, pressures, and censorships. The main question, rather, is, why did these networks fail to translate public pressure and mobilization into liberal democratic reforms? To answer this question, we should first look at how CSOs arrived at the Arab Spring. That is, to understand why most CSOs in the region lacked the necessary infrastructure for a democratizing role, it is important to understand how they have survived, adapted, and evolved over time in one of the most authoritarian regions in the world.

The Evolution of Civil Society in the Arab World

The history of civic life in the Middle East and North Africa can be divided into four phases. The first generation is the traditional, religious, and tribal-based civic networks and foundations, which were developed over centuries across the region. Modernization, the creation of independent states, and the encounter with Western ideas led to the development of the modern CSOs in the first half of the twentieth century. The third generation of CSOs was developed under robust authoritarian regimes from the 1950s to the 1980s. After decades of oppression, a new wave of civic movements and activism was born in the 1990s. A key feature of this fourth phase is the rise in participation of youth and women in CSOs.

Most analysts broadly define civil society as an associational space where a mélange of civic groups provide a conduit between state and citizens (see Yom 2005; Carapico 2019). This conceptualization is indeed broad and not very specific. As a result, in the context of the Arab world, identifying these CSOs is still a matter of debate. For Yom, to be counted as a CSO, groups must be "secular in ideology, civil in their behavior, legally recognized, and supportive of democratic reform" (2005, 18). Five groups meet these parameters: membership-based professional groups (such as syndicates), NGOs providing social services, public interest advocates (such as human rights activists and women's movements), labor unions, and informal social networks (such as recreational clubs or youth leagues). Carapico (2019) outlines a longer list of CSOs that includes, in addition to the groups mentioned previously, universities, interest groups, civic-minded parades, concerts, museums, charities, and philanthropies. Most of these groups meet Yom's parameters and fit in one of his five categories of CSOs, with the exception of the last two. Considering charities and philanthropies as CSOs is a matter of debate in the context of the Arab world because most charities and philanthropies have been historically religious in nature. And this is where the theoretical parameters of Arab civil society are contested: Are Islamic associations considered part of civil society?

For Yom (2005), they are not, because CSOs must be secular in ideology. As Carapico argues, for some orientalists, "Islamic cannot be simultaneously civil" (2019, 101). Similarly, charities and philanthropies rooted in ethnic, kinship, or tribal identities are not considered civic activism for these critics. This antagonistic perspective eliminates most religious charities, libraries, academies, and foundations, which ironically were the forebearers of Euro-American civil society. The question then becomes, do Islamic institutions, in contrast to the Judeo-Christian institutions, lack the concepts of civic engagement and the common good? Far from this, the Islamic concepts of *maslahah* (the common good), *khayriyyah* (welfare), *zakat* (a charitable tithe), *waqf* (endowments), and *sadaqah* (charity) are well developed and have historically been the foundations of the traditional "public civic realm" in the Arab world for several centuries (Carapico 2019, 101). Religious and tribal institutions indeed provided the earliest public civic space in the region. Religious endowments were a cornerstone of providing public goods and services from drinking fountains, public baths, and canal systems to mosques, schools, universities, and libraries. Informal networks of religious judges, scholars, and officials often interacted in rich public spaces. Informal networks of tradesmen evolved into small chambers of commerce regulating prices and offering services to members and their families. The most important feature of this traditional civic space was the decentralization of small clusters of these associational networks and foundations. The Ottoman Empire attempted several times to centralize these independent foundations under the Ministry of Awqaf in regions under its control. Later, colonial and postcolonial governments made similar attempts. But in all circumstances, these civic foundations resisted the pressure and tried to remain as autonomous as they could. In the absence of functioning modern states, these traditional civic foundations could deliver public goods and services to people (Carapico 2019).

The fall of the Ottoman Empire in the early twentieth century and inter-actions with European imperialist powers transformed the established social order in Arab societies. Capitalist enclaves emerged in large port cities like Alexandria, Basra, and Beirut. Tradesmen sent their children to schools in Europe. These Western-educated intellectuals along with the exponentially increasing number of university students expanded and shaped the space for civic activism in the region. Soon political parties with different ideologies from the Communists to Muslim Brotherhood emerged. Rapid moderniza-tion led to the creation of profession-based associations. Syndicates represent-ing different professions, from engineers and physicians to teachers and attorneys, emerged in parts of the region. In cities like Baghdad and Cairo, labor unions were organized to represent workers. In some rural areas, farmers organized their own associations. Student unions turned campuses into public spaces. Associational networks of writers, artists, and performers formed clubs, started schools, wrote manifestos, and published newspapers. While Cairo and Baghdad were the hotspots of this new social and civic activism in the 1930s and 1940s, modern CSOs grew in most of the Arab world (Carapico 2019). The new social activism was distinct from the traditional civic realm in two ways. First, it was not charity, philanthropy, or welfare-based. Rather, it expanded to most aspects of civic and public life. And second, it was not completely religious-based. While some of the modern associational networks were still faith-based (including some new charities or faith-based academic institu-tions), most were not.

The vibrant associational life resulting from the intellectual renaissance in the Arab world changed drastically after World War II when newly independ-ent and authoritarian governments sought to curtail this larger and more secular civil society. Riding on a wave of Arab nationalism, monarchs, military officers, and strongmen tried to control or suppress CSOs in order to constrain the public space, which was readily available for their opponents. Under the name of modernization, they launched aggressive attacks on powerful religious, judicial, academic, and commercial institutions. Soon they established their own ruling parties while banning all opposition parties from the Communists to Muslim Brotherhood. All independent institutions from banks and industries to universities, media enterprises, and even mosques were nationalized. With the nationalization of all industries, workers became state employees represented by national unions that were affiliated with the ruling parties. National leagues and youth and women's associations were fused into the ruling parties. And what remained of independent CSOs was curtailed by aggressive laws that targeted CSOs. Egypt was among the pioneers in enacting laws that effectively curtailed independent associations, providing a model for other Arab states to follow. For example, Law 49 of 1945 enabled Egypt's Ministry of Social Affairs to register, audit, and dissolve all associations at its discretion. And Law 34 of 1964 yielded the suspension of some 4,000 legally established associations (Carapico 2019, 106–107). The third generation of Arab CSOs was, as such, extremely weakened. They were barely breathing but not quite dead, and in the late 1980s and early 1990s, they resurrected once again.

Several developments in the 1980s and 1990s led to the emergence of the fourth generation of Arab CSOs. By the 1980s, the Arab nationalism project was losing its legitimacy. States' mismanagement of the economy under the banner of nationalism resulted in mounting debts. The 1987 global financial crisis put more economic burden on Arab states. Arab authoritarian leaders who were losing their legitimacy and popularity were under immense pressure for liberal economic reforms. With the fall of the Soviet Union, their western allies, and in particular the United States, saw less urgency in the full front support of authoritarian leaders. From Jordan and Morocco to Egypt and Algeria, monarchs and presidents had no choice but to embark on liberal economic reforms, which included austerity measures. Slashing public spending led to public frustration and mobilization, particularly among the poor and working class. Pressure by international donors for liberal reforms forced the troubled states to loosen up their tight grip over the public and civic space. Simultaneously, foreign donors increased their financial and organizational support for CSOs exponentially around the world. All these developments led to a new generation of civic activism that was largely concentrated in social movements, such as youth and women movements and issue-based NGOs rather than traditional organizations such as unions and syndicates.

Governments did not stay passive, however, and used different strategies to keep the new civil society under control. One strategy was to create state-backed NGOs (known as G-NGOs). The Tunisian government, for example, created several of these G-NGOs, such as Lawyers Without

Borders, which were infiltrated by the secret service tasked with monitoring and spying on activists. Another strategy was to weaken the new associations by blocking their access to foreign funds. The Egyptian government, for example, arrested dual citizen directors or accountants of several associations, such as the Women's Solidarity Association or the Ibn Khaldun Center, for bringing money into the country illegally. The third strategy was the use of legal lawsuits against CSOs or the passage of new laws to forbid these associations from engaging in labor advocacy or political campaigning (Carapico 2019, 107–108).

Despite governments' decades-long efforts to curtail, manipulate, or put pressure on CSOs, people continued to engage in civic activism through three public spheres. First, despite state manipulations, millions of people still registered as members of labor unions, professional syndicates, and social leagues and clubs. Moreover, when formal civic activism was banned, people participated in informal civic networks, from coffeehouses in Egypt and Tunisia to *diwaniya* in Kuwait and tribal networks in Iraq and Yemen.[2] Second, when governments shut down legal venues for civic engagement, protest activities (from protests against wars or rising prices to protest for political reforms) became a venue for people to get together and share ideas. Lastly, since the turn of the millennium, cyberspace has provided an expanding public sphere for civic activism (Carapico 2019). Compared to the traditional civic spaces, such as labor unions and syndicates, the state was less able to manipulate social media and blogs, providing a safe space for like-minded activists to organize and share information. Students, artists, bloggers, journalists, and human rights activists contributed significantly to the richness of this new public civic space. It was this new generation of the cyber civil society that eventually brought down some of the most established and powerful Arab leaders, by raising awareness and mobilizing millions of protesters across the region. Despite the unprecedented energy that these civil movements brought to the Arab civic sphere, they failed to function as a democratizing force. The failure of civil society in democratizing their societies is due to a combination of both noninclusiveness of constitutional reform processes as well as endogenous and exogenous causes, including lack of political capacity, public legitimacy, societal polarization, and prevailing undemocratic forces. The remainder of this chapter elaborates on these causes.

---

[2] *Diwan* is a room, a hall, or a reception area, usually adjacent to the main house, where guests gather. *Diwaniya* is a traditional culture of Gulf countries, particularly Kuwait, where guests gather in a *diwan* for coffee or tea and conversation (see Carapico 2019).

NONINCLUSIVE PROCESSES: JORDAN, MOROCCO, AND ALGERIA

CSOs can play a consequential role in the democratic transition only if they are allowed to or succeed in forcing themselves into partaking in the constitutional negotiations. Only inclusive and participatory constitution-drafting processes can guarantee that civil groups will have access to the process. Yet, as was argued in the previous chapter, most post–Arab Spring constitutional negotiation processes were essentially noninclusive and/or nonparticipatory. Inclusive processes matter because they signal a credible commitment by the dominant group, which most often is the incumbent. Allowing the main segments of society to take part in constitutional negotiations in a transparent manner increases the cost of breaching particular provisions of the bargain for any party.

Through inclusive processes, participating groups learn democratic negotiations, leading to trust and eventually compromise among the actors (Axelrod 1984; Jermanová 2020). This is where civil society comes into play. When the process is inclusive and participatory, CSOs can act as a conduit connecting political groups with the general public, especially in post-authoritarian transitioning societies where political parties are not well-established. By contrast, when the process is closed and civil society is kept out, CSOs cannot effectively reach out to the public or communicate with political groups.

Take, for example, Jordan where despite a seemingly representative process and the establishment of an NDC, the process was not genuinely participatory or inclusive. While some CSOs had representation in the NDC, the overall process was not inclusive as major opposition parties and CSOs were either excluded or opted not to join the NDC. In fact, major CSOs that organized the protests and called for reform, including the Al-Hirak Youth Movement, were excluded. The Workers' Union and some of the most important activists such as Laith Shbailat and Toujan Al Faisal were not invited either. Of the fifty-two members of the NDC, only four were women, and no youth activist was invited. Nonetheless, representatives of the invited CSOs actively participated in the NDC debates, providing important recommendations, mostly limited to human rights and economic development. However, these groups too were excluded from the RCCR that drafted the constitutional amendments. Lack of continuity and communication between the NDC and the RCCR undermined the minimal work that CSOs undertook during the process.

Although some CSOs were allowed to take a limited part in the national dialogue, without a genuinely inclusive and participatory process, they could not play a prominent role in shaping public opinion and steering the national dialogue. The limited inclusion of civil society in the NDC was part of a broader façade that encompassed the expansion of the number of CSOs as a regime survival strategy.[3] Despite their numerical expansion, CSOs have remained toothless and unable to make serious challenges on the state. The vast majority of Jordanian CSOs are still philanthropic, charity-focused, and community-based, a large number of which are Royal NGOs. Advocacy CSOs, focusing on democracy, human rights, or governance, comprise only a minority of civil society in the country (USAID 2016). Furthermore, these advocacy CSOs usually suffer from "short sightedness with regard to their goals, lack of strategic planning, weakness of their administrative bodies, and unqualified staff" (Jarrah 2009, 10). During the constitutional reforms, CSOs were not successful in their public outreach and failed to mobilize enough segments of the Jordanian society during the process. This is partly because of the identity and ideological cleavages within civic activists. While activists in Transjordanian areas, which for a long time have been considered as the regime's social base, were demanding social justice, Palestinian Jordanian activists focused more on political inclusion (Yaghi and Clark 2014). The regime capitalized on these cleavages and attempted to exacerbate the existing divisions by including some CSOs and excluding others. When the state keeps civil society inherently weak and limits the civic space through a noninclusive and nonparticipatory process, civil society cannot pose serious challenges to the authoritarian state.

Morocco's CSOs had an experience somewhat similar to their Jordanian counterparts. They have been among the most capable CSOs with an impressive record of grassroots works in, for example, establishing microcredit systems, founding community organizations, and investing in social development. However, before the 2011 uprisings, only a handful were politically active, including the Moroccan Association for Human Rights (known by the French acronym, AMDH), ATTC Maroc,[4] and Al-Adl Wal-Ihsan[5] (Benchemsi 2014). King Mohammed VI's announcement of a new constitution came as a pleasant surprise for these groups, which sought to constitutionalize democratic reforms.

The constitutional reform process in Morocco was perhaps slightly more inclusive than the process in Jordan. Recall from Chapter 4 that the process comprised two main commissions including the CCRC that had a mandate of

---

[3] By one estimate, the number of NGOs in Jordan has doubled between 1989 and 2005 (Jarrah 2009).

[4] ATTC Maroc is the Moroccan local branch of Association pour la Taxation de Transactions financières et pour l'Aide au Citoyens (ATTC), an NGO created in France in 1998 to oppose neoliberal globalization (Benchemsi 2014, 232).

[5] Arabic for Justice and Charity.

reaching out to major societal stakeholders such as political parties and civil society. The CCRC held fewer than 100 hours of hearings with all these groups, including only 48 hours with over 300 representatives of various civic associations, unions, organizations, movements, and activists (see Table 4.1). The most important civic movement at the time, the February 20 Youth Movement, which called for protest and democratic constitutional reform, was not even invited. Those CSOs that had the opportunity to reach out to the CCRC were only engaged in one-way communication. That is, rather than deliberation, these groups were only allowed to submit their suggestions and demands. As a result, CSOs and movements were not really part of the constitutional negotiation in Morocco because they were not allowed to fully participate, most likely because of the potential threat they posed to the regime's survival.

Similar to the case of Jordan, the number of CSOs had increased exponentially over the two decades before the Arab Spring. The Moroccan state had successfully divided civic movements and associations into insider and outsider lines, similar to its divide-and-rule strategy for controlling the opposition parties. However, the rise of the February 20 Youth Movement, with its horizontal and cross-ideological organizational structure, was perceived as a major challenge to the state, forcing it to exclude this new civil society actor.

The noninclusive and nonparticipatory process, thus, served the state well. February 20 Youth Movement failed to mobilize the Moroccan people around major constitutional issues and debates because neither were actively engaged in the constitutional negotiations. Over time, February 20 Youth Movement's public outreach faded as the public lost interest in democratic constitutional reforms. With a lack of public support, February 20 Youth Movement lost the struggle over Moroccan democratization.

Algeria showcases yet another example of how a noninclusive and nonparticipatory process undermines the role of civil society in constitution-making and democratic transitions. Algerian civil society, despite decades of war and armed conflict and total state control, emerged as a major voice for democratization during the 2011 uprisings. The origins of modern Algerian civil society go back to the pre-independence period when many civic activists absorbed the French notion of associational life and developed their own professional and associational organizations (Metz 1994). After independence, from 1968 to 1989, all mass associations and civic organizations went under the direct administration of the ruling party, the FLN. The legalization of political parties in 1989 brought an end to FLN's total control over civic associations and resulted in a proliferation of independent interest groups. Despite the civil war in the 1990s, during which the public sphere was rendered dangerous, thousands of CSOs were established to protect human rights and vulnerable populations (Northey 2018).[6] The new CSOs capitalized on this momentum during the 2011 uprising when they mobilized mass protests against the state. Under this mounting pressure, the state had no choice but to include some CSOs, for the first time, in the constitution-making process. However, even that concession was a façade.

As discussed in the previous chapter, the multiphased, long process included two parallel dialogues in the first phase (2011–2012). The first dialogue took place in the EGSC, an assembly of civil society representatives. Despite the enthusiastic participation of CSOs in the dialogue, they were utterly disappointed when in late 2011, the CNES published its report of the dialogue with civil society. The CNES's report only focused on local development and did not reflect many recommendations regarding democratic governance, elections, fundamental rights, and the role of the youth (Benyettou 2015). Furthermore, the state conducted a parallel national dialogue with political leaders and parties, thus separating the civic from the political sphere of the constitutional negotiations. Lack of communication with political parties due to the way the national dialogues were set up, on the one hand, and lack of public outreach due to a nonparticipatory process, on the other, negatively impacted the role of the newly revived Algerian civil society in constituting democratic reforms. Furthermore, the very slow and lengthy process spanning over five years disengaged the Algerian public from the constitutional debates.

Algeria, Morocco, and Jordan had different degrees of civil society engagement in the constitutional reform process. Yet, as they all show, when civil society fails in its public outreach efforts because of noninclusive and nonparticipatory processes, as most CSOs did following the 2011 uprisings, it cannot create public interest in constitutional issues beyond those pertaining to ideological cleavages, which already mobilize large segments of the society. Consequently, the general public will probably be less engaged in constitutional discussions. If, on the contrary, CSOs create a public sphere for constitutional debate, through a participatory and inclusive process, the constitutional design is more likely to address the concerns raised in these public fora. A constitutional design that addresses the social and political challenges is very likely to enhance democracy, which, in turn, generates further inclusion and participation.

There is, as such, some degree of endogeneity between the inclusiveness of the constitution-making process and the role of civil society in the process.

---

[6]   Currently, there are over 93,000 registered CSOs in Algeria (Northey 2018).

That is, inclusive and participatory processes are likely to empower CSOs to take a meaningful part in the constitutional debate. At the same time, it is likely that a strong and independent civil society will increase the pressure for a more inclusive process. Nonetheless, civil society will definitely be less active and effective in a noninclusive and nonparticipatory environment. Besides the characteristics of constitution-making processes, several endogenous and exogenous factors had negative impacts on the democratizing role of civil society during the Arab Spring. I explain the endogenous factors first.

ORGANIZATIONAL CAPACITY AND THE ENDOGENOUS PATHWAYS OF FAILURE

As discussed above, it was a new generation of CSOs that led the initial phase of the 2010–2011 uprisings across the region (Khatib and Lust 2014). When youth movements challenged their authoritarian leaders in 2010 and 2011, most traditional CSOs such as labor unions and professional syndicates did not initially mobilize their supporters. Even the UGTT did not initially call for a strike or public demonstration. Experiencing decades of repression and manipulation by the state, unions were reluctant to join a movement that they thought would not only fall apart soon but could also lead to more state retaliation. That is, for unions, the costs of joining the movement were much higher than the predicted benefits. But their cost–benefit analysis changed very quickly when they saw authoritarian regimes trembling, so they too joined the call for democratic reforms. Yet, with the exception of CSOs in Tunisia, all CSOs failed to accomplish their goals and could not successfully channel the democratic movements they started into democratic transitions. I argue that among the main reasons these CSOs failed in their mission for democratization were a lack of political experience and skills, organizational capacity, and lack of public legitimacy. That is, they remained what they were all along, movements rather than organizations with the power and skills of political negotiations.

Organizational Structure and the Capacity of Youth Movements

As Khatib and Lust (2014) argue, the locus of civic activism started to shift in the decade before the Arab Spring from the traditional CSOs to a new generation of civic movements such as youth, women, and diaspora movements. Having a horizontal organizational structure, these movements and networks could attract many groups with very different ideologies, resulting in their initial success in mobilizing millions of protesters across the region. However, the same organizational structure became a major obstacle soon after demo-cratic transitions began. A horizontal structure as well as the lack of organiza-tional capacity and political skills slowly led to political rifts within these movements and networks. Gradually, these rifts along with public demobil-ization pushed these new civil movements aside, marking the end of their impact on transitional processes across the region. Before elaborating on how these youth, women, and diaspora movements and networks failed to have a lasting impact on democratic transitions, it is important to first explain how they became the nexus of civic activism during the Arab Spring.

As discussed above, youth movements began to rise in most parts of the region and came to the forefront of public mobilization in 2011. In Egypt, the April 6 Youth Movement played a critical role in mobilizing protests against Mubarak. In Morocco, the February 20 Youth Movement mobilized unpre-cedented protests in Rabat and other major cities. In Jordan, the Al-Hirak Youth Movement was a major force behind protest mobilizations. And in Bahrain, the February 14 Youth Coalition became the major pro-democracy movement during the uprisings.

Women movements were also among the most prominent civic movements that mobilized dissent against the regimes during the protests. Women had become politically active in most parts of the region years before the Arab Spring. Even in some of the most conservative countries, like Saudi Arabia, women were increasingly mobilized to safeguard or gain new rights. In Kuwait, women's groups were among the pioneers in coordinating protest strategies like sit-ins. And in Libya, mothers and relatives of Libyan prisoners who were killed in the Abu Salim prison coordinated and led a protest that sparked the February 17 Revolution. Perhaps the most prominent female activist is Tawakkol Karman, a member of the Al-Islah Party and a 2011 Nobel Laureate, who led several demonstrations even before the Arab Spring reached Yemen.

Besides youth and women movements, diaspora movements became an integral part of the struggle for democratization in their countries. From Egypt and Tunisia to Libya and Syria, exiled opposition groups lobbied the inter-national community for more serious pro-democracy actions, raised funds for domestic pro-democracy groups, creating a support network for domestic groups, and spread information about the regime's wrongdoings and oppos-ition activities. After the fall of regimes in Tunisia, Egypt, Libya, and Yemen, some members of the diaspora communities moved back to their countries and played a significant role in the transitional politics, which followed the fall of dictatorial regimes in the region. Some formed political parties; some ran for elected offices; and others joined or formed NGOs.

These CSOs had ideological rifts within their ranks, which were major sources of weakness and strength for them. On the one hand, the divisions prevented these groups from having one single vision for their country. The diaspora groups of Syria, for example, were divided on whether they should negotiate with the regime or whether they should support international intervention. On the other hand, the fact that these movements brought together activists with different ideologies showed their capability in bridging across different ideologies to deliver a message, which could resonate with most people in the society. Women's movements in Egypt, for example, comprised both Islamist and secular activists, indicating that they could reach a larger number of women.

The ideological divisions within the new CSOs just a decade before the Arab Spring had led to a very diverse set of goals for these groups. This too was changing, however, as their demands and goals were becoming increasingly targeted. Focusing on economic and political inequalities, these groups demanded liberal reforms, which they increasingly believed should start with a democratic constitution. Shortly after 2011, most CSOs concentrated their efforts on finding constitutional remedies for the political and economic ills in their societies. Such targeted goals gave these groups unprecedented unity and power to shape the national debate on democratic changes.

The youth, women, and diaspora movements and other CSOs used different tools and methods to coordinate their activities in order to reach their goals. One of the most important methods of coordination, which received global attention, was the use of the Internet and social media. The use of cyberspace in the early days of the uprisings was so prominent that some misleadingly labeled it as the cause of the revolution (see Howard and Hussain 2013). Nonetheless, this medium was a major tool for helping like-minded activists communicate and become more politically engaged. Activists who were not formal members of any CSO, but rather were, for example, bloggers, became increasingly active through the organically grown loose networks. Other loose networks of activists that were politicized during and after the uprisings were sports clubs' fans. The most notable example is the Egyptian Ultras, hard-core soccer clubs' fans who were perhaps one of the largest groups to reclaim the streets of Cairo, Alexandria, and other major cities when the regime failed to restore order and disperse protesters.

A major difference between the old and the new CSOs, thus, is that the new groups formed their activism based on loosely connected informal networks. Another difference was that the new activism was more decentralized as most civic movements developed a horizontal organizational structure. These loosely connected informal networks of activism and the horizontal organizational structure helped the new civic movements bridge ideological divides, which have historically been a major obstacle for political parties and their affiliated CSOs (Khatib and Lust 2014, 9). Their coordination methods and organizational structure were crucial for these movements' success in mobilizing dissent across different sectors of their societies. Why then did these CSOs fail to play a prominent role in the transitional period, despite this initial success in "creating" revolutions across the region?

Part of the answer to the question, as several contributors to Khatib and Lust's (2014) edited manuscript also argue, is that what constituted a source of strength for these civil societies in mobilizing protests became their source of weakness for governance and political participation. First, the focus on issues rather than ideologies before and during the uprisings helped these groups consolidate cross-ideological coalitions and mobilized larger segments of society. However, the cross-ideological differences resurfaced after the revolutions, and "activists who previously worked together to achieve the common goal of tearing down the regime suddenly found themselves wanting very different futures" (Khatib and Lust 2014, 15). The horizontal organizational structure that most of these CSOs adopted only exacerbated the problem of lacking a unified ideology and political agenda during the transitional period when regimes fell, as was the case in Egypt. And where the regime did not fall, such as in Morocco, the horizontal organizational structure and the lack of a unified ideology among members of these movements helped the regime successfully utilize their old divide-and-rule strategies.

Second, working through loosely connected informal networks might have been an advantage before the uprisings, but it made coordination more difficult during the transitional period. Many activists knew each other through social media networks but had not met in person before the uprisings. Most importantly, however, membership in the new civic activities was skewed toward young, educated, and urban populations. Being detached from rural, older, poorer, and more conservative populations weakened these groups' appeals to the general population. After the uprisings and during the transitional period, it was the old political parties and their affiliated CSOs that filled this gap by building on their established patronage networks through community services and philanthropic activism. Subsequently, the established parties and CSOs played a more influential role in shaping public opinion in those regions.

Third, being grassroots civic movements, youth, women, and diaspora groups rarely formed new political parties after the revolutions. Neither did they organize politically to continue to push for their interests in the constitution writing and democratic process. In Morocco, the February 20 Youth

Movement decided to boycott the constitutional reform negotiations. Jordan's Al-Hirak Youth Movement and Bahrain's February 14 Youth Coalition did the same, calling the process a democratic façade and citing the regimes' unwillingness for real democratic reforms. While their claims were true, the youth movements' self-boycott further pushed them away from major political negotiations. Unlike these groups, Egypt's April 6 Youth Movement participated in the Constituent Assembly, although their representatives did not run as a party, and they did not win seats in the election. Nevertheless, following an agreement among opposition groups over the structure of the Assembly, they were appointed to the Constituent Assembly to represent the youth movements. Except for April 6 Youth Movement and a few other movements, most activists lacked political ambitions. Indeed, for many civil activists, a natural postrevolutionary demobilization pushed them to go back to their work, to their families, and to their normal life (Khatib and Lust 2014, 15).

For those activists who remained politically active and mobilized after the revolution, lack of political skills and experience was a major obstacle to achieving their goals. This deficit was the result of being politically excluded during the authoritarian rule and was a major reason why these groups could not play a more decisive role in transitional politics. Ahmed Maher, a cofounder of Egypt's April 6 Youth Movement, admitted that he signed up to join the Rights and Freedoms commission of the Constituent Assembly "partly because we [the youth] lack the knowledge about political institutions and how the state organizations function" (Ahmed Maher, interview by author, May 7, 2013). This lack of political experience and negotiation skills, along with a horizontal organizational structure and loosely connected affinities, was among the endogenous reasons why the new civic movements could not play a more prominent role in the constitutional negotiation process.

Egypt's youth movement showcases this endogenous factor. Civil society in Egypt was revived with the rise of the pro-democracy Kifaya Movement in 2004 and 2005. In 2004, almost a year before the scheduled presidential election in which Hosni Mubarak sought to run for his fifth six-year term and during the rising rumors that he was grooming his son Gamal as his successor, a group of pro-democracy movements rallied under the slogan *Kifaya* (Enough) to reject the prospect of Gamal Mubarak inheriting power. This movement comprised a fairly large number of small and new groups, including the Popular Campaign for Change, the Egyptian Movement for Change, Women for Democracy, Youth for Change, Journalists for Change, and Workers for Change, to mention a few. Between December 2004 and September 2005, when the presidential election was held, these groups, under the collective name of Kifaya Movement, organized mass demonstrations, attracting a young generation of Egyptians who saw Kifaya as their first collective political action (El-Mahdi 2014, 55).

With the regime cracking down on Kifaya particularly after the 2005 election, the movement faded from Egypt's political landscape. Yet activists continued their mission through several offshoot movements, including the Youth for Change, which was the country's first youth movement (El-Mahdi 2014). The April 6 Youth Movement, which became the most famous group organizing the 2011 protests was formed in 2008 by a group of young activists from the Youth for Change movement. On April 6, 2008, workers at a major textile industrial complex in El-Mahalla had called for a strike. A group of young activists, which later came to be known as the April 6 Youth Movement, created a Facebook group, recruited tens of thousands of members online, and managed to escalate the strike by turning it into a mass mobilization. There was no organic link between the April 6 group and the textile workers in El-Mahalla, and most members of the April 6 Youth Movement were not even from that city, but they both shared some common goals (El-Mahdi 2014).

Two years later, another Facebook group called "We are all Khaled Said" managed to mobilize thousands of young Egyptians in peaceful protests. This group was formed by a group of anonymous activists after the brutal death of a young Egyptian, Khaled Said, killed by undercover policemen in June 2010. Pictures of Said's deformed face after his death spread through social media and created national outrage. These groups and movements were joined by the Ultras, Egyptian soccer fan clubs, which were known to fearlessly confront security forces after soccer games.[7] The Ultras were very strong in numbers and were known to "own" the streets but had not been politically active before 2011. When April 6 Youth Movement and other movements called for protests in January 2011, members of the Ultras (individually or in small groups) rushed to the streets of Cairo and occupied the Tahrir Square, which eventually led to Mubarak's resignation. The Ultras became more organized after the revolution and by September 2011 became involved in protest activism as a collective (El-Madi 2014, 65).

These new civic actors shared some common traits, including their organizational structure, with the 2004–2005 Kifaya Movement, which awakened and politically charged most of the young activists. Kifaya was a horizontally structured network of smaller movements and individual activists. Kifaya's decisions were made through consensus in a steering committee composed of representatives from different groups including the Nasserites (Al-Karama

---

[7] Among the major Ultras, which became politically active, are the Ultras Ahlawy, Zamalek's Ultras White Knights, and Ismaily's Ultras Yellow Dragons (El-Mahdi 2014).

Party), the leftists (the Revolutionary Socialist Organization), liberals (Al-Ghad Party), Islamists (Al-Wasat Party), and several independent activists (El-Mahdi 2014, 56).[8] Kifaya, as such, was "a consortium" of civic-political activists, movements, and organizations, with no institutionalized formal procedures for coordination.

April 6 Youth Movement and other movements faced similar challenges. They were mostly based on loose networks, had a horizontal organizational structure, lacked coordination procedures or an anti-gridlock mechanism, and did not have enough organized grassroots support. These organizational challenges became a major source of weakness for these groups when they moved to electoral politics. During the post-Mubarak elections, none of the parties they established, including Al-Adl, Al-Wa'ee, Al-Tayyar Al-Masry, and Misr Al-Huriyaa, was a major political contender, and they easily lost to more established Muslim Brotherhood candidates and other groups with vertical organizational structures (El-Mahdi 2014). That is, an organizational structure that was their advantage during Mubarak's regime became their disadvantage after his ouster. Moreover, these groups and movements suffered from a lack of coordination. When, for example, Muslim Brotherhood put its constitution draft up for public referendum, these groups failed to coordinate a single strategy to oppose the draft. While some of these groups and even individuals from these groups publicly called for a boycott of the referendum, others believed a boycott would be ineffective and called for participating in the referendum to reject the draft constitution. Signaling different messages to their supporters, these CSOs failed to prevent the adoption of the draft constitution (Maboudi and Nadi 2016). Most importantly, however, these movements failed to provide a clear political alternative for Egyptians who felt they were stuck between the Islamists and the remnants of the old regime.

The organizational deficit of April 6 Youth Movement and other movements in Egypt and across the Arab region had a significant impact on civil society's failure to play a more consequential role in constitution-making and democracy-building after the uprisings. Hailed as the major force of democratization in the regions, some western countries including the United States and many international NGOs began funding and training these movements. This support came to a halt when authoritarian leaders regained their control over democratic movements. Nonetheless, the foreign support, in fact, presented another challenge for Arab civil society: the lack of public legitimacy.

---

[8]   With the exception of Al-Ghad Party, all of these parties were illegal.

The Question of Legitimacy for Civil Society

Besides lacking organizational capacity and political skills, many newer CSOs and even established professional and labor unions lacked independence from either authoritarian states or foreign donors and stakeholders. These particularistic pressures not only have prevented civil society from focusing on or attaining democratizing objectives but also have contributed to their lack of public legitimacy, allowing the state or their political rivals to repeatedly wage attacks on them.

As mentioned previously, the lack of organizational capacity and skills forced most of the newer CSOs to seek financial and technical support from international donors. This financial dependence on foreign actors has been a source of systematic attacks by governments and political rivals to delegitimize civil society. Governments seeking to constrain civic spaces engaged not only in legal campaigns or even physical harassment but also in spreading doubt about the legitimacy of CSOs (Brechenmacher and Carothers 2018).

Four arguments are commonly used in efforts to delegitimize CSOs. First, because most of their financial resources come from abroad, CSOs are accountable to foreign actors rather than domestic constituencies. In the Middle East, those CSOs that are not co-opted by the government are commonly framed as agents of Israel, the United States, or other "hostile" states. Second, because CSOs are self-appointed rather than elected, they do not represent the popular will. This is a common argument made by CSOs' political rivals (including political parties) in democracies or "hybrid" regimes with competitive elections since these groups see themselves more representative of the popular will. Ennahda deputies in the NCA, for example, initially believed and argued that CSOs are not representative of the whole Tunisian society and as such should not play a significant role in the constitutional negotiations (Badreldin Abdelkafi, interview by author, January 22, 2015). Third, because some CSOs have a political agenda, it is argued that they are not civic actors; rather, they are partisan political actors disguised as nonpartisan CSOs. Some CSOs in the Arab region are usually accused of being an unofficial arm of secular political parties. Others, specifically unions, are accused of pushing the agenda of leftist or nationalist parties. Furthermore, in ethnically divided societies, some regional CSOs are disregarded as agents of ethnic groups and advocate for their political goals. Lastly, it is commonly argued that civil society activists are elites who falsely claim to represent and fight for the poor and ordinary citizens. Western educational backgrounds, frequent foreign travels, lavish lifestyles, and high salaries of some civil society leaders are often used to claim that they are out of touch with the concerns of ordinary citizens (Brechenmacher and Carothers 2018).

These attacks on the legitimacy of CSOs are a common tool especially for populist leaders who ride the tide of nationalist, anti-elite, and majoritarian sentiments of the people and frame CSOs as corrupt, elitist, and foreign agents. Borrowing from the populist toolbox, many authoritarian leaders in the Middle East and North Africa have engaged in negative campaigns against civil society since the 1990s. These negative campaigns significantly increased the gap between CSOs and the general public, paving the way for authoritarian leaders, such as Hosni Mubarak, to enact legislation to further restrict the space for independent CSOs. Mubarak's regime co-opted most CSOs, and those that it could not co-opt or repress, it successfully framed as illegitimate. Even after Mubarak resigned, public skepticism about civil society persisted. While hundreds of new independent CSOs were established in the few years after Mubarak's fall, Egyptians were still concerned about civil society corruption and nepotism. Even in a country such as Tunisia, which transitioned to a democracy, popular skepticism about CSOs is still high (Cherif 2018). In post-Mubarak Egypt, both the Muslim Brotherhood government and the military saw the new CSOs as a potential enemy, and both continued the legitimacy attack on these groups. For example, when many civil society activists, such as the April 6 group, opposed the military coup d'état in July 2013, members were arrested for different charges including receiving money from foreign governments or even espionage.

While the newer CSOs suffer from dependence on foreign funds, the older and more established organizations including labor unions and professional syndicates suffer from another particularistic pressure, which led to popular skepticism both before and after the uprisings. Over several decades, Arab leaders made tremendous efforts to strip unions and syndicates of their independence and bring them under state control. Before the uprisings, these organizations had the reputation of being government-affiliated and corrupt. After the uprisings, this skepticism led to a proliferation of new unions leading to fragmentation and polarization within unions that further undermined the role of unions in facilitating democratic transition in countries like Egypt.

The history of labor unions and worker activism in Egypt showcases how the legacy of authoritarian control over unions had a negative impact on their work as a democratic mediator during the transitional period. The Egyptian Trade Union Federation (ETUF) had the monopoly of representing workers in Egypt from 1957 when it was established until the 2011 revolution (Beinin 2012). The ETUF, established by President Gamal Abdel Nasser as a tool to

TABLE 5.1 *Labor protection standards in the Arab world before the Arab Spring*

Country	De Facto Labor Standard
Algeria	51.5
Bahrain	48
Egypt	26.8
Jordan	45.3
Kuwait	32.8
Morocco	57.5
Oman	50.6
Qatar	56.8
Saudi Arabia	0.0
Syria	27.2
Tunisia	55.7
United Arab Emirates	0.0
Yemen	29.5
Regional Average	**37.1**

* *Source:* Cammett and Posusney (2010, 258)

control the workers, was the sole legal trade union in the country and an arm of the state for almost six decades (Beinin 2012; Bishara 2014). Consequently, the ETUF represented the state rather than the workers and sought to be co-opted rather than challenge the state (Bishara 2018).

While all authoritarian regimes co-opted and tried to control labor unions, the Egyptian state interference in union affairs is unique in the whole region. For example, it was commonly believed that Tunisia's Ben Ali asserted total control over UGTT leadership. After all, UGTT endorsed his campaign for reelection in 1995 and 1999. However, even when UGTT's leadership remained loyal to Ben Ali, the local branches asserted some level of independence (Bishara 2014). In Egypt, by contrast, Mubarak and his predecessors managed to control and co-opt even the local branches of ETUF. As Table 5.1 shows, before the Arab Spring, Egypt had one of the lowest de facto labor standards in the Arab world, only higher than oil-rich Gulf monarchies such as Saudi Arabia and the United Arab Emirates where no legal framework for labor protection existed (Cammett and Posusney 2010).[9]

[9] Labor protection standard is an indicator of 17 de facto collective labor rights, including freedom of association, collective bargaining, and the right to strike, and it ranges from 0 to 100 (see Cammett and Posusney 2010).

There are several reasons for ETUF's lack of independence, one of which is how the union federation was created. Whereas Tunisia's UGTT, for example, was established ten years before Tunisia gained independence and was a major actor in the country's struggle for independence, the ETUF was established by a socialist president as a means to control the workers' discontent a few years after Egypt gained independence. The ETUF, as such, did not earn any popular legitimacy, as UGTT did in Tunisia, and could not become a major political actor after independence. Moreover, the Egyptian state never lost control over the union, even outlawing strikes until 2003 (Bishara 2018). But the state's control over workers through the monopolistic union began to change a few years before the Arab Spring.

Parallel to the rise of pro-democracy movements, such as the Kifaya Movement, some worker activists began to organize and contest the monopoly of ETUF in 2007. The proliferation of protest activism by other civil society segments and Mubarak's neoliberal economic reforms since 2004 prompted workers from different sectors to organize street protests. In the fall of 2007, the Real Estate Tax Authority workers formed a national strike committee to coordinate their campaign for equal pay with tax workers who were directly employed by the Ministry of Finance and were receiving higher salaries. Thousands of real estate tax workers protested for eleven days, occupying the streets in front of the cabinet members' offices in downtown Cairo. The protest campaign was successful and yielded them a 325 percent salary increase. By 2008, over 60 percent of real estate clerical workers employed by local authorities across Egypt joined the Independent General Union of Real Estate Tax Authority Workers (IGURETA). In April 2009, the government eventually recognized IGURETA, breaking the nearly six decades of monopoly of ETUF. Shortly after that, healthcare technicians and teachers followed suit and formed their own independent unions by the end of 2010 (Beinin 2012).

The fall of Mubarak's regime accelerated workers' quest for establishing independent unions. By one estimate, 400 new independent unions were established in the first two years following Mubarak's departure from power (Bishara2018). While this union growth and activism was a byproduct of the regime's fall, unions, in general, failed to make an impact on the democratic transition. On the one hand, the ETUF was commonly known for being co-opted and rarely contested the regime's power. On the other hand, the newly independent unions were fragmented and unprepared to take the lead (Beinin 2012). Also, they did not have a nationally recognized leadership or sufficient organizational and financial resources. Moreover, unions did not have a united political or economic agenda and were unable to generate international or domestic networks of support beyond union members and their families. Many of the new unions were also internally fragmented and struggled to generate the funding necessary for their day-to-day operations. Rather than trying to unify the unions, ETUF joined the Supreme Council of Armed Forces (SCAF) to undermine the independence and the work of the new unions (Beinin 2012).

Struggling with these obstacles, the new labor movement failed to have a prominent presence in the emerging institutions following the 2011 revolution. Labor movements, instead, focused on street protests over their immediate grievances and, although they achieved some success in this area, failed to play any leadership role, as the UGTT did in Tunisia, after the revolution. The failure to forge political coalitions with sympathetic groups left labor movements and organizations without leverage to fend off attacks from their political opponents, which put them in a very weak position during the transitional period (Benin 2012). The failure of labor unions to make an impact during the transition was indeed the consequence of an authoritarian state legacy that undermined their organizational capacity, independence, and subsequently legitimacy.

As the case of Egypt shows, both labor unions and the newer CSOs suffered from a lack of legitimacy, albeit for different reasons. Rather than openly challenging the state, labor unions worked as an arm of the state for controlling workers' discontent. For the newer CSOs, years of legitimacy attacks by authoritarian states and dependence on foreign funds, on the one hand, and lack of grassroots support networks, on the other, led to popular skepticism about their legitimacy. This popular skepticism was another major obstacle for CSOs to play a more serious role in constitutional negotiations and the democratic transition in their countries. This popular skepticism hurt the majority of CSOs, including well-established labor unions, preventing them from forging cross-societal coalitions. Without societal coalitions, civil society in Egypt and beyond could not steer important national debates including constitutional negotiations in their societies.

INTRACTABLE DIFFERENCES AND THE EXOGENOUS PATHWAYS OF FAILURE

On the eve of the Arab Spring uprisings, most CSOs were fragmented, lacked organizational capacity, lacked financial and political independence, or were co-opted by the state. Besides these inherent sources of weakness, civil society in the Arab world suffered from several exogenous sources of weakness. Most importantly, civil society in the Arab world lacked institutionalization. As discussed previously, the institutionalization of CSOs is achieved through the establishment of both formal institutions, such as constitutional guarantees of fundamental rights of association and assembly, and informal practices, such as recognition of the operation of national and international human rights watchdogs (Arato 2000). This lack of institutionalization has been a common challenge for almost all CSOs in the regions for several decades. As the next chapter discusses, de jure constitutional guarantees for independence and freedom of associations have always been lacking. Rights to assembly and speech existed, but escape hatches allowed governments to violate those terms. And de facto practices created a culture of co-optation and obedience among many CSOs and their leadership. Consequently, lack of institutionalization hindered the role of CSOs during the Arab Spring transitional period.

Furthermore, lack of institutionalization inherently weakened most CSOs when facing other exogenous challenges such as societal cleavages or military interventions. Societal cleavages can undermine the work of civil society, as was the case in countries like Yemen and Libya. And undemocratic forces such as foreign or domestic military interventions often create a hostile environment for CSOs to function as a democratizing force, as was the case in Bahrain and Egypt. Overcoming these exogenous challenges is a daunting task, especially when most CSOs are weakly institutionalized. The following sections focus on these exogenous causes.

Societal Cleavages: Yemen and Libya

One contributor to a hostile environment for civil society is when societal cleavages have divided and polarized society. As was briefly discussed, societal, ideological, and ethnoreligious polarization is often spread to civil society and undermines the efforts of CSOs to build cross-group coalitions for democratic reforms (Brechenmacher and Carothers 2018). This is particularly the case for weakly institutionalized civil society in deeply divided societies. One of civil society's major challenges in such societies is overcoming mutual mistrust among different groups even when these groups share common concerns and grievances. This mistrust prevents civic actors from forming a strong democratic front for a change. Furthermore, authoritarian regimes often exploit divisions among civic activists to delegitimize them, repressing some challengers while co-opting others (Brechenmacher and Carothers 2018).

On the eve of the 2010–2011 uprisings, division among civic activists persisted along identity and longstanding societal cleavages in many countries (Khatib and Lust 2014, 13). In Bahrain and Syria, Sunni–Shia sectarianism was also a dividing factor among civic activists. In Saudi Arabia, in addition to divisions between Shia and Sunni CSOs, major divisions continued between "liberal" Sunnis and radical Sunni Islamists. Jordanian CSOs were also divided between Islamists and non-Islamists, in addition to the long-standing division between Palestinian and Transjordanian groups. Ideological polarization between Islamists and seculars dominated the activities of Egyptian and Tunisian civic actors. Even in a homogenous country such as Kuwait, mistrust prevailed between the tribes and the urbanites (Khatib and Lust 2014, 14).

Government leaders in Bahrain, Syria, Yemen, and other countries capitalized on the divisions and mistrust among civic actors to extend their survival. In Yemen, for example, where a vibrant civil society existed decades before the 2011 uprisings, civic activists could not create strong cross-group coalitions for democratic change after Saleh resigned. Civil society in Yemen was historically developed along two different lines. In the south, CSOs were developed through socialist, union-based activism in the 1960s, while in the north and east, charity-based activism funded by religious institutions and philanthropists constituted the majority of civic activism (Al-Sakkaf 2016). The political environment following the unification of Yemen in 1990 led to a renaissance for modern CSOs. In the first few years after the unification, activism mainly focused on party recruitment and mobilization. In an effort to expand their public outreach beyond their traditional support bases, major political parties started to develop their youth and civic organizations (Gasim 2014, 117). Parallel to these efforts, several independent CSOs began to organize. In a few years following the unification, over 700 CSOs registered with the Ministry of Social Affairs, receiving an annual stipend from the government (Al-Sakkaf 2016). Furthermore, in the 1990s, several international organizations started to fund civil-society-led development projects. As a result, some CSOs became experienced in fund-raising. As more funds became available to these CSOs, they were able to expand from local associations into national organizations. During this period, civil society in Yemen expanded to include several advocacy-based CSOs specializing in issues such as women's rights, children's rights, minorities, youth, water access, and environment protection (Al-Sakkaf 2016). Besides development- and advocacy-focused CSOs, a large number of research centers and think tanks were also established. By 2014, there were more than 8,000 registered CSOs, a large number of which were nationally representative (Al-Sakkaf 2016).

The flourishing of civil society and the evolution of its agenda from the local to the national level troubled Saleh's government. Consequently, the regime exploited the long-standing societal cleavages to divide its civic challengers. Besides the geographical divisions between the north and the south, Yemeni society is divided across tribal, clannish (Hashemite or not), and religious (Zeidi vs. Sunni) lines. Since their establishment, many CSOs kept close ties with one or several of these communities. This relationship gave many Yemeni CSOs a unique source of strength. Unlike those in Morocco, Jordan, Algeria, and other parts of the region, which failed in their public outreach efforts, CSOs in Yemen have been more engaged with their local communities.

These CSOs could not, however, utilize their community networks to build cross-group coalitions during the transitional period because they became entangled in the conflict between different regional and religious groups. Ironically, the very source of CSO's strength (i.e., local connections) became a source of their demise as the conflict between the north and the south expanded in 2015. In Yemen, CSOs are often labeled with the identity of their leaders. As the cross-group conflict was on the rise, mistrust between civic activists was also increasing (Al-Shami 2015). The civil war not only increased the divisions among civil activists but also had a devastating impact on the organizational capacity of CSOs, as many lost their funding. Shortage of water, food, fuel, transportation, and electricity also undermined these organizations' abilities to conduct meetings or carry out grassroots work (Al-Shami 2015). With societal divisions reproducing themselves within civil society and shortage of funding and basic goods, most CSOs failed to function as peace mediators and build cross-group democratic bridges.

Unlike in Yemen and most of the region, civil society was practically nonexistent during Muammar Qaddafi's rule in Libya (Khatib and Lust 2014). Qaddafi continued King Idris's 1952 policy to ban all political parties when he came to power after the 1969 coup. Qaddafi restricted the public civic space further by harshly punishing any expression of civic or political dissent. When, for instance, a group of student activists, in an act of defiance against the regime's attempt to establish government-backed unions, elected their own student unions, the government initially responded by arresting the activists. However, when a group of students from Tripoli and Benghazi universities continued to demonstrate in what was the first expression of civic dissent against Qaddafi's regime in April 1976, the government responded by sentencing many activists to long prison terms while publicly executing a number of them at both universities, with the executions being broadcasted live on television to send a clear message to all other potential dissidents across the country (Rajabany and Ben Shitrit 2014).

Despite the regime's severe repression, civic life survived through informal institutions and diaspora activists. The informal institutions for civic activism were mostly developed within tribes and tribal activism (Carapico 2019) as well as through artworks. For example, when the economy deteriorated between 1982 and 1985 and food shortage became a challenge for many Libyans due to the failure of the regime's economic policies, graffiti became a form of expression of dissent for many activists who could not express their opinion other ways. During these years, graffiti of bananas, apples, and chocolate appeared on the walls of the capital city of Tripoli with the sentence "Lest we forget" alluding to poverty and food shortages (Rajabany and Ben Shitrit 2014, 81). Since the 1990s, civic activism in exile became the major formal venue for the Libyan civil society. Young, educated, and tech-savvy Libyans living mostly in the West created a vibrant civil society in exile. However, these groups had little cross-communication and very weak ties with potential supporters in Libya (Rajabany and Ben Shitrit 2014).

Despite these challenges, only a year after the fall of Qaddafi's regime, civic activism was remarkably transformed from loosely connected diaspora movements and informal institutions to active, formal CSOs. Hundreds of CSOs were created within months following the 2011 rebellion. Soon after Qaddafi was ousted from power, the transitional government established the Ministry of Culture and Civil Society that along with a few international organizations including the United Nations Development Programme organized a workshop in February 2012 to create a legal framework for the work of CSOs. The main objective of the workshop was to develop legal procedures for the formation and internal governance, the funding, and the regulation of government supervision of CSOs (Rajabany and Ben Shitrit 2014). These goals were not completely achieved, and the transitional government retained its imposition of CSOs' funding restrictions.

Despite funding restrictions, lack of organizational capacity, and relevant experience, some CSOs became increasingly influential during the transitional process. One of these groups was the Libyan Civil Rights Lobby (LCRL), an interest group composed of several CSOs advocating for the freedom of expression. When the NTC issued the "Anti-Glorification Law" (or Law 37 of 2012), which criminalized any acts of speech against the February 17 Revolution, including speeches glorifying Qaddafi or his regime, the LCRL joined forces with other CSOs including Lawyers for Justice in Libya, Free Generation Movement, and Libya Outreach Group to contest the law. A month later and in a victory for these CSOs, the Libyan Supreme Court nullified the law, declaring it unconstitutional (Rajabany and Ben Shitrit 2014).

The impressive works of the newly established CSOs and their achievements in the first year since the transition were eventually nullified by rising tensions among different groups. Societal cleavages between the east and the west and between Islamists and seculars became a major obstacle for these CSOs to both remain impartial and build cross-sectional coalitions. Meanwhile, CSOs affiliated with the Amazigh, Touareg, and Tebu minorities who were feeling neglected focused only on advocating for minority rights. The armed conflict between the two governments in Tripoli and Tobruk that emerged after the downfall of Qaddafi has made coordination across regions almost impossible. With the civil war, the international community and donors also shifted their attention and funding sources to peace and conflict management rather than empowering CSOs.

Indeed, the forces of civil war have proved beyond the capacity of CSOs in Libya and Yemen. In Yemen, a vibrant and established civil society got caught in the civil conflict between the north and the south. Despite their strength in community links, many CSOs are considered to be agents of their ethnic groups (whether religious sects, tribes, or clans). In Libya, the young civil society was still lagging in its efforts for public outreach when the civil war between the east and the west rendered all its efforts ineffective. CSOs in both countries suffer from a lack of sufficient funding necessary for their daily operations. As Carapico (2019, 118) notes, "under circumstances of violence and desperation. . ., a national civic realm collapses."

The Power of Undemocratic Forces: Egypt and Bahrain

Another exogenous factor contributing to civil society's failure in fulfilling its democratizing role is the prevailing undemocratic forces such as the excessive influence or power of the armed forces and international influence. When strong armed forces intervene in the democratic transition or when regional and global powers come to the aid of an embattled authoritarian state, civil society is often silenced. This is particularly the case where civil society is not institutionalized. As the cases of Egypt and Bahrain demonstrate, lack of institutionalization leaves CSOs unshielded from undemocratic forces. In both countries, the weakly institutionalized civil society was no match for the power of undemocratic forces, which determined the future of democracy in their nations.

When Hosni Mubarak stepped down on February 11, 2011, the remnants of his regime remained in power. Most importantly, the military kept its control over the state throughout the transitional process. When Mubarak resigned, the power was transferred to the SCAF. Although SCAF eventually transferred the formal power to the elected President Morsi, its unmatched power over-shadowed all other groups. Only two years after the revolution, the military staged a coup, removing Egypt's first democratically elected president and suspending the constitution.

Egyptian civil society was divided in its response to the July 2013 coup. While some CSOs, particularly the secular, anti-Brotherhood groups, sided with the military, others that were against military intervention feared for their survival and opted to remain silent. Only a few pro-democracy civil society movements, including the April 6 Youth Movement, openly spoke against the military coup. The military, in response, successfully intimidated all dissent by civil society by repressing leaders of April 6 and other groups that expressed dissent. The remaining CSOs were not in a position to challenge the military's power or General El-Sisi's presidency.

As discussed previously in this chapter, Egyptian civil society was fragmented at the start of the uprisings. The old and established CSOs including the ETUF had a reputation for being co-opted by the state and representing the interests of the state rather than those of the workers. The ETUF worked with SCAF to undermine the work of newly created unions, associations, and civic movements (Beinin 2012). These new CSOs themselves suffered from a lack of organizational capacity, a unified political agenda, effective coordination strategies, and experience. Almost all CSOs also failed in their efforts for public outreach and communication with political stakeholders. These inherent weaknesses were partly because Egyptian civil society, despite its long history, had not been institutionalized. And the weakly institutionalized civil society movements such as the April 6 Youth Movement were no match for the power of the Egyptian military and were practically silenced after July 2013 because formal institutions and informal practices were not protecting them.

Similar to Egypt, Bahrain's civil society, mostly composed of young activists, was at the center of the 2011 uprisings. In Bahrain, however, civic activism has historically been divided along societal divisions. Shia activists often operated separately from Sunni activists. Moreover, Shia and Sunni civil society activists themselves were divided between religious and secular groups (Louër 2014). A few years before the 2011 uprisings, however, new cross-group, issue-based civil society came to the forefront of civic activism. The most important nonpartisan and nonsectarian civil society group was the Bahrain Center for Human Rights (BCHR). Since its inception in 2000, the Bahraini government saw the BCHR as a major dissident group and used all means to repress the group. Only four years after its establishment, the regime decided to revoke BCHR's authorization. Despite not being legally recognized, the association continued to work to promote human rights in Bahrain.

With the 2011 uprisings, the BCHR returned to the spotlight and became a major force for promoting democracy in the country. The regime responded with severe oppression, such as sentencing Abdulhadi Al-Khawaja, a BCHR member, to life in prison (Louër 2014). While the BCHR was a major source of spreading information about the protest events and the regime's brutal responses, it was the February 14 Coalition that organized the protests. The February 14 Coalition, however, shared many traits with other youth movements during the Arab Spring, such as Egypt's April 6 Youth Movement. They were all noninstitutionalized, decentralized, and lacked organizational capacity, political experience, or negotiation skills.

Like the BCHR, the February 14 Coalition was not recognized by the state as a legally operating organization. The lack of freedom and democratic institutions, such as independent courts, independent watchdogs, a free press, constitutional guarantees for rights to assembly, and freedom of association and speech allowed the state to undermine the work of civil society. Despite these democratic deficits, these CSOs created unprecedented pressure on the state, forcing the regime to request military assistance from the GCC. On March 14, 2011, the Peninsula Shield Force led by Saudi Arabia entered Bahrain and brought an end to the popular uprisings at the Pearl Roundabout, highlighting the importance of both military force and external intervention.

Following the fall of the movement, the Bahraini regime initiated a harsh campaign to limit the already constrained civic space in the country. Since 2011, for example, the regime made it illegal for CSOs to receive funding from overseas. Even when receiving funds from domestic sources, CSOs are now required to get approval from the Ministry of Social Affairs. The foreign military intervention, thus, further constrained the already limited civic space, undermining the role that civil society could potentially play. The young, unorganized, and weakly institutionalized civil movements and associations in Bahrain were no match for the Saudi troops and the Saudi support of the Bahraini regime.

As Bahrain and Egypt showcase, when undemocratic forces are at play, the civic space will be constrained, and civil society will be easily silenced. In Egypt, April 6 Youth Movement and other independent CSOs did not have the power and capacity to prevent the military takeover. Neither were the BCHR, the February 14 Coalition, and other CSOs in Bahrain capable of averting Saudi Arabia's military campaign. In both countries, interventions by undemocratic forces stifled civil society and ended the prospects for a successful transition to democracy.

CONCLUSION: WHEN CIVIL SOCIETY FAILS
TO MAKE A DIFFERENCE

As Arato (2000, 45) reminds us, "[I]t is now almost beyond dispute that the concept of civil society has played a major role in recent transitions to democracy...." During the Arab Spring, it was CSOs that took the lead in mobilizing mass protests against the authoritarian regimes. However, it did not take long for most of these groups to fail, one after another, to play a consequential role in the democratic transition. This chapter explored why Arab civil society failed to play an effective role in constitution-making and why it failed to facilitate democratization. It first examined why the characteristics of the constitution-making process matter if civil society is to succeed in its democratizing role. An inclusive and participatory process is a necessary (but not sufficient) condition for civil society to play an effective role in the democratic transition. As the cases of Jordan, Morocco, and Algeria show, when the process is not inclusive, CSOs cannot fulfill their democratizing role. Noninclusive, or even partially inclusive, constitution-making processes limit the civic space, making it difficult for civil society to influence the constitutional bargain from outside. When civil society is kept out of the bargain, it cannot contribute to the democratic quality of constitution, and without a democratic constitution, democratization cannot be achieved.

I also looked at both endogenous and exogenous factors impacting civil society's failure, which persist across the region. The first endogenous factor that hindered the work of most civic groups in the region was the lack of organizational capacity of CSOs. Most new civic movements that emerged during the Arab Spring had a horizontal and decentralized structure, which made consensus-building and strategy coordination extremely difficult. In Egypt, for example, the lack of political experience and negotiation skills as well as unified agenda hindered the civic movements' public outreach efforts as they could not offer a realistic alternative for many people who saw the military regime and the Muslim Brotherhood as the only options to choose from. The second endogenous factor leading to civil society's failure, which was also examined within the Egyptian context, was the CSOs' lack of public legitimacy, particularly among two groups. The first were those organizations (such as unions) that historically have been co-opted by the state and have been acting as an arm of the state in order to control civic dissents. And the second were those associations (such as human rights groups) that depend on funding from foreign donors and had to work under particularistic pressure. Both groups suffered from a lack of public legitimacy, which undermined their efforts during the transition.

This chapter also examined two exogenous factors that contributed to civil society's failure in playing a more prominent role in democratization. First, I discussed the negative impact of societal cleavages and conflict on the work of civil society. A review of Yemen and Libya underscores how under these circumstances, civil society cannot even perform its basic functions, let alone be an agent of democratization. Second, the powers of undemocratic forces, such as the military or international intervention, were assessed within the cases of Egypt and Bahrain. In both cases, the powers of undemocratic forces, which eventually determined the political outcome of the uprisings, were beyond the capacity of CSOs.

Under these circumstances, weakly institutionalized civil society is often destined to fail in its democratizing role. From relatively established, organized, and independent NGOs and unions to grassroots youth, women, and diaspora movements, civil society could not make a lasting impact on the democratic transition partly because they suffered from a lack of strong institutionalization including constitutional guarantees of civil society rights. Indeed, "civil society ha[s] to be securely institutionalized before becoming a key terrain of participatory politics in the long term" (Arato 2000, ix–x).

Constitutional negotiations in transitioning states are often rife with bitter divisions. During these constitutional moments, an independent and institutionalized civil society can function as a third-party arbiter and play an important role in steering public debates, facilitating negotiations, and establishing democracy. This role, however, is not possible if they are kept out of the constitutional process and negotiations. The Arab Spring, which in large part was instigated by civil society including youth movements, provided a unique opportunity for the Arab civil society to make an impact and facilitate the transition toward democracy. One after another, however, CSOs in the region failed in their efforts to facilitate democratization. The next chapter examines the consequences of civil society's failure by exploring how, in the absence of an effective civil society, the content of constitutions fails to address the most important societal concerns and political ills.

6

Pathways of Failure

The Importance of Constitutional Design

When Egypt's President Hosni Mubarak came to power in 1981, he had no incentive to change Anwar Al-Sadat's 1971 constitution because Al-Sadat's amendments shortly before his assassination in 1981 gave the new president what he wanted: no executive term limits (Brown 2002, 84–85). After three decades of Mubarak winning sham elections one after another, when Egyptian opposition groups forced him out, they focused on writing a new constitution that would institutionalize turnover of power and executive term limits. Indeed, both the 2012 and 2014 constitutions placed term limits on the executive. Yet, a year after President El-Sisi was elected for his second (and supposedly last) term in 2018, the Egyptian Parliament approved a constitutional amendment that, without abolishing term limits, allows El-Sisi to remain in power until 2030. By contrast, Tunisia, which also implemented presidential term limits, seems to have ended authoritarianism and successfully transitioned to democracy. Why did the Egyptian constitution fail to facilitate democratization, despite implementing democratic institutions similar to those adopted in Tunisia? The answer, this chapter argues, partially lies in Egypt's specific constitutional design. When constitutional designs fail to address the underlying societal and political ills in a polity, they will also fail to democratize.

This chapter looks at five distinct pathways of failed constitutional design that emerged after the Arab Spring. The first two pathways emerged as a result of constitutional designs failing to resolve the problem of authoritarianism. In Morocco and Jordan, constitutions did not limit the arbitrary powers of the monarchs. Rather than liberal constitutions, the embattled kings in Morocco and Jordan adopted documents, which do not limit their powers, by utilizing a legal language that lacks textual clarity, adopting contradictory provisions, and creating parallel institutions, which leave the door open for future manipulations through illiberal constitutional interpretations. In the cases of

Algeria and Egypt, despite adopting executive term limits, constitutions remain "nonbinding," allowing strongmen to manipulate the constitutional order without even lifting term limits and stay in power for years. Both of these "nonconstitutionalist" constitutional orders led to democratic backsliding because they did not address the underlying problem of unchecked executives with ultra-constitutional powers.

The other three pathways were specific to countries that were deeply divided across different lines. When these divisions resurfaced during the moments of constitutional negotiations, the "nonconsensual" constitutions that emerged failed to properly address them. In Bahrain and Syria, where an ethnoreligious minority rules against the majority's will, new constitutions failed to institutionalize power-sharing arrangements, as the authoritarian ruler did not see power-sharing as an option. Next, federalist and region-based power-sharing arrangements failed to prevent conflict in Yemen and Libya where regional cleavages, rivalries, and grievances were prominent issues. Lastly, the 2012 Constitution of Egypt failed to create a societal consensus in a country that was deeply divided across ideological and identity lines.

In all of these cases, the constitutional design could not resolve the predominant social and political problems in society, mostly because, as discussed in previous chapters, the constitution-making process was not inclusive or participatory, and independent CSOs were not able to influence the constitutional bargain. Before explaining each of these five pathways, I first briefly discuss why the content of constitutions matters for democratization.

DO CONSTITUTIONS REALLY MATTER?

Constitutions are (re)negotiated during the most exceptional moments of a nation's history. Elster (1995, 370–371) identifies eight situations for constitutional change including social and economic crisis, revolution, regime collapse, fear of regime collapse, defeat in war, reconstruction after war, creation of a new state, and liberation from colonial rule. Under these exceptional circumstances, constitutions play two fundamental roles. First, they establish the legal and political structure of state institutions, regulate the machinery of the government, and establish the legal limits of governmental powers. Second, they define and institutionalize the most fundamental beliefs, norms, and values of the political collectivity (Lerner 2011). To play these roles in transitional states, constitutions should be both democratic and consensual. By establishing the legal limits of governmental power, democratic constitutions can prevent democratic backsliding. And by defining the state's identity based on beliefs, norms, and aspirations that are shared by most societal groups, consensual constitutions can prevent conflict and contribute to democratic stability.

Constitutions that fail to fulfill these two roles will also fail in consolidating democracy. In transitional contexts, such undemocratic and nonconsensual constitutions are more likely to emerge in countries with a history of authoritarian legacy and/or where the society is deeply divided across regional, ethnic, religious, or ideological lines. Thus, it is imperative for these societies to write constitutions that address these underlying problems. The widespread protests in the Arab world in 2010–2011 were precisely about these problems. The question remains, however, how constitutions can resolve these two challenges.

The Challenge of Constitution-Making in Societies with Authoritarian Legacy

When public pressure for liberalization is mounting, many authoritarian incumbents initiate constitutional reforms. They often expand the provision of rights, share power with the legislative branch, make judicial reforms, facilitate multiparty and multicandidate elections, and sometimes even bind themselves with term limits. While these constitutional reforms look democratic, the documents are often designed in a way that allows future constitutional manipulations by the executives to reinstate the powers they relinquished through the very same reforms. These constitutional toolboxes, or "menu of manipulation" to use Schedler's (2002) term, often include strategies such as adopting poorly developed rights provisions and "escape hatch" clauses, which allow the state to limit those rights. They can also include establishment of parallel institutions to undermine the independence of the legislative or judiciary branches, using vague and sometimes contradictory provisions, and crafting succession mechanisms that do not hold the executive accountable (see Brown 2002).

Instead, democratic constitutions should institutionalize specific constraints on the authority of the government by creating a system of checks and balances that distributes power and authority among different branches of the government (Lijphart 2012). They should also include formal procedures for the protection of individual and group rights. By institutionalizing checks and balances and the protection of fundamental rights, constitutions can manifest the principles of constitutionalism (Friedrich 1950). This manifestation of principles of constitutionalism is, indeed, what distinguishes democratic constitutional systems from window-dressing or nonconstitutional constitutions (Brown 2002; Lerner 2011).

Simply adding new rights provisions in constitutions or sharing some power with other government branches does not necessarily make a constitution more democratic. As several recent constitutional reforms, like those in Algeria (2016), Turkey (2017), and Egypt (2019), show that even presidential term limits do not mean much as executives have been embarking on various constitutional innovations to extend their tenure in office without abolishing term limits.

As long as the authoritarian incumbent initiates constitutional reforms, even under pressures for liberalization, chances are that the constitution will not institutionalize real constraints on governmental powers. Without the inclusion of all major societal and political groups in the process, these constitutions have scant chances for success. This was a challenge that unraveled efforts to democratize Arab countries at the onset of the Arab Spring. The uprisings were a wake-up call for millions of people who were living under the mandate of constitutions that were merely tools for authoritarian control rather than manifestations of the principles of constitutionalism. Even where protesters were not chanting *Erhal* (Leave!) or *Ash-shab yurid isqat an-nizam* (The people want the fall of the regime) to force their authoritarian leaders to resign, they still demanded *hurriya* (political freedom), *adala ijtima'iyya* (social justice), and *karama* (dignity), the lack of which was rooted in authoritarianism. All over the region, protesters sought fundamental constitutional change as the remedy for the ills of Arab politics (Brown 2013). With the exception of the Tunisian constitution, however, all post–Arab Spring constitutional documents failed to resolve these underlying problems in their societies. The new constitutional bargains led, instead, to documents with unchecked executive powers, vague provisions about individual and group rights, and escape hatches that allow the state to violate its own rules. Constitutional reforms in Algeria, Egypt, Jordan, and Morocco are among the primary examples of such constitutions.

The Challenge of Constitution-Making in Deeply Divided Societies

Writing democratic constitutions is even a greater challenge for societies with a legacy of authoritarianism, which are also deeply divided. These divisions are mostly across ethnolinguistic, religious, or regional lines (where distinct groups are concentrated in specific regions) but can also include societies that are deeply divided across ideological lines such as secular versus religious identities. Under authoritarian rule, these cleavages are often muted with state repression. However, when authoritarian regimes fall and sometimes even when they do not fall but initiate constitutional reforms to extend their rule, these cleavages gradually move to the top of national debates. In these circumstances, the "high politics" of constitution-making awakens the silenced divisions, which most often become the main issues of discord in the constitutional bargain.

Constitution-making is an attempt to identify and formalize the most fundamental norms and values shared by the people. When there are competing visions for the identity of the state and when there are clashing societal norms and values, innovative constitutional solutions become inevitable if a conflict is to be avoided. Without consensual constitutional solutions, these disagreements will be inflated. Subsequently, constitutional negotiations, instead of becoming instruments of compromise, become a major source of conflict and escalating societal tensions (Lerner 2011). But what are the best constitutional solutions for such societies? As Lerner (2011) argues, the answer to this question depends on whether that society is segmented along ethnoreligious or geographical lines or whether competing identities are the major source of divisions.

When ethnoreligious divisions are the major source of discord, power-sharing can function as the institutional mechanism for preventing conflict and enhancing democracy. A very rich body of literature has suggested a variety of such power-sharing institutions. These institutional arrangements include federalism, consociationalism, different electoral systems (such as proportional representation), and constitutional guarantees for special group rights. Indeed, each of these arrangements might work only in a specific context. For example, federalism will work only where ethnic, religious, or linguistic groups are concentrated in specific territories. Consociationalism, by contrast, has even a less integrative approach to power-sharing by freezing those societal divisions and might, as such, work better in established democracies where there is less likelihood of civil conflicts. Similarly, proportional representation electoral systems might be appropriate in societies with several minority groups. Proportional representation is not territorial-based that can help with territorial-based divisions, but it is also a less integrative approach because it discourages different groups from reaching out to other communities. Lastly, constitutional protections for special group rights are more relevant in societies with multicultural or multinational identities.

Each of these institutional arrangements, depending on the source of societal divisions, can provide a power-sharing solution for those deeply divided societies. While there is no scholarly consensus over precisely which arrangements work best in various situations, it can be argued that the success of any of these arrangements depends on three conditions. First, these power-sharing arrangements should be clearly stated in the constitution and should be left out of ordinary legislative laws. In other words, constitutions should provide the formal basis for these arrangements. Second, these constitutional arrangements should be consensual. That is, all groups should agree on these arrangements. Lastly, these institutions become consensual only when the process of writing the constitution is inclusive. Without the inclusion of all interested groups in constitutional bargains, it is impossible to institutionalize consensual arrangements for power-sharing.

Power-sharing arrangements are, however, less relevant in societies that are deeply divided across ideological or identity lines. An example of these societal cleavages is the division between religious and secular groups in society. In these societies, federal solutions, consociationalism, electoral systems, or constitutional rights cannot resolve the societal divisions. When different groups in the society have different visions and definitions about the identity of the state and who "we the people" are, other constitutional innovations are needed. In her seminal work on making constitutions in deeply divided societies, Hanna Lerner (2011) argues that constitutions in such societies should avoid clear-cut decisions on controversial issues such as church–state relations and the definition of national identity in order to prevent conflict. Instead, by formulating vague, ambiguous, and contradictory provisions on these divisive issues, constitution drafters should defer decisions on controversial choices to the future. As Lerner (2011) argues, this "incrementalist" strategy will inevitably transfer these decisions from the constitutional sphere to the political sphere and hence lower societal tensions. As discussed in Chapter 3, the Tunisian constitution-makers used this approach in intentionally formulating contradictory and vague provisions on controversial issues such as the role of religion and Islamic Sharia, which had polarized other Arab nations such as Egypt.

As Lerner's (2011) "incrementalist approach" suggests, making democratic and consensual constitutions is a daunting task, particularly in deeply divided societies and in countries with a legacy of authoritarianism. These societies face several challenges that require constitutional solutions. If left unresolved in the constitution, as was the case in all Arab Spring constitutional reform cases with the exception of Tunisia, these issues or "ills," to use Brown's (2013) term, will hinder a successful and peaceful transition toward democracy. We can identify five patterns in the post–Arab Spring constitutional documents that failed to provide foundational remedies for the ills of Arab politics. The first two are constitutional texts in Jordan (2011), Morocco (2011), Algeria (2016), and Egypt (2014) that despite being much more liberal and democratic than their predecessors still failed to resolve the underlying problem of authoritarianism.[1] The other three are constitutions in societies that are deeply divided across ethnoreligious (Bahrain 2012 and Syria 2012), regional (Libya 2017 and Yemen 2015), and ideological/political identity (Egypt 2012) lines but failed to create societal consensus. The remainder of this chapter discusses these five failed pathways of constitutional design.

ARAB SPRING CONSTITUTIONS AND THE UNRESOLVED AUTHORITARIAN LEGACY

Most constitutions around the world, whether democratic or not, have a similar format and cover similar issues and topics: most of them have a preamble, where they formalize the most fundamental beliefs, norms, and values of the political collectivity; address the machinery of government, regulating state institution; guarantee individual and collective rights; and address the procedures for amending the constitution (Elster 1993). Despite their apparent resemblance to democratic constitutions, however, "nonconstitutionalist" constitutions are inherently different. The most common features of nonconstitutionalist constitutions in the Arab world are unchecked executives, escape hatches allowing the executive to violate the rules, and vague provisions about individual and group rights (Brown 2002). When Arab executives took on the mission of initiating constitutional reforms in the wake of the Arab Spring, they were meticulous about crafting a new constitutional order that looked democratic but did not attenuate their grip on power. The new constitutional orders were not very new, and the political ills of Arab polities (i.e., authoritarian legacy) remained without constitutional remedies, leading to two distinct pathways of constitutional failures in some Arab monarchies and republics.

Constitutions for All Seasons: Morocco (2011) and Jordan (2011)

Arab monarchies, in general, were more stable during the Arab Spring uprisings. Yet, besides Bahrain, the other two monarchies that felt the pressure for democratization were the resource-poor kingdoms of Morocco and Jordan. Both kingdoms promised major constitutional reforms, but the outcome of those reforms were unambitious constitutions, which kept all central powers in the palace. These constitutions are abundant with vague provisions, open

---

[1] I excluded the constitutions of Saudi Arabia and Oman from this analysis because these documents included the least ambitious reforms and never promised to make a substantive change in power-sharing or democratic institutions.

for interpretation by a judicial review, which is not independent of the executive. While these documents create a mirage of democratic reforms, they remain among the most nonconstitutional constitutions in the region.

Recall that King Mohammed VI of Morocco was the first Arab leader to announce a new constitution in response to public demands for political reform. There is speculation, for at least two reasons, that even the decision to write a new constitution was not genuinely in response to the public call for democracy. First, unlike his predecessors, King Mohammed VI had not changed the constitution since he ascended to the throne in 1999, and after a decade, some of his advisors thought it was time for him to have his own constitutional legacy. Additionally, on the eve of the Arab Spring, major institutional issues were rising to the top of the state's agenda. Three of the most important institutional issues that required constitutional solutions included: (1) the structure of power was not clear in the constitution; (2) the powers of the prime minister were not well-defined; and (3) elections and electoral system laws needed major revisions. Second, Morocco was witnessing a democratic regression since 2007, and a constitutional reform seemed to be a serious option for the king to rebrand himself as a reformer. Early in his reign, from 2000 to 2007, the king started an aggressive initiative for broad social, political, and economic reforms. These reforms started with Abderrahmane Youssoufi, Morocco's prime minister from 1998 to 2002. The reforms continued even after Youssoufi's resignation in 2002. But they came to a halt by 2007 around the same time when most of the Arab region witnessed a democratic regression. For these reasons, the palace was already thinking of a constitutional reform when the Arab Spring happened, which seemed only to accelerate the preplanned reforms (anonymous member of the CCRC, interview by author, January 30, 2019).

Perhaps this was the reason the king's March 9 speech and the reforms that he promised surpassed everyone's expectations. In particular, the king promised six broad reforms that exceeded expectations. First, he pledged that there would be broad consultation over the constitution with major groups including political parties, CSOs, lawyers, professors, and youth and women groups. This was important since the Moroccan opposition would participate in the constitution-making process for the first time since 1961 when Hassan II assumed power in the newly independent state. Second, the prime minister would be selected through electoral institutions, rather than being appointed by the king. The king also vowed that executive power, the role of political parties, and other institutions would be clearly defined. The king also promised that the parliament would be empowered, and the judiciary would be independent. Finally, he assured the public that civil rights would be expanded (anonymous member of the CCRC, interview by author, January 30, 2019).

Shortly after his speech, the king appointed nineteen independent members to the CCRC. These members had different political orientations and were in discord over several issues. At least, seven controversial issues surfaced during the CCRC's constitutional debates. The first two issues of discord over which members of the CCRC were almost evenly split were related to the identity of the Moroccan state. On the one hand, the more conservative members including Abdallah Saaf opposed the recognition of Tamazight as an official language, emphasizing the Arabic identity of the state, while the more reformist members including Nadia El-Barnousi accused their colleagues of being anti-Amazigh (anonymous member of the CCRC, interview by author, January 30, 2019). Eventually, the constitution recognized Tamazight as an official language. On the other hand, CCRC members clashed over the religious identity of the Moroccan people. Here, the major debate was over freedom of conscience with the conservative members projecting fear of Evangelization from the West and Shiaization from the east as major threats to the Islamic identity of Moroccans, while reformists emphasized freedom of choice (anonymous member of the CCRC, interview by author, January 30, 2019). The adopted constitution created a balance between freedom of religion and the Islamic identity of Morocco but struck out freedom of conscience.

Other issues of debate and discord included the powers and responsibilities of the prime minister and the question of whether the prime minister can dissolve the parliament and inform the king or whether only the king should have this power. On these issues, the majority of the CCRC members believed that the powers of the prime minister should not exceed those of the king. A few members, including Mohamed El-Touzi and Nadia El-Barnousi, opposed this arrangement and argued that a balance of power between the two should exist (anonymous member of the CCRC, interview by author, January 30, 2019). Another debate emerged regarding the independence of the judiciary. While most members wanted a provision stating that "the king guarantees the independence of the judiciary," a minority opposed this provision, arguing that if the judiciary is independent, it does not require the king's "guarantee" (anonymous member of the CCRC, interview by author, January 30, 2019). The CCRC members were in discord even over the process of changing the constitution. While few members, most notably Edris El-Yazmi, advocated for a participatory process as one of the major public demands, the majority disagreed, questioning the value of public consultations: "what do villagers and the illiterate know about the constitution?"

(anonymous member of the CCRC, interview by author, January 30, 2019). Lastly, a debate surfaced around a major controversial issue regarding the mechanism of adopting the constitution. Fearing that the king might change the draft constitution written by the CCRC, Amina Bouayach and Mohamed El-Touzi went public to say that the draft constitution cannot be unilaterally changed after the CCRC submitted it to the king. However, most CCRC members remained silent on this issue (anonymous member of the CCRC, interview by author, January 30, 2019). Eventually, the king changed the proposed draft three times, to modify provisions pertaining to the judiciary, before signing it into law after a public referendum in July 2011 (Ma'ati Monjib, interview by author, November 19, 2014).

It took just a few years after the adoption of the 2011 constitution for the opposition to realize that the king has once again outfoxed them. The new constitution did not lead to more democracy. Rather, it helped the king stay ahead of the game and successfully weather the Arab Spring. The constitution achieved its purpose for King Mohammed VI in three ways. First, it kept the core power in the palace. Second, it created parallel institutions to give the impression of empowering the parliament and political parties while essentially leaving the king as the ultimate decision-maker in the most important areas. And finally, the ambiguous language of the constitution left the door open for constitutional interpretations and, consequently, constitutional manipulations in the future. An example of each of these three constitutional strategies illustrates why the Moroccan constitution has failed to fortify democracy.

In the Moroccan constitution, the king is the state, and the state is the king. As Article 46 of the 2011 constitution puts it, "The person of the king is inviolable, and respect is due Him." The king is the head of the state (Article 42), the commander of the faithful who presides over the Superior Council of the Ulema (Article 41), the supreme head of the Royal Armed Forces (Article 53), and the president of the Superior Council of Security (Article 54). He still appoints the head of government from the political party that wins the HOR elections, appoints all members of the government on proposal of the head of government, and can terminate any member of the government or the whole government (Article 47). The king can promulgate laws (Article 50), issue *Dahir* or Royal Decree (Article 41), accredit ambassadors to foreign states, and sign and ratify all treaties (Article 55). He can also dissolve both chambers of the parliament (Article 51). Moreover, the king presides over the Superior Council of the Judicial Power (Article 56), has the right to pardon (Article 58), and can issue Emergency Law (Article 59). The king is the guarantor of the independence of the judiciary (Article 107), and yet he appoints the president and half of the members of the Constitutional Court (Article 130).

When it comes to the king's powers, the Moroccan constitution is very clear. However, when the constitution addresses checks and balances, the text suddenly turns vague and contradictory. As the above examples show, the king shares many powers with the executive, legislative, and judiciary branches. Yet the constitution institutionalizes parallel institutions that, in practice, strip these branches of their independence. Most notably, the constitution creates two executive councils: the Council of Government and the Council of Ministers. The prime minister presides over the Council of Government, which deliberates on most public policies and executive issues (Article 92). However, the final decisions are made in the Council of Ministers that is composed of the prime minister and government ministers and is presided over by the king (Article 48). Furthermore, it is the Council of Ministers that solely makes decisions on major issues such as the declaration of war, appointments of governors, or "the strategic orientations of the policy of the State" (Article 49). Given that the king has the power to terminate all members of the Council of Government, major executive decisions will practically be made only by the king.

Besides the parallel institutions, the constitution employs a very ambiguous language in certain provisions that makes constitutional review key to power distribution. This was one of the smartest strategies that the king employed. The Moroccan constitution was written at the onset of the Arab Spring after two powerful Arab presidents were overthrown by popular protests. The Arab Spring was a moment of uncertainty for most Arab leaders. Not knowing what would happen next, a vague constitutional language could be interpreted in different ways. If more Arab leaders were to lose power and the Moroccan opposition to gain more power and leverage, constitutional reviews could lead to a more liberal constitution without king Mohammed VI losing his power guaranteed in Articles 41–59. However, should the winds of the Arab Spring shift and the opposition lose power, the king would not need to change the constitution again (as Egypt had to do in 2019) to reinstate his constitutional powers. In that case, constitutional reviews by the appointed Constitutional Court could deliver what the king wants. This is precisely what happened in 2017.

By 2017, the winds of the Arab Spring had stopped; authoritarian leaders had regained control; civil wars were raging in Libya, Yemen, and Syria; and ISIS was feeding on these instabilities. In Morocco, the February 20 Youth Movement lost its momentum and the popular support it once enjoyed. Opposition parties were making more concessions to the state, and King

Mohammed VI felt more confident that he had the upper hand. Under these circumstances, the king began to change the rules of the game by reinterpreting those vague provisions. For example, Article 47 of the constitution articulates, "The king appoints the Head of Government from within the political party arriving ahead in the elections of the members of the HOR, and with a view to their results."

Although this text does not specify exactly who within the winning party should be appointed, the understanding (and practice since 2011) was that the king would appoint the secretary-general of the winning party, which is usually the head of that party's electoral list. However, in March 2017, the king changed the interpretation of Article 47 when he ousted Prime Minister Abdelilah Benkirane, who was the secretary-general of the moderate Islamist Justice and Development Party (JDP), only five months after the parliamentary election. This move came after Benkirane failed to form a functioning government. Rather than calling for new elections, the king appointed Saadeddine El-Othmani, another member of the JDP as the Prime Minister. Hence, the king changed how the law was implemented. The prime minister was supposed to be the head of the party, not "any member," because the king then could appoint the most loyal party member. The JDP at that time had one option and that was to oppose the king. If they had done so, they could have called for a new election. But fearing state reprisal, the party voted that it would not oppose the king's decision. By conceding to the king's will, JDP created a precedent for the king to appoint any member of the winning party to head the government (Ahmed Jazouli [senior expert in Democratic Governance, TALM Group], interview by author, January 31, 2019).

In sum, while the Moroccan constitution was more democratic than its precedents, it did not change the status quo. The constitution created a balance between different views on "identity" issues, such as the role of religion and the Amazigh rights. It provided more rights and freedoms and introduced reforms in functions of the government and the legislature. However, it kept most of the king's powers unchanged. It did so in a few ways such as very clear provisions on the king's powers as the head of the state, parallel institutions that undermine the independence of government and leave the king as the ultimate decision-maker, and vague language in certain provisions that allow the king to interpret the constitution however he sees fit.

In a similar fashion, the Jordanian constitutional reform of 2011 was framed as democratic progress for the country, while, in reality, it was far from being democratic. Recall from Chapter 4 that the constitutional reform package in Jordan affected at least one-third of the constitution. Forty-two provisions

pertaining to rights and freedoms, the executive authority, legislative authority, and the judiciary were changed. Almost a quarter of these amendments
were related to Chapter II that focuses on citizens' rights, freedoms, and
responsibilities. The 2011 constitution considers any infringement on public
rights and freedoms or sanctity of private life a crime punishable by law
(Article 7). The new changes also dismiss the arresting, detaining, or restricting the freedom of citizens except in accordance with provisions of the law
(Article 8). The amendments also forbid physical or moral torture and abuse
(Article 8), ensure freedom of movement (Article 9), and protect the privacy of
citizens by illegalizing the surveillance of mail correspondence, telegrams,
telephones, and any other means of communications except by judicial order
(Article 18). Lastly, the new changes provide for more protections of freedom
of opinion, expression, and scientific research (Article 15) and freedom of
assembly and association (Article 16).

The 2011 Constitution of Jordan, for sure, offers more protection of human
rights than its predecessor. It also introduced major democratic changes to the
state institutions. Among these democratic changes, Article 67 institutionalizes an independent electoral commission to oversee elections. Article 74 now
requires the whole government to resign within a week if the parliament is
dissolved by an executive order. Moreover, Article 73 seems to limit the king's
power by deleting a clause that used to allow him to postpone elections
indefinitely. This article now requires the king to hold elections within four
months if he dissolves the HOR. In the judiciary chapter of the constitution,
major changes were introduced with Articles 58–61, which institutionalize the
Constitutional Court, and Article 98, which establishes a Judicial Council to
be responsible for all judiciary affairs including the appointment, promotion,
relocation, and dismissal of judges.

These important changes give the impression that Jordan was on the right
track toward democratization. On the contrary, the constitutional reform
package helped King Abdullah II manage public demands for democratization without relinquishing power. Indeed, the 2011 constitution made important democratic reforms. However, what did not change was Chapter IV,
Section I (Article 28–40), which specifies the powers of the king. Not
a single amendment was introduced to this chapter. The king remains the
head of the state enjoying full immunity from any liability (Article 30). He is
the commander of all armed forces (Article 32) and is responsible for declaring
war and peace and signing all international treaties (Article 33). He ratifies
laws and promulgates them (Article 31). He issues orders for holding elections;
inaugurates, adjourns, and convenes the National Assembly; and can dissolve
both the HOR and the Senate (Article 34). He appoints and can dismiss all

members of the Senate (Article 36), the prime minister, and all ministers (Article 35). He has the power of Royal Decree (Article 40) and can pardon anyone (Article 38), and no death penalty can be executed without his approval (Article 39).

Rather than limiting the king's powers in some ways (as the Moroccan constitution *appears* to do), the Jordanian constitutional reform, in fact, concentrated even more powers in the king. Most importantly, the new Article 58 (Chapter V) institutionalized a Constitutional Court comprising nine members, all of whom are appointed by the king for a nonrenewable, six-year term. As the review of Morocco's constitution shows, in that country, the king is the state. In Jordan, by contrast, the constitution elevates the king to the extent that he appears to be even more powerful than the state itself (Bani Salameh and Ananzah 2015). For example, while the term "king" (and relevant adjectives) is mentioned seventy-three times in the constitution, the term "state" is mentioned thirty-three times, "nation" thirty-two times, and "people" only once. That is, the "king" is mentioned more than the "state," the "nation," and the "people," combined (Bani Salameh and Ananzah 2015).

The strategies that the kings of Morocco and Jordan used to reform their constitutions might seem different, but they were essentially the same and yielded similar outcomes. They both preserved the authority in the hands of the monarchs while giving the impression of being democratic. Neither of the two constitutional reforms opened a pathway toward democracy or constitutionalism. And they both failed to remedy the core political ills in their nations, which are excessive, and extra-constitutional powers that the kings have enjoyed for decades.

Electoral Authoritarian Constitutions: Algeria (2016) and Egypt (2014 and 2019)

Presidents are not hereditary monarchs, but in most Arab republics, they rule like kings. Constitutions in Arab republics, similar to those in monarchies, are abundant with loopholes and escape hatches that allow the executive to breach the constitutional agreement without fearing constitutional punishments. Rights and freedom laws are poorly designed, allowing the government to deny them to citizens. Courts are not completely independent, and parliaments mostly function to rubber-stamp the executive's decisions. Most importantly, there is no turnover of power, which is why in 2011 protesters particularly focused on executive term limits across many Arab republics. By the turn of the twenty-first century, almost all Arab presidents, from Yemen's Saleh and

Syria's Al-Assad to Egypt's Mubarak and Tunisia's Ben Ali, ruled without constitutional barriers including term limits.[2]

When protesters rose against these "presidents for life," they wanted an end to the tyranny of strong presidents in their countries. Tunisia, the only country to democratize, ended the problem of unchecked executives by adopting Article 75 that not only limits the presidency to two five-year terms but also prohibits any amendments to the number or length of presidential terms. Article 75 of Tunisia's constitution can perhaps serve as a model for all democratizing countries around the world, as over time, authoritarian presidents have learned how to stay longer in power without lifting presidential term limits in their constitutions. Authoritarians' "menu of manipulation" includes several forms of constitutional manipulations that allow the authoritarian presidents to buy themselves extra time in power. For example, the 2017 constitutional amendment in Turkey, which changed the government system from semi-presidentialism to presidentialism, allows President Recep Tayyip Erdoğan to potentially stay in power until 2029 without even abolishing presidential term limits. Similarly, the 2020 constitutional change in Russia, which changed term limits from "two consecutive terms" to "two terms" and nullified the terms served by all previous presidents, allows President Vladimir Putin to potentially stay in power until 2036, again without lifting term limits.

Clearly, a mere adoption of constitutional term limits does not prevent authoritarian presidents from overstaying in power. Other, and stricter, constitutional guarantees, like Tunisia's Article 75, are needed to prevent future constitutional manipulations that extend presidents' continuance in office. Algeria and Egypt, both of which suffered from a legacy of authoritarian presidents, did not provide such constitutional guarantees, which contributed to their failure to democratize. Both republics wrote seemingly democratic constitutions, and both adopted term limits, yet neither constitution resolved the underlying problem of authoritarianism.

The 2016 constitutional reform package in Algeria included seventy-four amendments and thirty-eight new inclusions. The 2016 revised constitution embodies more civil rights and liberties than its predecessor, including the recognition of the role of women and youth in the society (Article 31), free press (Article 41), and the Tamazight language (Article 3). However, these changes are far from being new and have surfaced several times during Algerian political history. For example, the amended constitution merely extends the government's commitment to the recognition of the Tamazight

---

[2] Among Arab republics, only Algeria's constitution had term limits, which Bouteflika removed in his 2008 constitutional amendments.

language as a national language, a commitment it made in the 2002 constitutional amendment, which permits it to be taught in particular regions of the country (Markey and Ahmed 2016).

Additionally, the new constitution now requires the president to nominate a prime minister from the largest party in the parliament, which is still controlled by the ruling FLN. This and other democratic-looking reforms did not facilitate a democratic transition but rather were designed to maintain the regime in power (Khettab 2016). For example, the constitutional reform package prevents Algerians with dual citizenship from running for public office. Under the revised constitution, the president must have permanent residency in Algeria for the last ten years, in addition to being a citizen of only Algeria. This amendment prevents many regime opponents, such as Rachid Nekkaz, a French Algerian and 2014 presidential candidate, from running for president. Another important change is the creation of an independent electoral commission, which is still headed by an appointee of the president (Article 170) and seems to have been introduced to counter the regime's challenges of low voter turnout and public mistrust in electoral institutions (Allouche 2016).

The most important change was, however, made to Article 74, which addresses the executive term limit. Shortly after Bouteflika was elected for a second term in 2004, he began to review his options for staying longer in office. In 2006, his government initiated the official discussions about potential constitutional changes, and in 2008, he amended the constitution just to abolish the two-term limit in Article 74. In 2016, Bouteflika amended Article 74 again, but this time to reinstate the presidential term limit. However, the new constitution allowed Bouteflika to finish his fourth term in 2019 and also to run for a fifth term, potentially extending his presidency until 2024.[3]

In a similar fashion, President El-Sisi amended Egypt's constitution in 2019 in order to extend his stay in power without lifting term limits. The constitutional reform package included changes to eleven articles of Egypt's 2014 constitution (Articles 102, 140, 160, 189–190, 193, 200, 204, 234, and 243–244) as well as eight new articles, which were added to the constitution. Similar to Algeria's constitutional reform, the amendments in Egypt were a wholesale package that included both democratic (for window-dressing purposes) and undemocratic changes. On the one hand, the new amendments create a gender quota requiring 25 percent of the HOR seats to be reserved for women. On the other hand, the constitutional amendments empower the

---

[3] Bouteflika resigned in 2019 after major protests erupted following his decision to run for reelections (see Chapter 7).

president to appoint the heads of judicial bodies, the president of the SCC, and the prosecutor general. Furthermore, the new constitution gives the president the chairmanship of the Supreme Council for Judicial Bodies and Entities. Other nondemocratic changes include the expansion of the role of the Armed Forces and the expansion of the jurisdiction of military courts over civilians. Furthermore, the new constitution brings back the upper house of the parliament with 180 seats, one-third of which are appointed by the president.

The most important amendment, however, was made to Article 140, which addresses the executive term limit. The amended constitution changes the term limit from two four-year terms to two six-year terms. El-Sisi was reelected in 2018 for the second term, and his presidency was scheduled to end in 2022. However, the newly introduced amendments extend the current president's term until 2024 and allow him to run for reelection that year and serve an additional six-year term until 2030.

Clearly, the constitutional term limits could not prevent authoritarian presidents in Algeria and Egypt from manipulating their constitutions in order to stay longer in power. Authoritarian executives in both countries employed constitutional manipulations that included some democratic reforms serving window-dressing purposes. Yet the main purpose of these constitutional reforms was to extend the executive's grip over power. The lesson from Algeria and Egypt is that the ouster of the head of state and institutionalization of executive term limits mean nothing if constitutions do not first address the underlying institutional problem, which is loopholes that can lead to manipulation. Authoritarianism in both Algeria and Egypt still runs deep, and the armed forces still call the final shots. Courts are not independent and cannot protect citizens when their rights and freedoms are violated by the government. Parliaments are sources of clientelism and tools for legitimizing the executives' decisions. With no constitutional remedy for these political ills, democratic backsliding will always be a threat. This threat became a reality in Algeria and Egypt just a few years after the high hopes that the Arab Spring could finally bring democratization to these nations.

Authoritarian presidents in Algeria and Egypt used different strategies than the monarchs in Morocco and Jordan, yet they all borrowed from the same authoritarian toolbox of constitutional manipulations. This constitutional toolbox included poorly developed, vague, and sometimes contradictory provisions pertaining to the protection of rights and freedoms, parallel institutions and other constitutional loopholes that undermine the independence of the judiciary and legislature, unchecked executive powers, and succession mechanisms that do not hold the executive accountable. As the cases of Morocco,

Jordan, Algeria, and Egypt illustrate, when the institutional origins of authoritarianism are not resolved, constitutional manipulations by authoritarian leaders are not difficult. Indeed, none of these democratic-branded constitutional reforms by authoritarian regimes created constitutionalist constitutions.

ARAB SPRING CONSTITUTIONS AND THE UNRESOLVED SOCIETAL CLEAVAGES

Constitution-making is a daunting task in deeply divided societies that are transitioning from authoritarian rule. Societal cleavages are so complex and often so context-specific that it is difficult to prescribe universal institutional design solutions. Nevertheless, when societies are segmented across ethnic or regional lines, power-sharing constitutional arrangements are inevitable if democracy is to thrive and cross-group conflict is to be diminished. When the Arab Spring reached deeply divided societies and when, in response, these nations tried to reform their constitutions, three pathways of failed constitutional designs emerged. First, in ethnoreligiously divided Syria and Bahrain, authoritarian leaders did not implement any power-sharing constitutional arrangements. Second, in Yemen and Libya where divided groups were concentrated in geographical regions, the federalist and power-sharing arrangements failed to prevent civil conflicts. Lastly, in Egypt where the society was polarized across ideological lines, the 2012 constitution failed to create societal consensus. All three pathways showcase constitutional designs that failed to resolve important societal cleavages and as such did not facilitate democratic transitions.

Ethnoreligious Cleavages: Syria and Bahrain

As ethnic conflict and democratic backsliding have both grown more frequent over the last couple of decades, the most common prescribed solution has been the adoption of power-sharing arrangements (Eisenstadt et al. 2019). Power-sharing gained cachet among policy practitioners after Arend Lijphart popularized it in the 1970s as consociationalism. The basic idea had an almost intuitive normative appeal; that including conflict "losers" in negotiating the new rules of the game, such as in moments of constitutional bargains, would better serve the interests of former regime opponents and the rest of society.

In his seminal work, *Democracy in Plural Societies*, Lijphart (1977) argues that culturally fragmented societies, such as Netherlands, Belgium, and Switzerland, enjoy stable democratic political systems because they share one particular system of government: power-sharing in a consociational form. According to Lijphart, "consociational democracy means government by elite cartel designed to turn a democracy with a fragmented political culture into a stable femocracy" (1969, 216). Such consociational systems of government share specific characteristics including a grand coalition government (between parties from different segments of society), segmental autonomy (in the cultural sector), proportionality (in the voting system and public sector employment), and minority veto (Lijphart 1977).

Following Lijphart (1977, 2012), several influential scholars (Linz1990; Norris 2008; Hartzell and Hoddie 2015) have argued in favor of power-sharing. Advocates of consociationalism strongly believe that political violence can be prevented in fragmented societies through democratic means and political institutions (Cohen 1997; Reynal-Querol 2002). Furthermore, Binningsbø (2005) finds that proportional representation or consociationalism helps decrease the recurrence of civil war and sustain a more lasting peace after a civil conflict is over. And since these political institutions can be engineered in fledgling democracies or divided societies, consociationalism is the best option for many people around the world (Selway and Templeman 2012).

Despite this optimism in the efficacy of consociationalism and its power in overcoming political instability in fragmented societies, several cases have proven otherwise. Prominent examples of failed consociational government systems include Lebanon with its fifteen years of civil war (1975–1990), Burundi that only experienced consociational power-sharing for one year (1993) before plummeting into a brutal civil conflict, and more recently Iraq and its ongoing sectarian conflict. Critics generally argue that consociationalism deepens cleavages instead of transcending them. According to Wilson and Wilford, "the fundamental problem with consociationalism is that it rests on precisely the division it is supposed to solve. It assumes that identities are primordial and exclusive rather than malleable and relational" (2003, 270). Others like Taylor (2006) and Dixon (2011) argue that consociationalism is an illiberal form of government that does not necessarily bring sustainable peace or democratic institutions.

Despite these criticisms and cases that show consociationalism might not be effective in preventing conflict, without consociationalism or other forms of power-sharing arrangements, a transition to democracy is unlikely. Consociationalism might be an illiberal form of democracy, which freezes societal divisions, but nonetheless, it offers the much-needed political and economic inclusion, which has been nonexistent in polities such as Syria and Bahrain. That is, despite its deficiencies, consociationalism can be an inclusive and democratic solution for the ethnically divided Syria and Bahrain, neither of which implemented any sort of power-sharing arrangements in their constitutional reforms.

In both Syria and Bahrain, large segments of the society are excluded from access to key political, military, economic, judicial, and bureaucratic positions because of their ethnicity or religion. While, in Syria, the Kurds and Sunni Arabs are excluded from power-sharing, in Bahrain, it is the Shia and Persian descendants who are the excluded groups. In both countries, the excluded groups comprise the majority of the population, and in both cases, they were the groups who rose against their regimes in 2011. While the two regimes made constitutional reforms to appease the protesters and in the case of Bahrain included more civil rights in the new constitution, these reforms were definitely not a step toward power-sharing. The regimes' unwillingness to share power is largely because they are demographically in a weaker position. Any ethnoreligious-based power-sharing arrangements would make the incumbent regime the "loser" in the bargain. And this has been the most important obstacle to democratization in both Syria and Bahrain.

Another major obstacle that has so far prevented a democratic bargain for power-sharing is the regional and international interests in the two countries. One of the most important regional rivalries, affecting both Syria and Bahrain, has been the sectarian conflict between Iran (and its proxy Shia militias across the region) and Saudi Arabia and United Arab Emirates (and their proxy Sunni militias). Moreover, Turkey and its military campaign against the Kurds in Syria, the United States' conflict with Iran and its naval base in Bahrain, and Israel's military campaign against Iran-backed Shia militias and Assad's regime all contribute to the sectarian divisions in the two deeply divided societies. Indeed, both Al-Khalifa and Al-Assad regimes have managed to play the sectarian card to mobilize their domestic as well as regional and international supporters in order to stay in power.

The winds of the Arab Spring storm might have calmed in Bahrain, and Assad might be winning the civil conflict in Syria, but the regimes in these countries are not and will not be stable unless there is a new and real power-sharing bargain. Among possible power-sharing solutions might be a consociational government system, much like the constitutional arrangements in Lebanon and Iraq. Although consociationalism has been fairly criticized in both Lebanon and Iraq and it is far from perfect, it is much more inclusive than the status quo. Indeed, the lack of national accountability has undermined government commitment to providing public goods in both countries, and sectarian conflict is still ongoing at varying intensity levels (Salamey 2009). However, the "inefficacy" of consociationalism in Iraq and Lebanon has been attributed to several causes, including a weak state

(Salamey 2009), the lack of a grand coalition and mutual veto arrangements particularly in Iraq (Abu Ltaif 2015), and changing demography particularly in Lebanon (Salamey 2009). While consociationalism has been inefficient in these two conflict-ridden Arab nations, the sectarian conflict itself cannot be solely attributed to consociational power-sharing arrangements. Perhaps, more importantly, regional or global interests have negatively contributed to increasing conflict in these countries. Salamey and Payne (2008), for example, argue that whenever external powers (i.e., Syria and France in the 1970s and Iran, Saudi Arabia, Syria, and France in the 2000s) tried to pursue their national interests by interfering in Lebanon's domestic issues, the country's political violence increased drastically, which had little (if not nothing) to do with consociational institutions in the country.

This book does not suggest that consociationalism is the best or the only solution for Syria or Bahrain. Rather, it contends that when societies are deeply divided across ethnoreligious lines, constitutional reforms will fail to democratize unless they formulate a power-sharing institutional design, such as a consociational government system. When a constitution fails to distribute political power and economic rents among different ethnic groups, it opens a pathway toward failed democratization.

Regional Cleavages: Yemen and Libya

Similar to Bahrain and Syria, ethnic or sectarian divisions are prevalent in Libya and Yemen. However, unlike in Bahrain or Syria, the most dominant societal cleavage in these countries has historically been across regional lines. Libya was a federalist state before Qaddafi abolished the 1951 federalist constitution following his 1969 coup. The three main regions in Libya include Cyrenaica (east), Tripolitania (west), and Fezzan (south). The Republic of Yemen has not been a federalist state, but it was formed after the unification of the Yemen Arab Republic (North Yemen) and the PDRY (South Yemen) in 1990. Naturally, constitutional negotiations that followed the fall of authoritarian regimes in the two countries centered on the preexisting regional grievances, rivalries, and divisions. During these constitutional bargains, different groups envisioned three different scenarios for the future: unitary, decentralized unitary, and federalist systems. Among the three options, federalism received the largest attention in both countries. Indeed, the global focus on federalism has been reemerging in recent years as a solution for silenced local and regional divisions (Galligan 2008).

As Watts argues, a federal political system refers to a system of government "in which, by contrast to the single central source of authority in unitary systems, there are two (or more) levels of government, thus combing elements of shared rule through common institutions and regional self-rule for the governments of constituent units" (1999, 6–7). A federal system is an appealing choice for transitioning states for several reasons. It can neutralize authoritarianism through power-sharing arrangements and the expansion of political participation. Moreover, in states with preexisting cultural, linguistic, and ethnic divisions, federalism has the capacity to strike a balance between unity and diversity. Federalism is argued to allow for regional differences under a unified national identity.

Yet empirical evidence shows that federalism can also foster divisions and lead to insufficient government decision-making (Williams et al. 2017). Although federalism provides institutional protection for ethnic minority groups, it has been criticized for the opportunity it provides for secession and self-autonomy. Under certain circumstances, federalism instigates conflict and provides the opportunity and institutions required for popular mobilization. The cases of southern American states during the Civil War and Canada's Quebec are good examples of such opportunities for secession (Galligan 2008). Thus, the success of federalism in transitioning states depends to a large extent on how it is implemented.

There is, however, no ideal model of federalism, and a successful implementation depends on the context. Although federalism has been implemented in different ways across the world, there are some institutions that are common to most federalist states, including written constitutions with procedural rigidity to amend, bicameral legislatures that include a strong federal chamber representing regions, constitutional courts with the power to protect the constitution through judicial review, and intergovernmental institutions that function to facilitate cooperation where there is shared jurisdiction (Galligan 2008). Critically, establishing a constitution is essential for a successful federation (Watts 1999, 99). During constitutional negotiations between different subunits, a consensus must be reached on three key issues. These three issues are the division of federal regions, the structure of the new federal system, and the distribution of power between different layers of the government as well as between the federal regions, with particular attention to the distribution of income and natural resources management (Mujais 2017; Williams et al. 2017). Without societal consensus on these three issues, a federal constitution will most likely fail in facilitating the transition to democracy. The main reason the 2015 draft constitution of Yemen failed to implement a federal political system was exactly because there was no societal consensus on any of these three issues.

Recall from Chapter 4 that in Yemen, the NDC's Outcome Document consisted of some 1,800 recommendations for transitioning the country to a federal political system. Surprisingly, this elaborate document did not outline how Yemen would be divided into federal regions. The NDC consisted of nine working groups that worked separately and submitted their recommendations. The NDC negotiations broke down in early August 2013 after southern representatives boycotted the remaining sessions due to deadlock in the Southern Issue Working Group. Eventually, the NDC authorized President Hadi to form a subcommittee of the Southern Issue Working Group, known as the 8+8 (or North-South) Committee, to develop a solution for the southern issue. After months of tense negotiations, the 8+8 Committee brokered a deal, called "A Just Solution," between different groups that avoided southern secession by creating a federal state with great autonomy for the regions, including the south (Gaston 2014, 3–4). Deadlock persisted, however, over the division of federal regions and whether Yemen should be divided into two, four, five, or six regions. Another agreement was reached to create an ad hoc committee, known as The Committee, whose members were mostly appointed by President Hadi, with the authority to determine the number and boundaries of the federal regions. In February 2014, the Committee announced that the existing provinces would be organized into six federal regions, including Sheba, Aljanad, Azal, and Tahamh in the north and Aden and Hadhramaut in the south. The boundaries of these regions were later specified in Article 391 of the 2015 draft constitution (Williams et al. 2017).

The draft constitution faced strong opposition over these regional divisions from the Houthis in the north and Al-Hirak in the south.[4] The regional division kept the Houthis disadvantaged because they were not given access to major political and urban centers such as Aden or Sa'ada, oil fields, or valuable seaports. Southern secessionists disapproved of the federal arrangements because they were given only two regions, which could undermine their secession efforts in the future (Williams et al. 2017). Both groups specifically criticized how this decision was made by a committee appointed by President Hadi, without considering their input.

The second key issue over which the draft constitution failed to create a societal consensus was the structure of the new federal system. The NDC Outcome Document, which was based on a national consensus, suggested three tiers: central government, regional governments, and *wilayas* for the new federal structure. However, the draft constitution created a five-tier

---

[4] As discussed in Chapter 4, opposition to the draft constitution and its federal arrangements sparked Yemen's civil war.

structure: central government, regional governments, and two local governments comprising *wilayas* and districts, in addition to the cities of Aden and
Sanaa, which received special status and autonomy equivalent to the regions
(Williams et al. 2017). This arrangement was again decided without a prior
societal consensus, and although it was not a major contentious issue directly,
it led to conflict over the distribution of income among these tiers.

The last major contentious issue was the distribution of power in the new
federal Yemen. On the one hand, the draft constitution established an asym-
metric power structure by giving the two southern regions a greater level of
influence over national politics. For example, Article 204 granted the south
special constitutional protections.[5] Furthermore, Article 424 guarantees the
southern regions of Aden and Hadhramaut 50 percent representation "in the
federal legislative authority and all leadership structures in the legislative,
judiciary and executive bodies including the army and security." And Article
139 determines that the two southern regions "shall be represented in the
Federal HOR based on the land and population formula at a share of 40%."
On the other hand, the draft constitution did not give the southern regions
what they most wanted: control over their natural resources. Article 356 of the
draft constitution established a National Revenue Fund to which all national
revenues including from oil and gas would be deposited. Article 357 stipulated
that the Revenue Division Act was to govern the distribution of revenues from
the National Revenue Fund "among the federal and regional governments,
wiliyas, districts and the cities of Sanaa and Aden." For many southern groups,
this arrangement was not acceptable and reminded them of Saleh's decades-
long control over gas and oil revenues and the exploitation of southern
resources by the northern elites in his patronage network (Williams et al. 2017).

The draft constitution of Yemen failed to successfully implement a federal
government system because the federal arrangements were not based on
a societal consensus. Without popular buy-ins on controversial issues such as
regional divisions, the structure of the federal system, and the allocation and
distribution of wealth and power, the federalist constitution of Yemen had no
chance of success in transitioning the deeply divided country to democracy.

Besides Yemen, the other regionally divided country that is still entangled
in a civil war is Libya. The draft constitution of Libya, like that of Yemen,
failed to provide effective power-sharing among different groups and regions.
Unlike Yemen, however, the Libyan draft constitution of 2017 opted for

---

[5] Article 204 of the 2015 draft constitution reads: "The State shall be committed to take necessary
legislative and executive actions to ensure fair representation of the South to achieve participation in federal executive authorities and institutions."

a unitary government system rather than a federal one. The draft constitution of Libya had three features that resulted in the breakdown of power-sharing efforts: a strong presidential system, a unitary government with limited decentralization, and a lack of group autonomy despite its minority rights protections.

The first fundamental issue that had been a source of contention since 2011 was the choice of government system. Following the 2011 uprisings, most countries emerging from decades of presidential tyranny favored the establishment of a semi-presidential system, believing that a divided executive power decreases the chances of authoritarian backsliding by "strong men." Libya, however, did not follow this regional trend from the very beginning. The 2011 interim constitution adopted by the NTC established a parliamentary system instead, which made Libya one of the few Arab countries with a parliamentary government. However, as security across the country started to deteriorate and Libya started to spiral into civil conflict, many people blamed the fragmented political parties and the parliament for the situation (Al-Ali 2017). The Constitution Drafting Assembly (CDA) later reached an agreement to establish a semi-presidential system and formalize it with an early draft constitution, which it published in December 2014. With the 2014 draft constitution, the CDA assured that it had no desire to create a powerful presidency. For example, Article 50 of the 2014 draft constitution stated that the president will be indirectly elected by the Shura Council, an arrangement that strips off popular legitimacy from the presidency. Furthermore, Article 74 limited the powers of the president by mandating him/her to appoint a prime minister from the electoral coalition that had the largest number of seats in the parliament (Article 74). Also, Article 68 left the president with very little power to dissolve the parliament.

Three years later, however, the CDA decided to establish a presidential system. After six years of violence, the 2017 draft constitution envisioned a strong presidency as the CDA was trying to find a solution (i.e., one man in charge) for the ongoing conflict (Al-Ali 2017). Article 100 of the final draft constitution stipulates that the president of the Republic will be directly elected. And Article 104 states that the president is solely responsible for forming a government and setting government policies. Perhaps, more importantly, the president is given a free hand in choosing the prime minister, as Article 113 allows the president to select any candidate with any party affiliation regardless of whether that candidate was elected to the parliament. And while Article 115 suggests that the parliament can withdraw confidence from the government, it needs a two-thirds vote threshold. The only protection that the parliament receives is from Article 109 that stipulates that the president can dissolve the parliament only after approval through a public referendum.

These excessive presidential powers are extremely dangerous, especially if evaluated in the light of a unitary government system with limited decentralization, which the draft constitution establishes. From the onset of constitutional negotiations, the choice between federal and unitary systems divided the Libyans. On the one hand, a group of Libyans (known as the "federalists") wanted a federal arrangement that could address the cross-regional inequalities and grievances (Al-Ali 2017). The federalists believed that by diffusing power, promoting shared rule, and increasing political participation, federal arrangements could successfully transition Libya toward democracy. Most ethnic minorities also had the same vision. They favored a federal system, believing that only federalism could give them the autonomy they desired. On the other hand, many others favored a traditional unitary system with some level of decentralization to promote shared rule and address regional inequalities. Similarly, an early draft of the constitution proposed two options: a unitary system with limited decentralization as well as a three-region federation (Al-Ali 2017).

The 2017 draft constitution opted for the first option. Article 144 created three levels of government, including the central government, governorates, and municipalities. And while Article 146 stipulates that governorates and municipal councils should be directly elected by popular vote, Chapter VI of the draft constitution that addresses decentralization remains vague, broad, and overly unambitious. For example, Article 143 states that "Local governance shall be based on the principle of expanded decentralization." But the principles of decentralization are left unexplained. The only provisions that bind the state to commit to regional equality are Articles 75 and 79, which stipulate that the seventy-eight seats of the upper chamber of the parliament should be distributed between the three regions (Article 75) and that any draft law related to local governance must be authorized by the upper chamber (Article 79).[6] Despite these two provisions, the unitary government system with limited and vague decentralization left the federalists and ethnic minorities disappointed with the draft constitution (Al-Ali 2017).

The nonfederalist constitutional arrangement was a major blow, particularly to the ethnic minority groups of Amazigh, Touareg, and Tebu, which sought an extensive autonomy in the constitution, similar to the Kurdistan

---

[6] Article 75 mandates that of the seventy-eight seats of the Senate, thirty-two seats should be reserved for the western region, twenty-six for the eastern region, and twenty for the southern region.

Regional Government in the Iraqi constitution (Al-Ali 2017). While Article 2 of the 2017 draft constitution recognizes the cultural and linguistic diversity of Libya and in fact considered the languages of these groups as cultural heritage for all Libyans to be protected and preserved, it falls short in recognizing them as official languages.[7] Similarly, Article 160 establishes the National Council for Protection of Cultural and Linguistic Heritage to protect and preserve the cultural and linguistic heritage of Libyan ethnic minorities but fails to give ethnic minorities an autonomy in preserving their languages through, for example, controlling their educational institutions. While these are indeed progressive provisions, considering Libya's constitutional history, they are criticized by ethnic minorities as insufficient (Al-Ali 2017).

Together, these three features of the 2017 draft constitution were greeted by significant discontent in the Libyan society. At first glance, the draft constitution appears to be ignorant of Libya's history as a federal state, its regional divisions and inequalities, and its ethnic diversity. It seems odd that a constitution addresses issues such as the right to sports or environmental concerns but fails to recognize the regional and ethnic grievances many Libyans face every day. These constitutional developments, however, came as a result of increased violence and in reaction to it. Nonetheless, the constitution's denial of major societal demands, such as regional and ethnic equality, delivered a crushing blow to the democratic transition process. By establishing a centralized unitary government, constitutional drafters ignored what caused conflict and violence in the first place, including regional and ethnic grievances and rivalries fueled by a security vacuum in the aftermath of the removal of Qaddafi and his extensively centralized and pan-Arabist rule.

In sum, the Libyan 2017 draft constitution opted for a unitary government system with limited decentralization and a strong presidency as a response to increasing conflict in the country. The draft constitution was, however, dead on arrival, as it failed to provide for the regional decentralization and group autonomy many wanted. By contrast, the Yemeni 2015 draft constitution established a federal system that most groups wanted. However, the terms of the federal arrangement, particularly the division of federal regions, the structure of the federal government, and the distribution of wealth and power, were not accepted by some groups in both the north and the south. Without popular buy-ins and societal consensus, the envisioned federalist system in the draft constitution fueled a civil war. Yemen's draft constitution, as such, serves as an example of federalist constitutional arrangements becoming the main driver of conflict if the constitution-making process is noninclusive.

---

[7] Article 2 states that "Arabic is the language of the state."

Ideological Cleavages: Egypt

Unlike regional cleavages in Libya and Yemen or ethnoreligious cleavages in Syria and Bahrain, which can be remedied through power-sharing constitutional arrangements, ideological divisions can hardly be tied to institutional arrangements. Indeed, Arab societies are divided across several ideological lines. But the most important ideological division has been the polarization between Islamists and non-Islamists (Brown 2017).[8] This societal division became a major source of constitutional debate as a result of the gradual "Islamic inflation" of the Arab constitutions in the second half of the twentieth century.[9] As a result of this "Islamic inflation," the absolute majority of Arab constitutions proclaim Islamic Sharia a source of legislation. It is not, however, the mere acknowledgment of Sharia, which is divisive in Arab societies; rather, issues closely related to religion such as gender equality or freedom of conscience fuel ideological division in these countries. Freedom of speech, religious minorities' rights, and the religion of the head of the state are among many other constitutional issues that are closely tied to the role of religion in politics and society.

These controversial issues have polarized those Arab societies in which there is a relative balance of power between Islamists and non-Islamists. By contrast, where one or the other group is more dominant, these issues become less divisive. For instance, in Saudi Arabia, which is a strongly Islamist state, or in Lebanon, which is a moderate secular country, these ideological divisions are less entrenched. In other societies segmented along these ideological lines, such as in Egypt or Tunisia, repressive authoritarian rule has silenced these divisions for decades. The Arab Spring in these countries opened the space for a public debate about these issues, and the heated (and transparent) constitutional debates polarized these societies to an unprecedented degree. While the Tunisian Constitution could dampen this increased societal division, the Egyptian Constitution of 2012 failed to do so. The question remains why the Egyptian constitution missed the opportunity to create societal consensus on these controversial issues.

[8]   The term "non-Islamists" is a broad category that includes seculars as well, but it is preferred to the latter term because many societal groups in the Arab world that oppose Islamism are in fact not secular.

[9]   As Brown (2017, 158) argues, the "Islamic inflation" of constitutions (i.e., the increasing number of constitutional provisions pertaining to the issue of Islamic Sharia) in the second half of the twentieth century was in part institutional, legal, fiscal, and ideological. But, most importantly, the increase in Islamic provisions happened because constitutions became public issues due to the spread of participatory processes and public constitutional knowledge in the last few decades.

As discussed in Chapter 4, Egyptian opposition groups were divided from the onset of the revolution. The opposition to Mubarak was divided into two main camps, each with a distinct vision about post-Mubarak's Egypt. On the one hand, the Islamists included a range of groups from the Muslim Brotherhood and its political party, Freedom and Justice, as well as the Al-Azhar University, to more conservative Salafi groups including the Noor party. Indeed, each of these groups had its own internal divisions. For instance, there was a clear division between the older generation of Muslim Brotherhood leadership, which was more conservative, and its younger leadership, which was more progressive. On the other hand, the non-Islamist camp was composed of numerous groups from Nasserists, Liberals, Secularists, and Marxists, to youth movements, such as the April 6 Youth Movement, and the Coptic Church. The hostility among these two camps was a major obstacle to consensus-building from the beginning of the transitional process. Rather than engaging in constructive negotiations on a road map for the future of Egypt, both groups were constantly accusing the other of unwillingness to cooperate, often filing lawsuits, and eventually trying to ally with the military in order to win this battle.

Inevitably, this division overshadowed constitutional negotiations. The Islamist and non-Islamist members of the Constituent Assembly were more cooperative in the first few months of the process. But the polarization in the Constituent Assembly increased over time. Starting in late August 2012, polarization among the Constituent Assembly members increased significantly as Islamists changed several draft articles without consulting other members (Ahmed Maher [co-founder of April 6 Youth Movement], interview by author, May 7, 2013). To cite just one instance, the Islamists-dominated Drafting Committee unilaterally changed the content of twelve different articles from the Freedoms and Rights chapter in late August 2012, leading to a major protest by the non-Islamist members (The Constituent Assembly 2012, 5–17).

Most of these changes focused on issues that were ideologically important for both groups. For example, Article 43 (Article 8 in the first draft) articulated that "Freedom of belief is inevitable, and the State shall guarantee the freedom to establish places of worship for the divine religions, as regulated by law if it does not violate public order." However, the Islamist-dominated Drafting Committee went beyond its mandate by unilaterally changing the content of the original provision proposed by the Rights and Freedoms Committee and revealing the new version to the Constituent Assembly in its meeting on August 28. As some of the Rights and Freedoms Committee members, including Amani Abul-Fadl, Abd El-Send Yamama, Manal El-Teiby, and Bishop Paul, noticed at that meeting that the original proposed article included the phrase "freedom to practice religious rites" and did not have the clause "if it does not violate public order." The non-Islamists argued that this and the other eleven proposed articles related to Freedoms and Rights that the Islamists changed would pose serious threats to individual and group rights and freedoms.

Following the pressure by the Freedoms and Rights Committee, the Drafting Committee released the second draft of the same article on August 29 but only added "freedom to practice religious rites" to the first draft. The non-Islamist members put more pressure to omit the clause "if it does not violate public order" as they argued this phrase could be used by the Islamists or the government to limit the freedom of belief on the grounds that the practice of those beliefs violates public order. Eventually, the Islamists yielded to this pressure by omitting this controversial clause in the third draft of this article, which was published on September 12. The non-Islamists argued that the omission of the controversial phrase regarding public order in this article reduced the power of Islamists to limit the freedom of religion and, therefore, indirectly enhanced the freedom of belief and religion of minorities.

Such compromises by Islamists were, however, very rare. As polarization between the two camps deepened over time, the Islamists became more defensive and less willing to compromise. The ideological division over such controversial issues polarized the Egyptian society. Perhaps the most polarizing provision in the constitution was Article 2 that stated that "Islam is the religion of the state and Arabic its official language. Principles of Islamic Sharia are the principal source of legislation." The Constituent Assembly carried over this article from the 1971 constitution (as amended in 1980), without any changes. When this text was published online for public feedback on September 24, it quickly became the most debated provision among the general public both on online platforms and on the street. Similarly, this article became a divisive issue in the Constituent Assembly. Prior to its publication, the Islamist and non-Islamist members of the Constituent Assembly had agreed upon the phrase, "Principles of Islamic Sharia are the principal source of legislation." However, since early September, the Islamist members tried to change it to "Rules of Islamic Sharia are the principal source of legislation." Since the twelfth general meeting of the Constituent Assembly on September 11, this issue became a source of debate between the Islamist and non-Islamist members in the Constituent Assembly meetings. While some seculars argued that the state is a legal body and it cannot have a religion, the conservative Islamists argued that Sharia in general, and not only its principles should be the source of law. They specifically wanted to change "principles of Islamic Sharia" (*mabadi' el-Shari'a*) that is broader to "rules of Islamic Sharia" (*ahkam el-Shari'a*), which is more specific. Despite the heated debates among both the general public and the Constituent Assembly members, this draft article did not change. Because it was such a polarizing issue, both groups feared that any changes to the provision will have political costs for them.

While the Islamists did not push to change Article 2, which attracted more public attention, they added Article 219 to the constitution defining the principles of Islamic Sharia. The official English translation of this article reads: "The principles of Islamic Sharia include general evidence, foundational rules, rules of jurisprudence, and the credible sources accepted in Sunni doctrines and by the larger community." This translation does not, however, do justice to the religious tone of the provision. A better translation would be: "The principles of the Islamic Sharia include its *adilla kulliya, qawa'id usuli* and *qawa'id fiqhiyya* and the credible sources accepted in the Sunni *madhhabs*." As Lombardi and Brown (2012) note, the terms in italics are very technical terms that are only used in Islamic scholarly texts. In a critical analysis of this provision, Lombardi and Brown (2012) argue that this article and "its jumble of phrases that seems to tie Egypt's constitution to traditional Islamic jurisprudence" were the results of an odd compromise between the Salafis and non-Islamists who had very strong and antagonistic positions on this provision. Nonetheless, Article 219 is most unique in all Arab constitutions for its religious language.

As Article 219 showcases, Muslim Brotherhood, in an attempt to rapidly write a constitution and put it out for vote, tried to accommodate other Islamist groups. Other examples include Article 4, promising Al-Azhar to be consulted in all matters of Islamic law. Another example is Article 73 that encompassed several human rights issues. The first draft of Article 73, proposed by the non-Islamist members of the Freedoms and Rights Committee, stated "Forced labor, slavery, trafficking of women, children, and human organs, and sex trade are prohibited and criminalized by law." As members of this committee, including Mohamed Selim El-Awa, reported in several Constituent Assembly meetings, many Islamists opposed this article claiming that there is no human trafficking and sex trade in Egypt. The Salafis in particular opposed the draft because it could prohibit marriage of minor girls, which has traditionally been practiced in many rural areas in Egypt. As a result, the Islamists changed "trafficking women, children, and human organs" to "violation of women and children rights," which was vague and less strict because it did not define what those "women and children rights" are. The Constituent Assembly's non-Islamist members opposed the unilateral change. Eventually, when the non-Islamist members started to withdraw from the CA, the Islamists changed the whole article to "All forms of oppression, forced exploitation of humans and sex trade are prohibited and criminalized by law," which was vague enough not to strictly prohibit marriage of minors.

As the ideological rift between the two antagonistic groups became wider over these controversial issues, the non-Islamists engaged in a series of boycotts and withdrawals from the Constituent Assembly in order to force the Muslim Brotherhood into more compromises. Following the unilateral actions of the Islamists and the changes they made to draft provisions written by other groups, a number of political figures from various non-Islamist groups signed a statement written by Hamdeen Sabbahi, a Nasserist politician, and reform campaigner Mohamed El-Baradei to boycott the Assembly for its incompetency in late September.[10] The statement announced that the Assembly suffers from "the absence of a basic understanding of things that concern the Egyptian citizen, such as basic freedom, economic and social rights" (Ahram Online 2012c). Withdrawals increased in mid-November with the members of the Coptic Orthodox Church resigning from the Assembly, stating "the constitution … in its current form does not meet the desired national consensus and does not reflect the pluralistic identity of Egypt, [which has been] entrenched across generations" (Egypt Independent 2012c). Other prominent non-Islamist members including Ahmed Maher from the April 6 Youth Movement, former Arab League Chief Amr Moussa, and liberal politician Ayman Nour withdrew from the Assembly after their demands were not met in the Assembly (Ahram Online 2012d).

Rather than responding to these boycotts by compromising on its ideological stance, the Muslim Brotherhood hastened to review, complete, and vote on every single article in one marathon session to approve the constitution before the Constituent Assembly could get dissolved by the SCC's ruling over an ongoing lawsuit. By November 2012, when the non-Islamists boycotted the Constituent Assembly meetings, the Muslim Brotherhood members allied with the military and the radical Salafis to write the constitution. As a result, they included provisions that would particularly please their allies. For example, to keep the military on their side, the Islamists removed the clause "no civilian shall be prosecuted in a martial court" from the text of Article 75 on the last day of the Constituent Assembly meetings, while this provision was one of the major public demands.

---

[10]   Among the non-Islamist groups signing the statement were the Egyptian Democratic Party, the Socialist Popular Alliance, the Free Egyptians Party, the Kifaya Movement, and the Egyptian Socialist Party.

When the constitution was put for a public referendum in December 2012, non-Islamist groups did not agree on a unified strategy to stop the constitution from going into effect. While some opposition groups called for a boycott of the referendum, others saw the campaign to participate and vote "no" as more effective. Sending different signals to their supporters, the non-Islamists were not able to stop the constitutional adoption process. Despite a low voter turnout of about 32 percent, the constitution was eventually adopted by 64 percent approval vote (Stamboliyska 2012). The *Tamarod* (rebel) campaign and the public-backed military intervention to remove President Morsi and suspend the constitution were a testimony that the constitutional document was not consensual. Rather, it was an Islamist-oriented document written by an Islamist-majority Constituent Assembly that disregarded the rights and demands of at least half of Egypt's population.

There are several reasons why the Egyptian revolutionary groups could not compromise and agree on a consensual constitution among which one can point to a lack of progressive Islamist leadership that could lead the Islamists toward more democratic values, a lack of balance of power between the opposition groups that could force them to compromise, a rushed process that hindered consensus-building, and the military and remnants of the *ancien régime* that undemocratically intervened in the negotiation process. When the opposition groups had two antagonistic visions of the constitution and could not reach an agreement over a middle ground, the outcome exacerbated polarization in society, leading to the ultimate failure of the constitution and its revocations only six months after it went into force. In essence, the Egyptian Constituent Assembly used the opposite of an "incrementalist approach." Rather than using an intentionally vague and contradictory language on controversial issues dividing the Egyptian society in order to avoid a winner-takes-all outcome, the constitution in its entirety had a more Islamist tone and alienated the non-Islamists' vision about the identity of state and society. When constitutional negotiations have clear losers and winners, there is no incentive for the losers to remain in the bargain, and rebellion or new constitutional bargains will become an inevitable solution down the road.

The failure of the constitutional reforms in Egypt, Libya, Yemen, Bahrain, and Syria to create societal consensus demonstrates the challenges of writing consensual constitutions in deeply divided societies, particularly when they are transitioning from authoritarianism. When societies are deeply divided across ethnoreligious, regional, or even ideological lines, constitutional bargains must be consensual if they are to facilitate democratic transitions. The new constitutions in these nations failed to achieve this goal. In Syria and Bahrain where most citizens are discriminated against based on their ethnoreligious identity, the "top-down" constitutions failed to institutionalize power-sharing arrangements. In Libya and Yemen, which suffer from regional cleavages and grievances, the federalist and power-sharing arrangements failed to prevent civil conflicts. And, in Egypt where society was polarized along identity lines, the new constitutional order failed to dampen those societal cleavages.

WHEN CONSTITUTIONAL CLARITY IS NORMATIVELY GOOD AND WHEN IT IS NOT

As Brown (2002) argues, constitutions in the Arab world are "nonconstitutionalist" as they have historically failed to limit the executives' arbitrary use of power, protect citizens and groups' rights, and build societal consensus over divisive issues. Over the past several decades, this nonconstitutionalism resulted in a series of political and societal challenges or ills, which ultimately led to widespread calls for constitutional reforms in the aftermath of the Arab Spring. As discussed in Chapter 1, only when constitutions address all of these issues does a pathway for democratization open up. These challenges can be divided into two groups: unchecked authoritarianism and societal cleavages.

A critical analysis of constitutional designs in Morocco, Jordan, Algeria, and Egypt (2014 and 2019) indicates that when the major political ill is unchecked authoritarianism, for a constitution to facilitate democratization, it ought to be clear and decisive in limiting the arbitrary powers of the head of state. That is, constitutions should avoid vague or contradictory language, parallel institutions with overlapping jurisdictions and responsibilities, and escape hatches that either allow illiberal interpretations of the constitution or leave the doors open for constitutional manipulations down the road. In all four cases studied here, the authoritarian incumbents carefully designed constitutions that lacked textual clarity and were abundant with such parallel institutions and escape hatches, allowing the incumbent to consolidate power. The constitution of Morocco, for example, uses a precise and clear language on the powers of the king. When addressing checks and balances, however, the document turns vague and contradictory, creating several parallel institutions that undermine the independence of other government branches. As discussed in Chapter 4, the king of Morocco, like other authoritarian leaders, managed to achieve this constitutional outcome through a noninclusive and nonparticipatory process, shutting out voices from different political and societal groups including CSOs.

The second major challenge that many Arab polities wrestled with was designing a consensual constitution for deeply divided societies. When societal divisions are a major obstacle to democratization, constitutional arrangements should reflect a societal consensus. As discussed in the previous chapters, the optimal means to reach societal consensus is through participatory and inclusive constitution-making processes. Only when the process is inclusive and societal groups agree upon a constitutional solution for the societal cleavages that divide them will the constitution succeed in facilitating democratization. The specificity of the democratic and consensual constitutional solutions, however, depends to a large extent on the sources of societal divisions.

In this chapter, I distinguished between two sources of societal divisions. When ethnoreligious or regional divisions are the primary sources of conflict, power-sharing constitutional arrangements (e.g., consociationalism or federalism) adopted through an inclusive process can facilitate democratization. None of the four cases studied in this chapter (i.e., Bahrain, Syria, Libya, and Yemen) could constitutionalize consensual power-sharing arrangements, mostly because the constitutional negotiation processes were noninclusive. By contrast, when society is divided across ideological lines, as was the Egyptian society in 2012, power-sharing arrangements such as consociationalism, federalism, or minority rights cannot be the solution. The solution, this chapter contends, is to avoid a winner-takes-all approach. Rather, the constitution should be satisfying enough for all groups to accept. In other words, the constitutional design should be the second-best choice for most groups. To achieve this, the constitution should adopt an "incrementalist" approach, that is, use broad, vague, and often contradictory language in order to avoid a clear interpretation that might please one societal group but alienate the others (Lerner 2011). This is where constitutional ambiguity is normatively good as it is more likely to prevent the exacerbation of societal polarization. As discussed in Chapter 3, this was the approach that Tunisia followed in writing controversial provisions regarding the role of Islam in politics and society. By contrast, the Muslim Brotherhood in Egypt took a winner-takes-all approach that alienated at least half of the Egyptian society with the 2012 constitution, ultimately leading to the suspension of that constitution in just six months.

As the cases of Egypt, Bahrain, Syria, Libya, and Yemen show, crafting democratic and consensual constitutions in deeply divided societies is very challenging. These challenges are multifaceted. First, societies are divided along different lines, and there are no universal, one-size-fits-all solutions for creating consensual constitutions in these societies. Second, a legacy of authoritarianism often yields weak and sometimes nonfunctional political institutions that are incapable of implementing power-sharing or consensual agreements. Furthermore, authoritarian regimes often manipulate societal divisions using divide-and-rule strategies that create inherent mistrust among different groups. Finally, when authoritarian leaders are ousted, the resulting power and security vacuums can destabilize deeply divided nations, and this destabilization can hinder compromise and consensus-building.

To arrive at a consensual and democratic constitution, it is imperative for these nations to include all societal groups in the constitutional bargain. When major groups are excluded from the bargain, constitutions often fail to root out authoritarianism and societal divisions. From Egypt and Algeria to Syria and Bahrain, all constitutions studied in this chapter failed to facilitate democratization because they did not resolve the political and societal ills in their societies. As a result, Arab constitutions for the most part remained nonconstitutionalist, paving the way for democratic backsliding that started to take off only a few years after the start of the Arab Spring.

7

Lessons from the "Fall" of the Arab Spring

The Arab Spring marked a defining moment for many people in the Middle East and North Africa who, for the first time, took their political fate into their own hands. In that sense, the Arab Spring was unique. For the first time in the Arab world's history, grassroots movements focusing on political change created revolutionary waves across most part of the region. Four seemingly indestructible dictators were overthrown within a few months across the region. Those presidents and kings who were lucky enough to remain in power offered various concessions to the protesters in an unprecedented manner. Shortly after the start of the uprisings, constitutional reforms became a central part of people's struggle for political reforms. Yet, with the exception of Tunisia, all Arab Spring constitutional reforms failed to bring about democratic change.

I have endeavored in this book to explain the causes of these failed efforts and present an approach to democratization where an inclusive and participatory constitution-making process and a democratic and consensual constitutional design facilitate democratization. In this approach, an independent and institutionalized civil society is the key to consensus-building. As the previous three chapters have shown, the lack of inclusive processes, strong and independent civil society, and democratic and consensual constitutional designs during the course of constitutional reforms created distinct pathways of failed democratization. In this chapter, I compare and contrast these failed pathways with Tunisia's successful pathway in order to answer a question that has puzzled many for almost a decade now: Why did Tunisia succeed in democratizing, but the rest of the Arab world failed to do so? Next, and as concluding remarks, I offer some lessons from the Arab Spring. After spending most of this book explaining the causes of the Arab Spring failure, it is imperative to note that despite being a failed democratization project, the Arab Spring created a new repertoire for change in an exceptionally authoritarian region. The mistakes and bad choices and decisions made then will continue to live as lessons learned by people who for the first time were empowered to bring about democratic change from below.

"THINGS FALL APART": THE ARAB SPRING AS A FAILED DEMOCRATIZATION PROJECT

Ben Ali's departure from power was not something even the most optimistic Tunisian protesters could imagine. Yet his departure made people in other Arab countries believe that their country could be a second Tunisia. Soon after Ben Ali fled his country, Egyptians recognized that they could force out their own "president for life." When Egypt's Mubarak resigned only a few weeks after massive public pressure, the once unthinkable became a reality for the rest of the Arab world. Determined to take their political fate into their own hands, ordinary people all over the Arab world borrowed the revolutionary symbols and practices from Egypt and Tunisia and chanted *Al-sha'b yurid isqat al-nizam*! (The people want the overthrow of the regime!) In Yemen and Libya, protesters gained what they chanted for, and the dream seemed to become reality. However, a few years after the Arab Spring, the course of events shifted drastically.

Slowly, the Arab Spring events turned ugly. In Egypt, a military coup backed by a popular rebellion against the democratically elected President Morsi ended the dream for a democratic Egypt. In Bahrain, a military campaign led by Saudi Arabia crashed the democratic movement. Civil wars engulfed Libya, Yemen, and Syria claiming the lives of tens of thousands of civilians. The rise of the Islamic state and other terrorist groups led to more instability and violence. War, conflict, and instability led to famine in countries such as Yemen and Syria and economic downturns in countries with tourism-based economies such as Egypt and Tunisia. In other parts of the Arab world where the uprisings did not lead to regime collapse or instability (from Algeria to Morocco and Jordan), authoritarian leaders regained confidence and reversed most of the democratic concessions they made in 2011 and early 2012, practically nullifying the democratic gains of the Arab Spring for their nations.

Indeed, the lives of millions of people in the region are worse off since 2011. The only exception to this "tragedy" is Tunisia, which became the only functioning democracy in the Arab world (Feldman 2020). Even in Tunisia, democracy could not resolve major challenges including economic problems and terrorism, disillusioning most people with democracy and its outcomes. Nonetheless, Tunisia's success in institutionalizing a functioning democracy raises the question of why other Arab nations failed to achieve what they hoped for. As Brownlee et al. (2013) ask, "why the modest harvest?"

A plethora of studies have attempted to explain the failure of the Arab Spring in democratizing the region. Egypt received a special treatment with many studies trying to identify the crucial factors that led to the failure of democratic transition in the most populated Arab country. Some of the factors that received scholarly attention include the power of the military, the relative imbalance between political forces including the Islamists and non-Islamists (Brownlee et al. 2015), the lack of a clear design for transition (Brown 2013), weak CSOs as well as the lack of a progressive Islamist leadership (Stepan and Linz 2013), and the country's global and geopolitical importance (Mednicoff 2014).

Meanwhile, the broader literature on the Arab Spring mostly focused on elite negotiations or structural explanations of authoritarian regime durability (see, e.g., Kamrava 2014; Lynch 2014; Brownlee et al. 2015; Elbadawi and Makdisi 2017; Ketchley 2017; Volpi 2017). Building mostly on theories of democratization and social movements, several seminal studies of the Arab Spring disregarded constitutional reform efforts in the region, which were crucial aspects of the same democratization processes.[1] For example, the influential and insightful book of Brownlee et al. (2015) offers a structural explanation of authoritarian regime break-down leading to democratic reforms in the course of the Arab Spring without any discussion of how or why constitutional movements in the region failed to facilitate democratization.

This book tried to offer a different approach to the study of democratization and popular uprisings in the Arab world by focusing on the link between constitution-making and democratization. Recent scholarship in comparative constitutional studies has shown that there is a potentially significant relationship between constitution-making processes and the content of constitutions on one hand and democratization on the other (see, e.g., Eisenstadt et al. 2017a). Building on these studies and using illustrative cases, I tried to establish a causal mechanism through which constitution-making processes might explain why Tunisia managed to democratize, whereas the rest of the Arab world failed in their democratization efforts.

---

[1] There is a rich literature on the Arab Spring constitutions, but most of these studies focus on single cases and do not offer a general causal link between constitution-making and democratization.

THE ARAB SPRING: PATHWAYS OF SUCCESS AND FAILURE

I built the argument in this book on three propositions. First, constitutional negotiations have a higher prospect of success in establishing democracy in transitioning states if they resolve social, ideological, and political dilemmas. Second, constitutions can resolve these problems best through a participatory and inclusive process. Third, the link that connects constitution-making processes to the resolution of these dilemmas is civil society. Without the engagement of independent and institutionalized civil groups and associations during constitutional moments, new constitutions might face hurdles in establishing democracy. In Chapter 2, I offered empirical evidence, using cross-national statistical analyses of constitutional reforms from around the world (1974–2015) and from the Middle East and North Africa (1861–2020), showing the importance of participatory and inclusive constitution-making processes for the democratic content of constitutions. Chapter 3 then laid out Tunisia's path to democracy focusing on my three main propositions. In Chapters 4–6, I focused on the failed pathways to democracy showing why and how noninclusive and nonparticipatory processes, weakly institutionalized civil society, and undemocratic and nonconsensual constitutional designs failed to facilitate (or even hindered) democratization in the rest of the Arab world. Here, I compare and contrast Tunisia's successful path to democracy to a few failed pathways in relation to this book's three propositions.

Constitution-Making Processes

I argued in this book that the inclusion of major political blocs, ethnic groups, civil society associations, and societal interests in the constitution-making process legitimizes the constitution and increases its democratic quality. Inclusive and participatory processes are more likely to empower marginalized groups, enable an independent civil society to play a more prominent role in the negotiations, and facilitate democratization. As discussed in Chapter 3, only Tunisia's constitutional process included these aspects. All other constitutional reforms in the aftermath of the Arab Spring failed to adopt inclusive and participatory processes. In Chapter 4, I identified four distinct noninclusive and nonparticipatory constitution-making processes, including "populist," "window-dressing," "closed," and "conflict" processes. As summarized in Table 7.1, none of these processes were capable of ushering in democracy in Arab countries.

Similar to an inclusive and participatory process (e.g., Tunisia), a populist constitution-making process is marked with broad public mobilization and

TABLE 7.1 *Pathways of success and failure: constitutional process*

Process	Cases	Inclusion	Participation	Constitutional Outcome	Democratization
Inclusive and Participatory	Tunisia (2014)	All major groups are included in the process.	Civil society and the general public are genuinely consulted.	Democratic and consensual constitution is adopted.	+
Populist	Egypt (2012)	Major stakeholders are excluded from the constitutional bargain or boycott the process.	Massive public mobilization and participation	A nonconsensual constitution is adopted.	–
Window-Dressing	Jordan (2011) Morocco (2011) Egypt (2014) Algeria (2016)	Only co-opted groups are included with major opposition groups not being invited or rejecting the offer to join in the process.	Limited consultation with the general public and civil society but the state mostly seeks to demobilize people	Adopted constitutions are more liberal than their predecessors but remain nondemocratic.	–
Closed	Bahrain (2012) Syria (2012) Oman (2011) KSA (2013) Egypt (2019)	All opposition groups are excluded.	No public consultation	Adopted constitutions remain authoritarian.	–
Conflict	Yemen (2015) Libya (2017)	Some stakeholders are excluded from the constitutional bargain or boycott the process.	Limited consultation with the general public and civil society	No constitution is adopted.	–

consultation. However, this popular mobilization is mostly intended to legitimize a constitution written by the majority. Moreover, unlike inclusive and participatory processes, a populist process is a nondemocratic, exclusionary process identified by a majority rule. Egypt's 2012 constitutional reform is an illustrative example of a populist process. Throughout the rushed constitutional process that lasted only six months, the general public was massively mobilized to participate in the constitutional debate, but the process did not ensure the inclusion of public input because representatives of major societal interests boycotted the process (Maboudi and Nadi 2016). While the outcome of this process was a democratic constitution (at least compared to its predecessor), it was far from being a consensual constitution. Expectedly, such a constitutional bargain could not last long.

The second pathway of constitution-making that is unconducive to democratic outcomes is the window-dressing process. As the term itself conveys, a window-dressing process only mimics inclusive and participatory processes. Unlike in Tunisia where the constitutional negotiation was genuinely participatory and inclusive, authoritarian leaders in Morocco, Jordan, Egypt (2014), and Algeria that were under immense popular pressure for democratization opted to reform their constitutions through *seemingly* participatory and inclusive processes. The challenged executives in these states carefully designed these processes by inviting some moderate societal and political stakeholders while excluding major opposition groups from the constitutional negotiations. Despite the exclusion of major stakeholders and opponents, the state propaganda apparatus managed to brand the constitutional reform process as inclusive and participatory. Not only these processes failed to facilitate democratization in their nations, by mimicking the characteristics of inclusive and/or participatory reforms, window-dressing and populist constitution-making processes posed a major challenge to democratic movements.

In contrast to window-dressing processes, which are nominally branded as inclusive and/or participatory, closed processes are completely exclusive with no input from any societal or political group. Closed processes as such are the total opposite of inclusive and participatory processes. The closed constitutional reform process was the mode of constitution-making in oil-rich, stable monarchies with no history of constitutionalism (Oman and Saudi Arabia), in states where a minority ethnic group ruled and was unwilling to share power (Bahrain and Syria), and in countries marked by democratic backsliding (Egypt 2019). In none of these cases did a real constitutional negotiation ever take place. Not surprisingly, the outcomes of these processes were constitutions written by and for the incumbent leaders, which did not change the authoritarian status quo.

Lastly, conflict constitutional reforms involve a noninclusive process in ethnically or regionally divided nations where the process of crafting the constitution only exacerbates the existing conflict. Similar to window-dressing processes, conflict constitutional processes involve limited consult-ation with the general public and civil society. Most importantly, however, by excluding major societal groups, specifically ethnic minorities, conflict con-stitutions are nonconsensual. In that sense, conflict constitutional reform processes have some resemblance with populist constitutions. Contrary to populist constitutions, however, conflict constitutional processes are limited to countries with severe ethnic divisions, a security vacuum, and a lack of political institutions, as is the case in Yemen and Libya. In these deeply divided societies, noninclusive constitutional bargains increased the political tensions. Rather than creating societal consensus and paving the way for democracy, the noninclusive processes became the source of prolonged violence and civil conflict.

To summarize this comparison, with the exception of the Tunisian constitutional reform process, Arab Spring constitutional reforms were nei-ther inclusive nor participatory. But what was the impact of these noninclu-sive and nonparticipatory processes on democratization? I argued in this book that characteristics of the process have a significant impact on the role that CSOs can play in the constitutional bargains and on the content of constitutions that emerge from these bargains. The inclusion of societal and political groups including minorities in the process is likely to empower CSOs. When enabled, CSOs can direct the constitutional bargain toward democratic and consensual constitutions that can ultimately facilitate democratization.

Civil Society Organizations

Civil society in the Arab region successfully mobilized dissent during the 2011 uprisings. In particular, youth and women movements surprised many international and domestic audiences by leading massive peaceful protests against their authoritarian regimes. From Jordan's Hirak Shababi (or Youth Movement) to Egypt's April 6 and Morocco's February 20 Youth Movements successfully mobilized millions of people in their countries. Despite their initial success, these movements failed to bring liberal reforms or facilitate democratic transitions and soon lost their momentum and popular support. Civil society's failure in transforming uprisings into liberal democracy was partly because most constitutional bargain processes were set up in a way that confined CSOs.

Evidence from Tunisia indicates that only when the constitutional negotiation process is inclusive and participatory, civil society can play a serious
role in constitution-making. When, by contrast, constitution-making is characterized by majority or incumbent rule without minority rights ("populist"
process), counter-majoritarian civic groups are often silenced in the process.
As I discussed in Chapter 4, all CSOs' representatives in the Egyptian 2012
Constituent Assembly withdrew from the Assembly and boycotted the constitutional referendum in protest to Muslim Brotherhood's unilateral
constitution-making strategy, which served only their own political base.
Somewhat similarly, in window-dressing processes, only select groups of
CSOs are consulted. This consultation is usually conducted through a one-
way communication with these co-opted groups only being allowed to submit
their recommendation, rather than sitting at the negotiation table.
Furthermore, as was the case in Jordan, Morocco, Algeria, and Egypt (2014),
major independent CSOs were excluded. The participation of CSOs in
"conflict" constitution-making is more extensive and real than in window-
dressing processes. Yet, as was the case in Yemen and Libya, the noninclusive
characteristics of these processes along with ethnic and regional conflicts
rendered their participation ineffective. Lastly, closed constitution-making
is, by definition, antithetical to civil society participation in constitutional
negotiations.

As elaborated in Chapter 5, I do not contend that these constitution-making
characteristics are the sole reason for civil society's failure to make an impact
on constitutional negotiations and democratic transitions. Indeed, in the wake
of the Arab Spring, CSOs in the region suffered from several endogenous
and exogenous sources of weakness. First, major CSOs lacked the necessary
organizational capacity and structure. A common characteristic of these CSOs
was their horizontal and decentralized structure. Many of these associations
were created by merging several smaller movements with divergent ideologies.
What united them was the common purpose of overthrowing their authoritarian regimes. As was the case in Egypt, after success in reaching their initial
goal, these relatively new CSOs failed to play a serious role during the
transitional period precisely because of their horizontal and decentralized
decision-making structure. Lack of political experience and negotiation skills,
political ambitions, unified agenda, and effective public outreach soon alienated the people on the street with these civic groups.

Additionally, other CSOs, including the older and more established groups
that had the necessary organizational capacity, lacked public legitimacy. Most
unions across the region have been historically co-opted by the state and
known to be acting as an arm of the state to control civic dissents, rather

than being the voice of the people. Others that were independent of the authoritarian states, including human rights groups, were dependent on funding from foreign donors. Being the target of authoritarian states' delegitimization campaigns for decades due to their foreign ties, these groups also struggled to generate public legitimacy and support that undermined their efforts during the transition.

Furthermore, with no formal and informal institutional protections including constitutional guarantees, civil society was at best weakly institutionalized in most parts of the region when the uprisings started. Weakly institutionalized CSOs that lacked the organizational capacity or public legitimacy had to function in a hostile political environment characterized by societal cleavages and conflict or military and international intervention. In such hostile environments, most civic groups cease to carry out even their most basic functions.

It was, thus, not surprising that most CSOs in the regions failed to play a significant role during the Arab Spring. From the relatively more established, organized, and independent NGOs and unions to unorganized grassroots youth, women, and diaspora movements, civil society could not make a lasting impact on the democratic transition partly because constitution-making processes were noninclusive and nonparticipatory and partly because they suffered from lack of strong institutionalization, lack of organizational capacity, and lack of public legitimacy.

Constitutional Designs

When the constitutional bargain process is noninclusive and nonparticipatory and when civil society fails to operate as a democratizing force, the constitutional outcome is not likely to remedy the political and societal ills of authoritarianism. Chapter 6 addressed several of these constitutional design issues in the post–Arab Spring constitutions. First, in monarchies, such as Morocco and Jordan, where the most important demand by protesters was establishing a constitutional monarchy in which the king has only a ceremonial role, the new constitutions did not change the status quo. In both countries, only a select group of CSOs were allowed to participate in window-dressing constitutional reform processes. Major opposition groups, figures, and CSO representatives were either not allowed to participate or chose to boycott the sham process. With no real bargain between the opposition and the state, these constitutional reforms only served the troubled monarchs who wanted to appease the angry protesters by appearing serious about liberal reforms. While the newly designed constitutions were indeed more liberal than their predecessor by expanding several rights and freedoms, they did not change the authoritarian regime. For starters, the constitutional reforms in both countries left the powers of the kings intact. Moreover, the inclusion of several contradictory and vague provisions regarding the balance of power between different branches of the government including judicial independence left the door open for the monarchs to manipulate the constitutional order down the road.

A similar strategy was used by authoritarian presidents who were under immense pressure for democratization. In countries such as Egypt and Algeria where people protested for ending the regimes of "presidents for life," the incumbents had no choice but to institutionalize the presidential term limit. However, the noninclusive constitutional negotiation processes allowed the incumbents to design new constitutions that, despite installing term limits, would not shut the door on their political ambitions. Both Egypt (after the 2013 coup) and Algeria adopted their new constitutions through window-dressing processes, which only seemed to be inclusive or participatory. In both cases, however, major opposition groups and CSOs were excluded from the constitutional bargain. With the representatives of dissenting voices not being present at the negotiation table, the adopted constitutions could not change the underlying causes of authoritarianism (i.e., unchecked executive powers) in these countries. The result of noninclusive and nonparticipatory processes in the Arab republics of Algeria and Egypt was that despite adopting executive term limits, the constitutions remain "nonbinding," allowing strongmen to manipulate the constitutional order without even abolishing term limits and stay in power for years. Both of these "nonconstitutionalist" constitutional orders led to democratic backsliding as they failed to address the underlying problem of unchecked executives with ultra-constitutional powers. By contrast, Tunisia's inclusive and participatory process yielded a constitution that seems to have ended the problem of "presidents for life" by adopting Article 75 that not only limits the presidency to two five-year terms but also prohibits any amendments to the number or length of presidential terms. This provision, which was unanimously supported by almost all political groups and CSOs, highlights the benefits of inclusive and participatory processes for democratization.

The robustness of authoritarianism in the Arab world has not been only due to unchecked executive powers. From Syria and Bahrain to Libya and Yemen, several authoritarian leaders stayed in power using divide-and-rule strategies and the manipulation of existing ethnoreligious and regional cleavages. In Syria and Bahrain where the authoritarian incumbents were from ethnic minority groups and ruling against the majority's will, new constitutions failed to reconcile social divisions through power-sharing arrangements. In a desperate move to mitigate the situation, the Al-Assad and Al-Khalifa regimes commissioned new constitutions. Yet, since they did not see power-sharing as a real option, they opted for a closed constitution-making process. The appointed constitutional reform commissions in both countries had no intention of making a real change to the status quo, just to buy some time for the incumbents. While some opposition groups were invited to participate, most groups including CSOs boycotted the sham process. This, however, did not prevent the incumbents from adopting the constitutional changes and framing them as major democratic reforms in the land. Simultaneously, both regimes invited militias from their foreign allies in order to suppress the protesters.

Even in Libya and Yemen where the authoritarian regimes' collapse triggered transitional processes, the drafted constitutions failed to address the societal grievances, which were for long suppressed under the authoritarian regimes. In both countries, the constitution-making process was initially inclusive and participatory with civil society being actively engaged in the negotiations. Gradually, however, the security vacuum and foreign interventions turned regional and group rivalries into armed conflict. With flames of the conflict raging, civic groups and ethnic minorities were pushed out of the bargain process. As the processes became less inclusive, the constitutional outcome became less consensual, triggering even more conflict. The federalist and region-based power-sharing arrangements failed to prevent conflict in Yemen and Libya, partly because the noninclusive bargaining processes could not generate societal buy-ins. Without societal buy-ins, no power-sharing constitutional arrangements can establish peace or facilitate democratization.

Similarly, in ideologically polarized societies, noninclusive processes often fail to create societal consensus over divisive issues. When society is divided across ideological issues such as the role of religion, as was the Egyptian society in 2012, the only solution to creating societal consensus is to avoid a winner-takes-all approach in the constitutional bargain. That is, the constitutional design should be sufficiently satisfying for all groups to accept. As Lerner (2011) argues, to achieve this, the constitution should adopt an "incrementalist" approach, that is, using broad, vague, and often contradictory language regarding those divisive and polarizing issues in order to avoid a clear interpretation that might please one societal group but alienate the others. Such "incrementalist" constitutions can be designed only through inclusive and participatory processes, as was the case in Tunisia when the NCA adopted contradictory provisions regarding the role of Islam in politics and society. By contrast, the Muslim Brotherhood-controlled Constituent Assembly of Egypt utilized a populist constitution-making process with massive popular mobilization to amplify the majoritarian voices while silencing minority and dissenting voices through a noninclusive constitution-drafting approach. The result was a constitution that was viewed as Islamist by many Egyptians who did not want to live under its mandate. The Muslim Brotherhood's winner-takes-all approach, which alienated at least half of the Egyptian society with the 2012 constitution, ultimately lead to the failure of that constitution.

In sum, these five pathways of failed constitutional design provide reasonable evidence that noninclusive and nonparticipatory processes generate "democratically inferior" constitutional texts, and this, in turn, has undermined democratization in these nations. The empirical evidence from the successful and failed pathways of constitution-making presented in this book indicates that there is good reason to think that the characteristics of constitution-making processes have an important impact on both the democratic content of constitutions and democratization. Where the constitution-making process was both inclusive and participatory, as was the case only in Tunisia, it yielded democratic outcomes. The genuine public participation legitimized the process and created a sense of ownership of the constitution among citizens, two very important steps toward building constitutionalism and rule of law in transitioning countries. And the inclusiveness of the process transformed interpersonal relationships between different groups, enhanced intergroup trusts, and strengthened cross-partisan ties, which ultimately facilitated constitutional agreements (Jermanová 2020). By contrast, where the constitutional bargain processes were noninclusive and nonparticipatory, and civil society failed to play a prominent role, the resulting constitutions lacked public legitimacy. Rather than enhancing intergroup trusts, the noninclusive processes alienated large segments of society with the constitution. Ultimately, these "democratically inferior" constitutions failed to institutionalize democratic reforms.

THE ARAB SPRING: A TRAGEDY?

Apart from the ouster of four dictators and the establishment of a new democracy in Tunisia, the Arab Spring failed to fulfill the dreams of protesters for democratic governance as the grassroots efforts to establish democracy in the Arab world failed one after the other. Indeed, the Arab Spring as a democratizing project was mostly a tragic failure. Yet, as Feldman (2020) argues, this "tragedy" brought about some important changes with profound implications for the future of the Arab world. Feldman (2020) identifies two major changes, which the Arab Spring caused.

First, as a result of the 2010–2011 uprisings and their aftermaths, national identification based on Arab nationalism has collapsed. Many Arab leaders, from Qaddafi to Hussein and Al-Assad, had utilized pan-Arabism as their ideological mission in order to unify their divided nations and stay longer in power. The Arab Spring changed that perception. While it is true that the wave of the uprisings across many and only Arab countries demonstrated the existence of transnational political identification, it is also fair to say that in many post–Arab Spring countries, the sense of unifying Arab identity has been undercut by ethnoreligious divisions that emerged as a result of the uprisings (Feldman 2020). From Libya and Yemen to Syria and Bahrain, the collapse of national identity means that authoritarian leaders can no longer utilize Arab nationalism to project national unity within their countries (Feldman 2020, xiv).

Second, the Arab Spring uprisings fundamentally changed political Islam (i.e., a broad range of individuals, groups, movements, and ideas that aspire to transform the state and society through constitutional orders grounded in Islamic Sharia), which for several decades was branded by Islamist groups in many Arab countries as the alternative (to pan-Arabism) unifying ideology. Indeed, political Islam was increasingly under public scrutiny years before the Arab Spring. Popular skepticism of Sharia-based governance in the Arab world was partly due to the interventionist policies of the Islamic Republic of Iran and partly due to the rise of Islamic terrorism in the region. But before the Arab Spring, the idea of Sharia-based governance was never put to the test in most Arab countries. The Arab Spring and the electoral victories of Islamist political parties in several countries including Morocco, Tunisia, and Egypt were a real test for the resilience of political Islam. However, the Muslim Brotherhood's collapse in Egypt following a massive popular rebellion against its government, along with Ennahda's self-transformation into a liberal Islamic party in Tunisia and the rise of the Islamic State in Syria, marked an end to democratically oriented political Islam (Feldman 2020).

To these two changes, one can add the emergence of new repertoires of protests for grassroots-based movements capable of transforming their political regimes. Prior to the Arab Spring, pro-democracy movements were small, disorganized, and generally considered incapable of making real change. The Arab Spring changed that perception for both the governments and the general public.

The Arab Spring as a Repertoire

In 2019 and 2020, massive protest movements erupted in Sudan, Algeria, Iraq, and Lebanon. These movements resembled, in many ways, those of the Arab

Spring. They were all mass-based, peaceful movements aimed at overthrowing long-standing dictators or corrupt leaders. They all wanted an end to the inefficient and corrupt governments. In Sudan and Algeria, protesters succeeded in overthrowing the dictators, and in Iraq and Lebanon, they forced prime ministers to resign. Protesters in all four countries saw real constitutional reforms as crucial for meeting their demands, triggering constitutional reforms in Sudan and Algeria and informal constitutional talks in Iraq and Lebanon.

These protest movements started with the Sudanese Revolution when a series of demonstrations against the increasing costs of living broke out in several cities in late December 2018. The protests quickly turned into demands for major economic reforms and the stepping down of Omar Al-Bashir, Sudan's ruler for thirty years. Despite using violence against the peaceful protesters, Al-Bashir was not able to suppress the protests. In late February 2019, he declared a state of emergency, dissolving both national and regional governments. But the state of emergency was not effective either, as protests continued into April when the military stepped in and overthrew Al-Bashir through a coup d'état. The civil disobedience continued against the Transitional Military Council (TMC) forcing its leadership to sign an Interim Constitutional Declaration and a political agreement with Forces of Freedom and Change (FFC), a wide political coalition of civilian and rebel groups, in August that year. The agreements involved a three-year transitional period leading to the transfer of power to a civilian and democratically elected government. Despite the agreement between the TMC and FFC, protests against the military or the ruling coalition have not stopped as of the end of 2020.

Almost simultaneously with the protests in Sudan, the Algerian protesters created their own revolution to overthrow President Abdelaziz Bouteflika, a goal they failed to achieve during the Arab Spring. Algeria's so-called Revolution of Smiles started in mid-February 2019, six days after Bouteflika announced his candidacy for a fifth presidential term. Similar to the Arab Spring uprisings, the 2019 protests in Algeria, which later came to be known as the Hirak Movement, consisted of peaceful demonstrations demanding the immediate resignation of Bouteflika. As public pressure was mounting, President Bouteflika announced, on March 11, 2019, that he will not seek reelection and will postpone the presidential election. But protesters did not accept this as they chanted "No Tricks, Bouteflika." On March 31, Bouteflika named a caretaker government, and the next day, he announced that he will resign on April 28. That did not quiet the protesters who wanted his immediate resignation. Eventually, under pressure from the military, Bouteflika resigned on April 2. Similar to what happened in Sudan, protests in Algeria did not stop with the ouster of the dictator. Many civic and political groups including the Forces of the Democratic Alternative alliance and the Justice and Development Front called for boycotting the presidential election, which was scheduled for December 12 that year. Their demand was simple: no election should be held before a radical change to the regime. Despite the boycotts and protests, the presidential election was held, and the FLN candidate, Abdelmadjid Tebboune, emerged as the victor.[2] Shortly after assuming power, Tebboune appointed a CRC composed of seventeen constitutional experts to amend the constitution in order to meet the demands of Hirak. Among different constitutional reform proposals, Tebboune called for an "immutable and intangible" two presidential term limits, a major demand by protesters. Protesters rejected the move and called for an elected constituent assembly to be in charge of drafting a new constitution, which the regime rejected. The new constitution came into force after approval in a public referendum on November 1, 2020. Despite being a progressive document, the new constitution has not satisfied the protesters who continued to press for more reforms.

A few months after the fall of dictators in Sudan and Algeria, protests erupted simultaneously in Iraq and Lebanon, two countries that were not seriously impacted by the Arab Spring. The Iraqi protests (known as the Tishreen Revolution) started on October 1, 2019, mostly in central and southern provinces in Iraq. The protests in Lebanon (known as the October Revolution) started a few days later on October 17 all over the country. Protesters had a very wide range of demands from fighting corruption and unemployment and providing sufficient public services and improving the standard of living to ending foreign intervention. However, one specific demand was shared among almost all protesters in both countries: constitutional reforms to end the sectarian and confessional system of government. Indeed, the "constitutional sophistication" of the Iraqi and Lebanese protesters resembled that of the Arab Spring protesters. In both countries, the protesters saw the root of corruption and government inefficiency in their sectarian government systems and wanted an end to it. Under pressure from angry protesters on the street, prime ministers of both countries resigned.[3] Despite this achievement, the Iraqi and Lebanese protesters were not

---

[2] The turnout was under 40 percent, the lowest in Algeria's presidential election history since independence.

[3] Saad Hariri resigned as the prime minister of Lebanon on January 21, 2020, and Iraqi Prime Minister Adil Abdul-Mahdi resigned from his post on May 6, 2020.

ultimately able to force constitutional reforms to end the confessional systems in their countries, partly because of the COVID-19 pandemic that allowed the governments to impose curfews and limit gatherings in the name of controlling the pandemic.

It is perhaps too early to tell the democratic impact of the protest movements in Sudan, Algeria, Iraq, and Lebanon. Yet we can derive at least two conclusions from these movements. First, these protests are proof that the Arab Spring remained "an unfinished business." The massive grassroots uprisings, which started more than ten years ago, could not resolve the democracy deficit in the region. People who hoped that constitutional reforms could find remedies for the political and societal ills of authoritarianism were ultimately disappointed with the constitutional outcomes. Apart from Tunisia where the new constitution seems to have institutionalized democracy, most constitutional reforms failed to change the authoritarian status quo. Even worse, in some countries, such as Yemen and Libya, constitutional reforms fueled the civil conflict. The renewed societal interests in constitutional reforms in Sudan, Algeria, Iraq, and Lebanon should serve as a reminder that the ills of authoritarianism require constitutional remedies. But constitutional reforms cannot achieve this goal if the process of the constitutional bargain is not inclusive and participatory.

The second conclusion we can arrive at is that while the Arab Spring project has remained unfinished, the grassroots movements for constitutionalism, rule of law, and democratization have left a powerful legacy. The Arab Spring created a repertoire for change that will remain in the historical memory of Arab countries. Citizens in many Arab countries still feel empowered and capable of making change and determining their own fate. Some Arab leaders will have difficulty projecting the same image of indispensability they used to enjoy before the Arab Spring. Protesters remember the time when they overcame the collective action problem and know that they are capable of doing it again. They learned from the many mistakes they made. As was the case in Sudan and Algeria recently, protesters have learned not to stop with the ouster of the authoritarian leaders, and that change comes only when the regime is completely transformed. They also have learned not to be fooled by constitutional tricks and window-dressing reforms. The Arab Spring might have failed, but eventually, there will be new opportunities for change. When those opportunities finally emerge, the lessons learned from the Arab Spring will come to aid people to fulfill their self-determination dream.

Bibliography

Abdessadok, Zineb. 2017. "Libya Today: From Arab Spring to Failed State." *Al-Jazeera*, May 30. Retrieved from www.aljazeera.com/indepth/features/2017/04/happening-libya-today-170418083223563.html.

Abu Ltaif, Eduardo. 2015. "The Limitations of the Consociational Arrangements in Iraq." Ethnopolitics Paper No. 38. Belfast: The Exeter Centre for Ethnopolitical Studies and Centre for the Study of Ethnic Conflict, Queen's University.

Adams, John. 2000. "Thoughts on Government." In *The Revolutionary Writings of John Adams*. Selected and with a Foreword by C. Bradley Thompson. Indianapolis: Liberty Fund (Original work published 1776).

Ahmed, Dawood and Moamen Gouda. 2014. "Measuring Constitutional Islamization: The Islamic Constitutions Index." *Hastings International and Comparative Law Review* 38 (1): 1–74.

Ahram Online. 2012a. "Constituent Assembly to Launch Constitution Awareness Campaign on Wednesday with LE100,000 Budget." *Ahram Online*, October 7. Retrieved from http://english.ahram.org.eg/News/54997.aspx.

2012b. "NDP Offshoots Campaign against Egypt's Constitution." *Ahram Online*, October 7. Retrieved from http://english.ahram.org.eg/News/55009.aspx.

2012c. "Political Forces Sign on ElBaradei Call for Constituent Assembly Boycott." *Ahram Online*, September 29. Retrieved from http://english.ahram.org.eg/News/54250.aspx.

2012d. "Revolutionary Youth Group Leader Quits Constituent Assembly." *Ahram Online*, November 18. Retrieved from http://english.ahram.org.eg/News/58501.aspx.

2013. "Egypt Court Suspends Parliamentary Elections." *Ahram Online*, March 6. Retrieved from http://english.ahram.org.eg/News/66280.aspx.

2019. "Egypt Parliament Passes Constitutional Amendments, Extends President's Term Limit." *Ahram Online*, April 19. Retrieved from http://english.ahram.org.eg/News/330131.aspx.

Al-Ali, Zeyd. 2017. *Libya's Final Draft Constitution: A Contextual Analysis*. Stockholm: International Institute for Democracy and Electoral Assistance.

Alesina, Alberto, Arnaud Devleeschauwer, William Easterly, Sergio Kurlat, and Romain Wacziarg. 2003. "Fractionalization." *Journal of Economic Growth* 8: 155–194.

Al-Jazeera. 2012. "Syria Holds Vote on New Constitution." *Al-Jazeera*, February 26.
     Retrieved from www.aljazeera.com/news/middleeast/2012/02/201222645055510841
     .html.
     2019. "Egypt Opposition Urges Voters to Reject Constitutional Amendments." *Al-Jazeera*, April 18. Retrieved from https://aje.io/bguev.
Alley, April L. 2013. "Tracking the 'Arab Spring': Yemen Changes Everything... And
     Nothing." *Journal of Democracy* 24 (4): 74–85.
Allinson, Jamie. 2015. "Class Forces, Transition and the Arab Uprisings: A Comparison
     of Tunisia, Egypt and Syria." *Democratization* 22 (2): 294–314.
Allouche, Yasmina. 2016. "What Algeria's Constitutional Reforms Really Mean."
     Middle East Monitor, February 15. Retrieved from www.middleeastmonitor.com
     /20160215-what-algerias-constitutional-reforms-really-mean/.
Almond, Gabriel A. and Sidney Verba. 1963. *The Civic Culture: Political Attitudes and
     Democracy in Five Nations*. Princeton, NJ: Princeton University Press.
Al-Sakkaf, Nadia. 2016. *The Tragedy of Yemen's Civil Society*. Washington, DC:
     Washington Institute for Near East Policy (February 19).
Al-Sayyid, Mustafa Kamil. 1995. "A Civil Society in Egypt?" In *Civil Society in the
     Middle East*, Volume 1, ed. Augustus Richard Norton. Leiden: Brill Academic,
     269-293.
Al-Shami, Mohammad. 2015. "Youth and Civil Society: The Missing Powers in Yemen."
     Viewpoint No. 82. Washington, DC: Wilson Center Middle East Program.
Altan-Olcay, Ozlem and Ahmet Icduygu. 2012. "Mapping Civil Society in the Middle
     East: The Cases of Egypt, Lebanon and Turkey." *British Journal of Middle Eastern
     Studies* 39 (2): 157–179.
Angrist, Michele. 2012. "War, Resisting the West, and Women's Labor: Toward an
     Understanding of Arab Exceptionalism." *Politics & Gender* 8 (1): 51–82.
     2013. "Understanding the Success of Mass Civic Protest in Tunisia." *Middle East
     Journal* 67 (4): 547–564.
Antoun, Richard T. 2000. "Civil Society, Tribal Process, and Change in Jordan: An
     Anthropological View." *International Journal of Middle East Studies* 32 (4):
     441–463.
Aranson, Peter H. 1988. "Procedural and Substantive Constitutional Protection of
     Economic Liberties." In *Public Choice and Constitutional Economics*, ed. James
     D. Gwartney and Richard E. Wagner. Greenwich: JAI Press, 285-313.
Arato, Andrew. 1995. "Forms of Constitution Making and Theories of Democracy."
     Cardozo Law Review 17: 191–231.
     1996. "Civil Society, Transition and Consolidation of Democracy." Paper Presented
     at International Conference Democratic Transitions in Latin America and in
     Eastern Europe: Rupture and Continuity. Paris (March 4–6).
     2000. *Civil Society, Constitution, and Legitimacy*. Plymouth: Rowman and
     Littlefield.
Aristotle. 2013. *Aristotle's Politics*. Translated and with Introduction by Carnes Lord,
     2nd ed. Chicago, IL: University of Chicago Press (Original work written circa
     350 BCE).
Attasi, Basma. 2012. "Debating Syria's Draft Constitution." *Al-Jazeera*, February 16.
     Retrieved from www.aljazeera.com/indepth/features/2012/02/201221615517760425
     .html.

Avritzer, Leonardo. 2012. "Democracy Beyond Aggregation: The Participatory Dimension of Public Deliberation." *Journal of Public Deliberation* 8 (2): 1–20.

Axelrod, Robert. 1984. *The Evolution of Cooperation*. Cambridge, MA: Basic Books.

Banani, Mohamed Saed. 2012. *Dastour 2011: Qera'a tarkibiyya men khelal ba'dh el-sohof* [The Constitution of 2011: A Synthetic Reading Through Some News Papers]. Casablanca: Dar Al-Salam.

Bani Salameh, Mohammed Torki and Azzam Ali Ananzah. 2015. "Constitutional Reforms in Jordan: A Critical Analysis." *Digest of Middle East Studies* 24 (2): 139–160.

Banks, Arthur S. and Kenneth A. Wilson. 2014. *Cross-National Time-Series Data Archive*. Jerusalem: D. International.

Bannon, Alicia L. 2007. "Designing a Constitution-Drafting Process: Lessons from Kenya." *The Yale Law Journal* 116 (8): 1824–1872.

Barany, Zoltan. 2011. "The Role of the Military." *Journal of Democracy* 22 (4): 24–35.

Barber, Benjamin. 1984. *Strong Democracy*. Berkeley, CA: University of California Press.

BBC News Middle East. 2012. "Egypt's Muslim Brotherhood Denounces Parliament Ban." *BBC News Middle East*, June 16. Retrieved from www.bbc.co.uk/news/wo rld-middle-east-18474624.

Beaumont, Peter. 2019. "Death Toll in Yemen War Reaches 100,000." *The Guardian*, October 31. Retrieved from www.theguardian.com/world/2019/oct/31/death-toll-in -yemen-war-reaches-100000.

Beinin, Joel. 2012. *The Rise of Egypt's Workers*. Washington, DC: Carnegie Endowment for International Peace.

  2016. *Workers and Thieves: Labor Movements and Popular Uprisings in Tunisia and Egypt*. Stanford, CA: Stanford University Press.

Bell, Bethany. 2012. "Egypt Parties End Deadlock Over Constitutional Panel." *BBC NEWS Middle East*, June 8. Retrieved from www.bbc.co.uk/news/world-middle-east-18360403.

Bellin, Eva. 2004. "The Robustness of Authoritarianism in the Middle East: Exceptionalism in Comparative Perspective." *Comparative Politics* 36 (2): 139–157.

  2013. "Drivers of Democracy: Lessons from Tunisia." Middle East Brief 75. Crown Center for Middle East Studies, Brandeis University.

Benchemsi, Ahmed. 2012. "Morocco: Outfoxing the Opposition." *Journal of Democracy* 23 (1): 57–69.

  2014. "Morocco's Makhzen and the Haphazard Activists." In *Talking to the Streets: The Transformation of Arab Activism*, ed. Lina Khatib and Ellen Lust. Baltimore, MD: John Hopkins University Press, 199–235.

Benomar, Jamal. 2004. "Constitution-Making after Conflict: Lessons for Iraq." *Journal of Democracy* 15 (2): 81–95.

Benyettou, Wissam. 2015. *Will Algeria Start 2016 with a New Constitution? Long-Awaited Constitutional Revision and the Road to Democratic Transition*. Stockholm: International Institute for Democracy and Electoral Integrity.

Bernstein, Zoe. 2014. "Stuck in a Jordanian Winter: Why the Arab Spring Failed to Result in Lasting Regime Change in Jordan." Undergraduate Honors Thesis. Boulder: Department of International Affairs, University of Colorado.

Bessinger, Mark. 2008. "A New Look at Ethnicity and Democratization." *Journal of Democracy* 19 (3): 85–97.

Binningsbø, Helga Malmin. 2005. "Consociational Democracy and Post-Conflict Peace: Will Power-Sharing Institutions Increase the Probability of Lasting Peace after Civil War?" Paper Presented at 13th Annual National Political Science Conference. Hurdalsjøen: Centre for the Study of Civil War, International Peace Research Institute, Oslo.

Bishara, Dina. 2014. *Labor Movements in Tunisia and Egypt: Drivers vs. Objects of Change in Transition from Authoritarian Rule.* SWP Comment, 1/2014. Berlin: Stiftung Wissenschaft und Politik -SWP- Deutsches Institut für Internationale Politik und Sicherheit.

2018. *Contesting Authoritarianism: Labor Challenges to the State in Egypt.* New York: Cambridge University Press.

Brechenmacher, Saskia and Thomas Carothers. 2018. *Examining Civil Society Legitimacy.* Washington, DC: Carnegie Endowment for International Peace.

Brenan, Geoffrey and James M. Buchanan. 1985. *The Reason of Rules.* Cambridge: Cambridge University Press.

Brett, Roddy and Antonio Delgado. 2005. *The Role of Constitution-Building Process in Democratization: Case Study of Guatemala.* Stockholm: International Institute for Democracy and Electoral Integrity.

Brown, Nathan. 2002. *Constitutions in a Nonconstitutional World: Arab Basic Laws and the Prospects for Accountable Government.* Albany, NY: State University of New York.

2012. *The Egyptian Political System in Disarray.* Washington, DC: Carnegie Endowment for International Peace.

2013. "Constitutional Reform in the Arab Spring: A New Beginning or an Unhappy Ending?" *Yale Law School Legal Scholarship Repository*, 33–54.

2017. *Arguing Islam after the Revival of Arab Politics.* Oxford: Oxford University Press.

Brown, Nathan and Michele Dunne. 2013. *Egypt's Draft Constitution Rewards the Military and Judiciary.* Washington, DC: Carnegie Endowment for International Peace.

Brownlee, Jason. 2007. *Authoritarianism in an Age of Democratization.* Cambridge: Cambridge University Press.

Brownlee, Jason, Tarek Masoud, and Andrew Reynolds. 2013. "Tracking the 'Arab Spring': Why the Modest Harvest?" *Journal of Democracy* 24 (4): 29–44.

2015. *The Arab Spring: Pathways of Repression and Reform.* Oxford: Oxford University Press.

Buchanan, James M. and Roger L. Faith. 1987. "Secession and the Limits of Taxation." *American Economic Review* 77: 1023–1031.

Bunce, Valerie. 2003. "Rethinking Recent Democratization: Lessons from the Postcommunist Experience." *World Politics* 55 (1): 167–192.

Burke, Edmund. 1999. *Reflections on the Revolution in France.* Oxford: Oxford University Press (Original work published 1790).

Cammett, Melani and Marsha P. Posusney. 2010. "Labor Standards and Labor Market Flexibility in the Middle East: Free Trade and Freer Unions?" *Studies in Comparative International Development* 45 (2): 250–279.

Carapico, Sheila. 2019. "Civil Society." In *Politics and Society in the Contemporary Middle East*, 3rd ed., ed. Michele P. Angrist. Boulder, CO: Lynne Rienner, 99-120.

Carey, John M. 2009. "Does It Matter How a Constitution Is Created?" In *Is Democracy Exportable?*, ed. Zoltan Barany and Robert G. Moser. Cambridge: Cambridge University Press, 155-177.

The Carnegie Endowment. 2011. *Guide the Egypt's Transition*. Washington, DC: Carnegie Endowment for International Peace.

The Carter Center. 2014. *Constitution Report: The Constitution-Making Process in Tunisia*. Atlanta, GA: Carter Center.

Chambers, Simone. 2003. "Deliberative Democratic Theory." *Annual Review of Political Science* 6 (1): 307–326.

2004. "Democracy, Popular Sovereignty, and Constitutional Legitimacy." *Constellations* 11 (2): 153–173.

Chayes, Sarah. 2014. *How a Leftist Labor Union Helped Force Tunisia's Political Settlement*. Washington, DC: Carnegie Endowment for International Peace.

Cheibub, Jose Antonio. 2007. *Presidentialism, Parliamentarism, and Democracy*. Cambridge: Cambridge University Press.

Cheibub, Jose Antonio, Jennifer Gandhi, and James Raymond Vreeland. 2010. "Democracy and Dictatorship Revisited." *Public Choice* 143 (1–2): 67–101.

Cherif, Youssef. 2018. "Delegitimizing Civil Society in Tunisia." In *Examining Civil Society Legitimacy*, ed. Saskia Brechenmacher and Thomas Carothers. Washington, DC: Carnegie Endowment for International Peace. Available at https://carnegieendowment.org/2018/05/02/examining-civil-society-legitimacy-pub-76211

Cohen, Frank. 1997. "Proportional versus Majoritarian Ethnic Conflict Management in Democracies." *Comparative Political Studies* 30 (5): 607–630.

Cohen, Jean L. and Andrew Arato. 1992. *Civil Society and Political Theory*. Cambridge, MA: Massachusetts Institute of Technology Press.

The Constituent Assembly. 2012. "Al-ijtema' al-'asher lel-jam'iya al-ta'sisiya" [The Tenth Meeting of the Constituent Assembly]. *The Constituent Assembly*, Cairo, August 28. Retrieved from dostour.eg/ ‫الاجتماع-الجلسات/محاضر/الجمعية_جلسات‬ ‫العاشر-الاجتماع - 371 /الخامس‬

Coppedge, Michael. 2012. *Democratization and Research Methods*. Cambridge: Cambridge University Press.

Cottrell, Jill and Yash Ghai. 2007. "Constitution Making and Democratization in Kenya (2000–2005)." *Democratization* 14 (1): 1–25.

Cross, Ester and Jason Sorens. 2016. "Arab Spring Constitution-Making: Polarization, Exclusion, and Constraints." *Democratization* 23 (7): 1292–1312.

Cummings, Kate. 2014. "Tunisians Cast Their Online Votes for a New Constitution." *Democracy International*. (8 January 2014).

Dahl, Robert. 1971. *Polyarchy: Participation and Opposition*. New Haven, CT: Yale University Press.

1998. *On Democracy*. New Haven, CT: Yale University Press.

2005. *Who Governs? Democracy and Power in an American City*, 2nd ed. New Haven, CT: Yale University Press.

Davenport, Christian. 2012. "The Arab Spring, Winter, and Back Again? (Re) Introducing the Dissent-Repression Nexus with a Twist." *International Interactions* 38 (5): 704–713.

Diamond, Larry. 1999. *Developing Democracy: Towards Consolidation*. Baltimore, MD: John Hopkins University Press.

Dixon, Paul. 2011. "Is Consociational Theory the Answer to Global Conflict? From the Netherlands to Northern Ireland and Iraq." *Political Studies Review* 9 (3): 309–322.

Downs, Anthony. 1957. *An Economic Theory of Democracy*. New York: Harper and Row.

Dryzek, John S. 2000. *Deliberative Democracy and Beyond: Liberals, Critics, Contestations*. Oxford: Oxford University Press.

Egypt Independent. 2012a. "Awareness Campaign to Familiarize People with Coming Constitution." *Egypt Independent*, August 28. Retrieved from www .egyptindependent.com/news/awareness-campaign-familiarize-people-coming-constitution.

2012b. "Constituent Assembly Announces First Draft of New Constitution." *Egypt Independent*, October 10. Retrieved from www.egyptindependent.com/news/con stituent-assembly-announces-first-draft-new-constitution.

2012c. "Egyptian Churches Withdraw from Constituent Assembly." *Egypt Independent*, November 17. Retrieved from www.egyptindependent.com/news/e gyptian-churches-withdraw-constituent-assembly.

Eisenstadt, Todd A., A. Carl LeVan, and Tofigh Maboudi. 2015. "When Talk Trumps Text: The Democratizing Effects of Deliberation during Constitution-making, 1974–2011." *American Political Science Review* 109 (3): 592–612.

2017a. *Constituents before Assembly: Participation, Deliberation, and Representation in the Crafting of New Constitutions*. Cambridge: Cambridge University Press.

2017b. *Constitutionalism and Democracy Dataset, Version 1.0*. Washington, DC: American University's Digital Research Archive. Last modified June 1, 2017. Available at http://doi.org/10.17606/M63W25.

Eisenstadt, Todd A. and Tofigh Maboudi. 2019. "Being There Is Half the Battle: Group Inclusion, Constitution-Writing, and Democracy." *Comparative Political Studies* 52 (13–14): 2135–2170.

Eisenstadt, Todd, Tofigh Maboudi, and Ife Olawole. 2019. "Consensual Constitution-Writing Over Consensus Institutions: The Power of Inclusion through Group Rights in Mitigating Conflict." Paper Presented at the American Political Science Association's 115th Annual Meeting. Washington, DC (August 29–September 1).

Elbadawi, Ibrahim and Samir Makdisi (eds.). 2017. *Democratic Transitions in the Arab World*. Cambridge: Cambridge University Press.

El-Behairy, Nouran. 2012. "FJP Launches Referendum Campaign." *Daily News Egypt*, December 9. Retrieved from www.dailynewsegypt.com/2012/12/09/fjp-launches-referendum-campaign/.

Elkins, Zachary, Tom Ginsburg, and Justin Blount. 2009. "Can We Trust Legislators to Write Constitutions?" Paper Presented at the Latin American Studies Association Annual Conference. Rio de Janeiro.

Elkins, Zachary, Tom Ginsburg, and James Melton. 2009. *The Endurance of National Constitutions*. Cambridge: Cambridge University Press.

2014a. *Characteristics of National Constitutions, Version 2.0*. Comparative Constitutions Project. Last modified April 18, 2014. Available at www .comparativeconstitutionsproject.org/index.htm.

2014b. "The Content of Authoritarian Constitutions." In *Constitutions in Authoritarian Regimes*, ed. Tom Ginsburg and Alberto Simpser. Cambridge: Cambridge University Press, 141–164.

El-Madani, Mohamed, Edris El-Maqrawi, and Salwi El-Zarhouni. 2012. *Derasa naqdiyya lel-dastour al-maqrebi lel-'am 2011* [A Critical Study of the Moroccan Constitution of 2011]. Stockholm: International Institute for Democracy and Electoral Integrity.

El-Mahdi, Rabab. 2014. "Egypt: A Decade of Ruptures." In *Talking to the Streets: The Transformation of Arab Activism*, ed. Lina Khatib and Ellen Lust. Baltimore, MD: John Hopkins University Press, 52–75.

Elster, Jon. 1993. "Constitution Making in Eastern Europe: Rebuilding the Boat in the Open Sea." *Public Administration* 71 (1–2): 169–217.

　　1995. "Forces and Mechanisms in the Constitution-Making Process." *Duke Law Journal* 45: 364–396.

　　1997. "Ways of Constitution-Making." In *Democracy's Victory and Crisis*, ed. Axel Hadenius. Cambridge: Cambridge University Press, 123–142.

　　2000. "Arguing and Bargaining in Two Constituent Assemblies." *University of Pennsylvania Journal of Constitutional Law* 2 (2): 345–421.

　　2012. "The Optimal Design of a Constituent Assembly." In *Collective Wisdom: Principles and Mechanisms*, ed. Hélène Landemore and Jon Elster. Cambridge: Cambridge University Press, 148–172.

Enein, Ahmed Aboul. 2012. "Human Rights Activist Manal El-Teiby Withdraws from Constituent Assembly." *Daily News Egypt*, August 16. Retrieved from www .dailynewsegypt.com/2012/08/16/human-rights-activist-manal-el-teiby-withdraws-from -constituent-assembly/.

Epple, Dennis and Thomas Romer. 1989. "Mobility and Redistribution." Working Papers in Economics, E-89–26. Stanford, CA: Hoover Institution.

Fares, Qais. 2014. *The Syrian Constitution: Assad's Magic Wand*. Washington, DC: Carnegie Endowment for International Peace.

Feldman, Noah. 2020. *The Arab Winter: A Tragedy*. Princeton, NJ: Princeton University Press.

Fiorina, Morris P. 1999. "Extreme Voices: A Dark Side of Civic Engagement." In *Civic Engagement in American Democracy*, ed. Theda Skocpol and Morris Fiorina. Washington, DC: Brookings Institute Press.

Fishkin, James A. 2009. *When the People Speak: Deliberative Democracy and Public Consultation*. Oxford: Oxford University Press.

Fliegelman, Oren. 2016. "The Question of Education in the 2014 Tunisian Constitution: Article 39 and its Ambiguous Values." *Middle East Law and Governance* 8 (1): 1–31.

Franck, Thomas M. and Arun K. Thiruvengadam. 2010. "Norms of International Law Relating to the Constitution-Making Process." In *Framing the State in Times of Transition: Case Studies in Constitution Making*, ed. Laurel Miller. Washington, DC: United States Institute of Peace Press, 20–56.

Friedrich, Carl J. 1950. *Constitutional Government and Democracy: Theory and Practice in Europe and America*. Boston, MA: Ginn.

Fruhstorfer, Anna and Alexander Hudson. 2021. "Majorities for Minorities: Participatory Constitution Making and the Protection of Minority Rights." *Political Research Quarterly*. Available at https://doi.org/10.1177/1065912920984246.

Galligan, Brian. 2008. "Comparative Federalism." In *The Oxford Handbook of Political Institutions*, ed. Sarah A. Binder, R. A. W. Rhodes, and Bert A. Rockman. Oxford: Oxford University Press, 261–280.

Gasim, Gamal. 2014. "Explaining Political Activism in Yemen." In *Talking to the Streets: The Transformation of Arab Activism*, ed. Lina Khatib and Ellen Lust. Baltimore, MD: John Hopkins University Press, 109–135.

Gaston, Erica. 2014. *Process Lessons Learned in Yemen's National Dialogue*. Washington, DC: United States Institute of Peace.

Gause, Gregory. 2013. "Kings for All Seasons: How the Middle East's Monarchies Survived the Arab Spring." Analysis Paper No. 8. Doha: Brookings Doha Center.

Geha, Carmen and Frédéric Volpi. 2016. "Constitutionalism and Political Order in Libya 2011–2014: Three Myths about the Past and a New Constitution." *The Journal of North African Studies* 21 (4): 687–706.

Genauer, Jessica. 2020. "Comparing Inclusion in Constitution-making in Egypt, Tunisia, and Iraq." *The Journal of North African Studies*. Available at https://doi.org/10.1080/13629387.2020.1759424.

Ghai, Yash. 2012. *The Role of Constituent Assemblies in Constitution Making*. Stockholm: International Institute for Democracy and Electoral Integrity.

Ghorbal, Samy. 2016. "Rachid Ammar, homme fort de la Tunisie: 'L'armée ne tire pas'" [Rachid Ammar, Strong Man from Tunisia: "The Army Does Not Fire"]. *L'OBS avec Rue89*, November 14. Retrieved from www.nouvelobs.com/rue89/rue89-monde/2011 0116.RUE0362/rachid-ammar-homme-fort-de-la-tunisie-l-armee-ne-tire-pas.html.

Ginsburg, Tom. 2003. *Judicial Review in New Democracies*. Cambridge: Cambridge University Press.

Ginsburg, Tom, Zachary Elkins, and Justin Blount. 2009. "Does the Process of Constitution-Making Matter?" *The Annual Review of Law and Social Science* 5: 201–223.

Ginsburg, Tom and Tamir Moustafa. 2008. *Rule by Law: The Politics of Courts in Authoritarian Regimes*. Cambridge: Cambridge University Press.

Ginsburg, Tom and Alberto Simpser. 2014. "Introduction: Constitutionalism in Authoritarian Regimes." In *Constitutions in Authoritarian Regimes*, ed. Tom Ginsburg and Alberto Simpser. Cambridge: Cambridge University Press, 1–17.

Gluck, Jason. 2015. "Constitution-Building in a Political Vacuum: Libya and Yemen in 2014." In *Annual Review of Constitution-Building Processes: 2014*, ed. Melanie Allen, Elliot Bulmer, Tom Ginsburg, Jason Gluck, Yasuo Hasebe, Yuhniwo Ngenge, and Roberto Toniatti. Stockholm: International Institute for Democracy and Electoral Integrity, 43–58.

Gordon, Michael R. 2014. "Kerry Makes Surprise Stop in Tunisia." *New York Times*, February 18. Retrieved from www.nytimes.com/2014/02/19/world/africa/secretary-of-state-john-kerry.html.

Goui, Bouhania. 2015. "Algerian Angst: Can It Agree on Constitutional Change?" *Arab Reform Initiative*. Retrieved from www.arab-reform.net/sites/default/files/Algerian %20angst,%20can%20it%20agree%20on%20constitutional%20change.pdf.

Grossman, Herschel I. and Suk Jae Noh. 1988. "Proprietary Public Finance, Political Competition, and Reputation." Working Paper # 2696. Cambridge, MA: National Bureau of Economic Research.

Haddad, Yvonne Yazbeck. 1998. "Islam and Gender: Dilemmas in the Changing Arab World." In *Islam, Gender and Social Change*, ed. Yvonne Yazbeck Haddad and John Esposito. Oxford: Oxford University Press, 3-29.

Hafez, M. Hosam. 2019. *Syria New Constitutional Committee: Enlightened UN Diplomacy or Repositioning the Assad Regime?* Doha: Al-Jazeera Centre for Studies.

Hakala, Pekka. 2013. *Cautious Reforms in Saudi Arabia*. Brussels: Directorate-General for External Policies, European Parliament.

Hart, Vivien. 2003. *Democratic Constitution Making*. Washington, DC: United States Institute for Peace.

Hartshorn, Ian M. 2017. "Organized Interests in Constitutional Assemblies." *Political Research Quarterly* 70 (2): 408–420.

Hartzell, Caroline A. and Matthew Hoddie. 2015. "The Art of the Possible: Power Sharing and Post-Civil War Democracy." *World Politics* 67 (1): 37–71.

Higley, John and Richard Gunther. 1992. *Elites and Democratic Consolidation in Latin America and Southern Europe*. Cambridge: Cambridge University Press.

Hirschman, Albert. 1970. *Exit, Voice, and Loyalty: Responses to Decline in Firms, Organizations, and States*. Cambridge, MA: Harvard University Press.

Hobbes, Thomas. 1968. "Leviathan." In *Classics of Moral and Political Theory*, ed. M. Morgan. Harmondsworth: Penguin, 581–735 (Original work published 1651).

Hodzi, Obert. 2013. *One Step Forward, Two Steps Back: Constitution-Making and Voter Education in Zimbabwe*. Oxford: Oxford Human Rights Hub. Available at http:// ohrh.law.ox.ac.uk/one-step-forward-two-steps-back-constitution-making-and-voter -education-in-zimbabwe/

Horowitz, Donald. 1985. *Ethnic Groups in Conflict*. Berkeley, CA: University of California Press.

2008. "Conciliatory Institutions and Constitutional Process in Post-Conflict States." *William and Mary Law Review* 49 (4): 1213–1248.

2013. *Constitutional Change and Democracy in Indonesia*. Cambridge: Cambridge University Press.

2014. "Reconsidering the Transition Paradigm: Discussion with Diamond, Larry, Francis Fukuyama, Donald Horowitz, and Marc Plattner." *Journal of Democracy* 25 (1): 86–100.

Howard, Philip N. and Muzammil M. Hussain. 2013. *Democracy's Fourth Wave? Digital Media and the Arab Spring*. Oxford: Oxford University Press.

Hudson, Alexander. 2018. "When Does Public Participation Make a Difference? Evidence from Iceland's Crowdsourced Constitution." *Policy & Internet* 10 (2): 185–217.

2021. "Political Parties and Public Participation in Constitution Making: Legitimation, Distraction, or Real Influence?" *Comparative Politics* 53(3): 501–524.

Ibrahim, Ekram. 2012. "Administrative Court Non-Decision Gives Assembly Ample Time to Finish Constitution." *Ahram Online*, October 23. Retrieved from http://english .ahram.org.eg/NewsContent/1/64/56348/Egypt/Politics-/Referral-to-court-buys-more- time-for-Egypts-embatt.aspx.

Ikhwan Web. 2012. "Hossam Ghariani: Constituent Assembly and New Constitution Statistics Speak for Themselves." *Ikhwan Web*, December 4. Retrieved from www .ikhwanweb.com/article.php?id=30451.

International Commission of Jurists. 2015. *The Draft Libyan Constitution: Procedural Deficiencies, Substantive Flaws*. Geneva: International Commission of Jurists. Retrieved from www.refworld.org/pdfid/57ee86814.pdf.

Jamal, Amal and Anna Kensicki. 2016. "A Theory of Critical Junctures for Democratization: A Comparative Examination of Constitution-Making in Egypt and Tunisia." *The Law & Ethics of Human Rights* 10 (1): 185–222.

Jarrah, Sameer. 2009. "Civil Society and Public Freedom in Jordan: The Path of Democratic Reform." Working Paper No. 3. Washington, DC: Saban Center for Middle East Policy at the Brookings Institution.

Jean-François, Bayart. 1993. *The State in Africa: The Politics of the Belly*. London: Longman.

Jermanová, Tereza. 2020. "From Mistrust to Understanding: Inclusive Constitution-Making Design and Agreement in Tunisia." *Political Research Quarterly*. Available at https://doi.org/10.1177/1065912920967106.

Johnson, Darin E. W. 2015. "Beyond Constituent Assemblies and Referenda: Assessing the Legitimacy of the Arab Spring Constitutions in Egypt and Tunisia." *Wake Forest Law Review* 50: 1007–1056.

2017. "Conflict Constitution-Making in Libya and Yemen." *University of Pennsylvania Journal of International Law* 39 (2): 293–354.

Kamrava, Mehran (ed.). 2014. *Beyond the Arab Spring: The Evolving Ruling Bargain in the Middle East*. Oxford: Oxford University Press.

Kellner, Douglas. 2016. "Media Spectacle and the North African Arab Uprising: Some Critical Reflections." In *Spectacle*, ed. Bruce Magnusson and Zahi Zalloua. Seattle, WA: University of Washington Press, 18–64.

Kennedy, Merrit. 2019. "Egypt Approves Constitutional Changes that Could Keep Sissi in Office Until 2030." *National Public Radio (NPR)*, April 23. Retrieved from www.npr.org/2019/04/23/716408260/egypt-approves-constitutional-changes-that-could-keep-el-sissi-in-office-until-2.

Ketchley, Neil. 2017. *Egypt in a Time of Revolution: Contentious Politics and the Arab Spring*. Cambridge: Cambridge University Press.

Khatib, Lina and Ellen Lust (eds.). 2014. *Talking to the Streets: The Transformation of Arab Activism*. Baltimore, MD: John Hopkins University Press.

Khettab, Djamila Ould. 2016. "Algeria Set to Approve New Constitution." *Al Jazeera*, February 2. Retrieved from www.aljazeera.com/news/2016/01/algeria-set-approveconstitution-160131141538778.html.

Knell, Yolande. 2012. "Egypt Court Suspends Constitutional Assembly." *BBC News Middle East*, April 10. Retrieved from www.bbc.co.uk/news/world-middle-east-17665048.

Kuran, Timur. 2004. "Why the Middle East Is Economically Underdeveloped: Historical Mechanisms of Institutional Stagnation." *The Journal of Economic Perspectives* 18 (3): 71–90.

Ladd, Everett C. 1996. "The Data Just Don't Show Erosion of Americas 'Social Capital.'" *The Public Perspective* 7 (4): 1, 5–22.

Laessing, Ulf. 2011. "Saudi Arabia Says Won't Tolerate Protests." *Reuters*, March 5. Retrieved from www.reuters.com/article/us-saudi-protests/saudi-arabia-says-wont-tolerate-protests-idUSTRE72419N20110305.

Landemore, Hélène. 2012. "Democratic Reason: The Mechanisms of Collective Intelligence in Politics." In *Collective Wisdom: Principles and Mechanisms*, ed. Hélène Landemore and Jon Elster. Cambridge: Cambridge University Press, 251–289.

2013. *Democratic Reason: Politics, Collective Intelligence, and the Rule of the Many.* Princeton, NJ: Princeton University Press.

2016. "What Is a Good Constitution? Assessing the Constitutional Proposal in the Icelandic Experiment." In *Assessing Constitutional Performance*, ed. Tom Ginsburg and Aziz Huq. Cambridge: Cambridge University Press, 71-98.

2017. "Inclusive Constitution Making and Religious Rights: Lessons from the Icelandic Experiment." *The Journal of Politics* 79 (3): 762–779.

Law, David D. and Mila Versteeg. 2011. "The Evolution and Ideology of Global Constitutionalism." *California Law Review* 99 (5): 1163–1257.

Lerner, Hanna. 2011.*Making Constitutions in Deeply Divided Societies.* New York: Cambridge University Press.

Lesch, David W. 2011. The Arab Spring – and Winter – in Syria. *Global Change, Peace & Security* 23 (3): 421–426.

Levi, Margaret. 1996. "Social and Unsocial Capital: A Review Essay of Robert Putnam's Making Democracy Work." *Politics & Society* 24 (1): 45–55.

Lewis, Peter M. 1992. "Political Transitions and the Dilemma of Civil Society in Africa." *Journal of International Affairs* 42 (1): 31–54.

Lijphart, Arend. 1969. "Consociational Democracy." *World Politics* 21 (2): 207–275.

   1977. *Democracy in Plural Societies: A Comparative Exploration.* New Haven, CT: Yale University Press.

   2012. *Patterns of Democracy: Government Forms and Performance in Thirty-Six Countries*, 2nd ed. New Haven, CT: Yale University Press.

Linz, Juan J. 1990. "The Perils of Presidentialism." *Journal of Democracy* 1 (1): 51–69.

Linz, Juan J. and Alfred Stepan. 1996. *Problems of Democratic Transition and Consolidation: Southern Europe, South America, and Post-Communist Europe.* Baltimore, MD: Johns Hopkins University Press.

Locke, John. 1988. *Two Treatises of Government*, Student ed., Cambridge Texts in the History of Political Thought. Cambridge: Cambridge University Press (Original work published 1690).

Lombardi, Clark and Nathan J. Brown. 2012. "Islam in Egypt's New Constitution." *Foreign Policy*, December 13. Retrieved from http://mideast.foreignpolicy.com/p osts/2012/12/13/islam_in_egypts_new_constitution.

Louër, Laurence. 2014. "Activism in Bahrain: Between Sectarian and Issue Politics." In *Talking to the Streets: The Transformation of Arab Activism*, ed. Lina Khatib and Ellen Lust. Baltimore, MD: John Hopkins University Press, 172–198.

Lust, Ellen and Lina Khatib. 2014. *The Transformation of Arab Activism.* Washington, DC: POMED Policy Brief Series.

Lynch, Marc (ed.). 2014. *The Arab Uprising Explained: New Contentious Politics in the Middle East.* New York: Columbian University Press.

Maboudi, Tofigh. 2019. "Democratization and the Evolution of the Foreign Policy Content of North African Constitutions." *Journal of North African Studies* 24 (4): 558–578.

   2020a. "Participation, Inclusion, and the Democratic Content of Constitutions." *Studies in Comparative International Development* 55 (1): 48–76.

   2020b. "Reconstituting Tunisia: Participation, Deliberation, and the Content of Constitution." *Political Research Quarterly* 73 (4): 774–789.

Maboudi, Tofigh and Ghazal P. Nadi. 2016. "Crowdsourcing the Egyptian Constitution: Social Media, Elites, and the Populace." *Political Research Quarterly* 69 (4): 716–731.

Maddy-Weitzman, Bruce. 2012. "Is Morocco Immune to Upheaval?" *Middle East Quarterly* 19 (1): 87–93.

Madison, James. 1961. *The Federalist Papers*, ed. Clinton Rossiter. New York: New American Library (Original work published 1787).

Magalhães, Pedro C. 2015. "Explaining the Constitutionalization of Social Rights: Portuguese Hypotheses and a Cross-National Test." In *Social and Political Foundations of Constitutions*, ed. Denis J. Galligan and Mila Versteeg. Cambridge: Cambridge University Press, 432–468.

Mahjoub, Rim. 2016. "From Division to Consensus: The Role and Contribution of the Consensus Committee." *United Nations Development Programme*, Constitution of Tunisia, Part 2, September 26. Retrieved from www.arabstates.undp.org/con tent/dam/rbas/doc/Compendium%20English/Part%202/25%20Rym%20Mahjoub %20EN.pdf.

Mahmoud, Khalid. 2018. "Libya: MPs Refuse to Recognize the Constitution Drafting Assembly." *Asharq Al-Awsat*, February 21. Retrieved from https://aawsat.com/eng lish/home/article/1182411/libya-mps-refuse-recognize-constitution-drafting-assembly.

Mansbridge, Jane, James Bohman, Simone Chambers, Thomas Christiano, Archon Fung, John Parkinson, Dennis F. Thompson, and Mark E. Warren. 2012. "A Systemic Approach to Deliberative Democracy." In *Deliberative Systems: Deliberative Democracy at the Large Scale*, ed. John Parkinson and Jane Mansbridge. Cambridge: Cambridge University Press, 1–26.

March, James and Johan Olsen. 1994. *Democratic Governance*. New York: Free Press.

Markey, Patrick and Hamid O. Ahmed. 2016. "Algerian Lawmakers Pass Constitutional Reforms, Opposition Dismiss." *Reuters*, February 7. Retrieved from www .reuters.com/article/us-algeria-politics/algerian-lawmakers-pass-constitutional-reforms-oppositiondismissidUSKCN0VG0KC.

Marks, Monica L. 2014. "Convince, Coerce, or Compromise? Ennahda's Approach to Tunisia's Constitution." Analysis Paper No. 10. Doha: Brookings Doha Center.

Marulanda, Ivan. 2004. *The Role of Constitution-Building Processes in Democratization: Case Study of Colombia*. Stockholm: International Institute for Democracy and Electoral Integrity.

Mecham, Quinn. 2014. "Bahrain's Fractured Ruling Bargain: Political Mobilization, Regime Response, and the New Sectarianism." In *Beyond the Arab Spring: The Evolving Ruling Bargain in the Middle East*, ed. Mehran Kamrava. Oxford: Oxford University Press, 341–371.

Mednicoff, David. 2014. "A Tale of Three Constitutions: Common Drives and Diverse Outcomes in Post-2010 Arab Legal Politics." *Temple International & Comparative Law Journal* 28: 215–251.

Meisburger, Timothy M. 2012. "Getting Majoritarianism Right." *Journal of Democracy* 23 (1): 155–163.

Metz, Helen Chapin (ed.). 1994. *Algeria: A Country Study*. Washington, DC: Federal Research Division, the Library of Congress.

Miller, Laurel and Louis Aucoin (eds.). 2010. *Framing the State in Times of Transition: Case Studies in Constitution Making*. Washington, DC: United States Institute of Peace Press.

Mir-Hosseini, Ziba. 1999. *Islam and Gender: The Religious Debate in Contemporary Iran*. Princeton, NJ: Princeton University Press.

2003. "The Construction of Gender in Islamic Legal Thought and Strategies for Reform." *Hawwa: Journal of Women of the Middle East and the Islamic World* 1 (1): 1–29.

Moehler, Devra C. 2008. *Distrusting Democrats: Outcomes of Participatory Constitution Making*. Ann Arbor, MI: University of Michigan Press.

Molina, Irene Fernandez. 2011. "The Monarchy vs. the 20 February Movement: Who Holds the Reins of Political Change in Morocco?" *Mediterranean Politics* 16 (3): 453–441.

Morrow, Adam and Khaled Moussa Al-Omrani. 2012. "New Revolution against New Constitution." *Inter Press Service*, January 27. Retrieved from www.ipsnews.net/2 013/01/new-revolution-against-new-constitution/.

Mostafa, Randa. 2019. "National Dialogue on Constitutional Amendments Includes No Opposition Voices." *Mada Masr*, March 21. Retrieved from https://madamasr .com/en/2019/03/21/feature/politics/national-dialogue-on-constitutional-amendments -includes-no-opposition-voices/.

Moustafa, Tamir. 2007. *The Struggle for Constitutional Power: Law, Politics, and Economic Development in Egypt*. Cambridge: Cambridge University Press.

Muasher, Marwan. 2011. *Jordan's Proposed Constitutional Amendments – A First Step in the Right Direction*. Washington, DC: Carnegie Endowment for International Peace.

Mudde, Cas. 2013. "Are Populists Friends or Foes of Constitutionalism?" Policy Brief. Oxford: The Foundation for Law, Justice and Society.

Mujais, Ayat. 2017. "The Dos and Don'ts of Federal Constitutions: A Case Study on Yemen." *American University International Law Review* 33 (1): 287–309.

Negretto, Gabriel. 2013. *Making Constitutions: Presidents, Parties, and Institutional Choice in Latin America*. Cambridge: Cambridge University Press.

Netterstrøm, Kasper L. 2015. "The Islamists' Compromise in Tunisia." *Journal of Democracy* 26 (4): 110–124.

2016. "The Tunisian General Labor Union and the Advent of Democracy." *Middle East Journal* 70 (3): 383–398.

Niskanen, William. A. 1990. "Conditions Affecting the Survival of Constitutional Rule." *Constitutional Political Economy* 1 (2): 53–62.

Norberg, Nicholas. 2018. "A Primer on Syria's Constitutional Committee." *Lawfare*, December 22. Retrieved from www.lawfareblog.com/primer-syrias-constitutional- committee.

Norris, Pippa. 2008. *Driving Democracy: Do Power-Sharing Institutions Work?* New York: Cambridge University Press.

North, Douglass C. and Barry R. Weingast. 1989. "Constitutions and Commitment: The Evolution of Institutions Governing Public Choice in Seventeenth-Century England." *The Journal of Economic History* 49 (4): 803–832.

Northey, Jessica Ayesha. 2018. *Civil Society in Algeria: Activism, Identity and the Democratic Process*. London: I. B. Tauris.

Norton, Augustus R. 1993. "The Future of Civil Society in the Middle East." *Middle East Journal* 47 (2): 205–216.

1995. "Introduction." In *Civil Society in the Middle East*, Volume 1, ed. Augustus Richard Norton. Leiden: Brill Academic, 1-25.

O'Donnell, Guillermo A. and Philippe C. Schmitter. 1986. *Transitions from Authoritarian Rule. Tentative Conclusions about Uncertain Democracies.* Baltimore, MD: John Hopkins University Press.

Ordeshook, Peter C. 1992. "Constitutional Stability." *Constitutional Political Economy* 3 (2): 137–175.

Ottaway, Marina. 2011. *Tunisia: The Revolution is Over, Can Reform Continue?* Washington, DC: Carnegie Endowment for International Peace.

Parolin, Gianluca P. 2015. "Constitutions against Revolutions: Political Participation in North Africa." *British Journal of Middle Eastern Studies* 42 (1): 31–45.

Pateman, Carole. 1970. *Participation and Democratic Theory*. Cambridge: Cambridge University Press.

2012. "Participatory Democracy Revisited." *Perspectives on Politics* 10 (1): 7–19.

Petrucci, Filippo and Marisa Fois. 2016. "Attitudes towards Israel in Tunisian Political Debate: From Bourguiba to the New Constitution." *The Journal of North African Studies* 21 (3): 392–410.

Phillips, Christopher. 2012. *After the Arab Spring: Power Shift in the Middle East? Syria's Bloody Arab Spring.* London: LSE Research Online.

Pickard, Duncan. 2012. *Lessons from Constitution-Making in Tunisia*. Washington, DC: Atlantic Council, Issue Brief.

Pitkin, Hanna F. 1967. *The Concept of Representation*. Berkley, CA and Los Angeles: University of California Press.

Plotke, David. 1997. "Representation is Democracy." *Constellations* 4 (1): 19–34.

Prashad, Vijay. 2012. *Arab Spring, Libyan Winter*. Edinburgh: AK Press.

Przeworski, Adam. 1986. *Capitalism and Social Democracy*. Cambridge: Cambridge University Press.

1991. *Democracy and the Market: Political and Economic Reforms in Eastern Europe and Latin America*. Cambridge: Cambridge University Press.

2014. "Ruling against Rules." In *Constitutions in Authoritarian Regimes*, ed. Tom Ginsburg and Alberto Simpser. New York: Cambridge University Press, 21–35.

Putnam, Robert D. 1993. *Making Democracy Work: Civic Traditions in Modern Italy*. Princeton, NJ: Princeton University Press.

2000. *Bowling Alone: The Collapse and Revival of American Community*. New York: Simon and Schuster.

Rajabany, Intissar K. and Lihi Ben Shitrit. 2014. "Activism and Civil War in Libya." In *Talking to the Streets: The Transformation of Arab Activism*, ed. Lina Khatib and Ellen Lust. Baltimore, MD: John Hopkins University Press, 76–108.

Rashwan, Nada Hussein. 2012. "Egypt's Constituent Assembly Convenes Tuesday with Future Still in Doubt." *Ahram Online*, June 27. Retrieved from http://english .ahram.org.eg/NewsContent/1/64/46274/Egypt/Politics-/Egypts-constituent-assembly -convenes-Tuesday-with-.aspx.

Reese, Aaron. 2013. "Sectarian and Regional Conflict in the Middle East." Middle East Security Report 13. Washington, DC: Institute for the Study of War.

Reynal-Querol, Marta. 2002. "Ethnicity, Political Systems, and Civil Wars." *Journal of Conflict Resolution* 46 (1): 29–54.

Roeder, Philip G. and Donald Rothchild (eds.). 2005. *Sustainable Peace: Power and Democracy after Civil Wars*. Ithaca, NY: Cornell University Press.

Rousseau, Jean-Jacques. 1997. "The Social Contract." In *The Spirit of Laws; On the Origin of Inequality; On Political Economy; The Social Contract*. Edinburgh: Encyclopedia Britannica, 387–439. (Original work published 1763).

Russell, Peter H. 1993. *Constitutional Odyssey: Can Canadians Become a Sovereign People?*, 2nd ed. Toronto: University of Toronto Press.

Russia Today. 2012. "Islamist Constitution Spurs Controversy in Egypt As Protests Grow." *Russia Today*, November 30. Retrieved from http://on.rt.com/ru6gxi.

Rustow, Dankwart A. 1970. "Transitions to Democracy: Toward a Dynamic Model." *Comparative Politics* 2 (3): 337–363.

Salamey, Imad. 2009. "Failing Consociationalism in Lebanon and Integrative Options." *Journal of Peace Studies* 14 (2): 83–105.

Salamey, Imad and Rhys Payne. 2008. "Parliamentary Consociationalism in Lebanon: Equal Citizenry vs. Quotated Confessionalism." *The Journal of Legislative Studies* 14 (4): 451–473.

Samuels, Kirsti. 2006. *Constitution Building Processes and Democratization: A Discussion of Twelve Case Studies*. Stockholm: International IDEA.

2007. "Separation of Powers." In *The Oxford Handbook of Comparative Politics*, ed. Carles Boix and Susan C. Stokes. Oxford: Oxford University Press, 703–726.

Sarkin, Jeremy. 1999. "The Drafting of South Africa's Final Constitution from a Human-Rights Perspective." *The American Journal of Comparative Law* 47 (1): 67–87.

Schedler, Andreas. 2002. "Elections without Democracy: The Menu of Manipulation." *Journal of Democracy* 13 (2): 36–50.

Schmitz, Charles. 2014. "Yemen's National Dialogue." Policy Paper Series 2014–1. Washington, DC: Middle East Institute.

Schumpeter, Joseph A. 1942. *Capitalism, Socialism, and Democracy*. New York: Harper & Brothers.

Seeley, Nicholas. 2011. "Jordan Aims to Avoid Unrest with Dialogue on Sweeping Reforms." *The Christian Science Monitor*, 23 March. Retrieved from www .csmonitor.com/World/Middle-East/2011/0323/Jordan-aims-to-avoid-unrest-with -dialogue-on-sweeping-reforms

Selway, Joel and Kharis Templeman. 2012. "The Myth of Consociationalism? Conflict Reduction in Divided Societies." *Comparative Political Studies* 45 (12): 1542–1571.

Shugart, Matthew S. and John Carey. 1992. *Presidents and Assemblies*. Cambridge: Cambridge University Press.

Silverstein, Gordon. 2008. "Singapore: The Exception That Proves Rules Matter." In *Rule by Law: The Politics of Courts in Authoritarian Regimes*, ed. Tom Ginsburg and Tamir Moustafa. Cambridge: Cambridge University Press, 73-101.

Smith, Graham. 2009. *Democratic Innovations: Designing Institutions for Citizen Participation*. Cambridge: Cambridge University Press.

Spencer, Richard. 2014. "Egypt Votes Overwhelmingly for Military-backed Constitution." *The Telegraph*, January 16. Retrieved from www.telegraph.co.uk/n ews/worldnews/africaandindianocean/egypt/10575772/Egypt-votes-overwhelmingly -for-military-backed-constitution.html.

Stamboliyska, Rayna. 2012. "Egypt's Constitutional Referendum Results." *Jadaliyya*, December 25. Retrieved from www.jadaliyya.com/pages/index/9234/.

Stepan, Alfred. 2000. "Religion, Democracy, and the 'Twin Tolerations.'" *Journal of Democracy* 11: 37–57.

2001. *Arguing Comparative Politics*. Oxford: Oxford University Press.

Stepan, Alfred and Juan Linz. 2013. "Democratization Theory and the Arab Spring." *Journal of Democracy* 24 (2): 15–30.

Stepan, Alfred and Graeme B. Robertson. 2004. "Debate: Arab, Not Muslim, Exceptionalism." *Journal of Democracy* 15 (4): 140–146.

Stevenson, Reed and Erika Solomon. 2011. "Protestors Doubt Bahrain Dialogue Will End Crisis." *Reuters*, July 1. Retrieved from www.reuters.com/article/us-bahrain-dialogue /protestors-doubt-bahrain-dialogue-will-end-crisis-idUSTRE7602MR20110701.

Stowasser, Barbara. 1993. "Women's Issues in Modern Islamic Thought." In *Arab Women: Old Boundaries, New Frontiers*, ed. Judith E. Tucker. Bloomington, IN: Indiana University Press, 3-28.

Sunstein, Cass R. 2001. *Designing Democracy: What Constitutions Do*. Oxford: Oxford University Press.

Szmolka, Inmaculada. 2015. "Exclusionary and Non-Consensual Transitions versus Inclusive and Consensual Democratizations: The Cases of Egypt and Tunisia." *Arab Studies Quarterly* 37 (1): 73–95.

The Tahrir Institute. 2019. *TIMEP Brief: 2019 Constitutional Amendments*. Washington, DC: Tahrir Institute for Middle East Policy (TIMEP).

Taylor, Rupert. 2006. "The Belfast Agreement and the Politics of Consociationalism: A Critique." *The Political Quarterly* 77 (2): 217–226.

Teorell, Jan. 2010. *Determinants of Democratization: Explaining Regime Change in the World, 1972–2006*. Cambridge: Cambridge University Press.

Tétreault, Mary Ann. 2011. "The Winter of the Arab Spring in the Gulf Monarchies." *Globalizations* 8 (5): 629–637.

Tharoor, Ishaan. 2010. "A Brief History of Yemen: Rich Past, Impoverished Present." *Time*, November 1. Retrieved from http://content.time.com/time/world/article/0, 8599,2028740,00.html.

de Tocqueville, Alexis. 1969. *Democracy in America*, ed. J. P. Mayer, trans. George Lawrence. Garden City, NY: Anchor Books (Original work published 1835).

Tsebelis, George. 2002. *Veto Players: How Political Institutions Work*. Princeton, NJ: Princeton University Press.

Tushnet, Mark. 2000. "The Constitution of Civil Society." *Chicago-Kent Law Review* 75 (2): 379–416.

United Nations Development Programme (UNDP). 2013a. *Dialogue National Sur Le Project de La Constitution: Rapport General* [National Dialogue on the Constitutional Project: General Report]. Tunis: UNDP.

2013b. *Athar al-hewar al-wadani 'ala al-mosawedat al-mashru' al-dastour al-thalethah: Qeraa tahliliyah* [The Impact of the National Dialogue on the Third Draft of the Constitution: A Critical Study]. Tunis: UNDP.

United States Agency for International Development (USAID). 2016. *Jordan: Civil Society Assessment Report*. Washington, DC: USAID.

Vandewalle, Dirk. 2014. "Beyond the Civil War in Libya: Toward a New Ruling Bargain." In *Beyond the Arab Spring: The Evolving Ruling Bargain in the Middle East*, ed. Mehran Kamrava. Oxford: Oxford University Press, 437–457.

Verba, Sidney, Kay L. Schlozman, and Henry Brady. 1995. *Voice and Equality: Civic Voluntarism in American Politics.* Cambridge, MA: Harvard University Press.

Volpi, Frédéric. 2017. *Revolution and Authoritarianism in North Africa.* Oxford: Oxford University Press.

Wagner, Richard E. 1987. "Parchment, Guns, and the Maintenance of Constitutional Contract." In *Democracy and Public Choice*, ed. Charles K. Rowley. New York: Basil Blackwell, 105-121.

Wampler, Brian. 2012. "Participation, Representation, and Social Justice: Using Participatory Governance to Transform Representative Democracy." *Polity* 44 (4): 666–682.

Warren, Mark and Dario Castiglione. 2004. "The Transformation of Democratic Representation." *Democracy and Society* 2 (1): 20–22.

Watts, Ronald L. 1999. *Comparing Federal Systems*, 2nd ed. Montreal: McGill-Queen's University Press.

Weingast, Barry. 1997. "The Political Foundations of Democracy and the Rule of Law." *American Political Science Review* 91 (2): 245–263.

Weyland, Kurt. 2013. "Latin America's Authoritarian Drift: The Threat from the Populist Left." *Journal of Democracy* 24 (3): 18–32.

Wiarda, Howard J. 2012. "Arab Fall or Arab Winter?" *American Foreign Policy Interests* 34 (3): 134–137.

Widner, Jennifer A. 2004. "Country Report: Zambia 1991." Constitution Writing and Conflict Resolution Project. Princeton, NJ: Princeton University.

2005. "Constitution Writing and Conflict Resolution." *The Round Table* 94 (381): 503–518.

2008. "Constitution Drafting in Post-Conflict States Symposium." *William and Mary Law Review* 49: 1513–1541.

Wiktorowicz, Quintan. 2000. "Civil Society as Social Control: State Power in Jordan." *Comparative Politics* 33 (1): 43–61.

Williams, Paul, Tiffany Sommadossi, and Ayat Mujais. 2017. "A Legal Perspective on Yemen's Attempted Transition from a Unitary to a Federal System of Government." *Utrecht Journal of International and European Law* 33 (84): 4–22.

Wilson, Robin and Rick Wilford. 2003. *Northern Ireland: A Route to Stability?* Belfast: ESRC.

Wing, Susanna D. 2008. *Constructing Democracy in Transitioning Societies of Africa: Constitutionalism and Deliberation in Mali.* New York: Palgrave McMillan.

World Bank. 2013. *World Development Indicators*, ed. Washington, DC: World Bank.

Worrall, James. 2012. "Oman: The 'Forgotten' Corner of the Arab Spring." *Middle East Policy* 19 (3): 98–115.

Yaghi, Mohammed and Janine A. Clark. 2014. "Jordan: Evolving Activism in a Divided Society." In *Talking to the Streets: The Transformation of Arab Activism*, ed. Lina Khatib and Ellen Lust. Baltimore, MD: John Hopkins University Press, 236–267.

Yom, Sean. 2005. "Civil Society and Democratization in the Arab World." *Middle East Review of International Affairs* 9 (4): 14–33.

Zoubir, Yahia H. 2015. "The Democratic Transition in Tunisia: A Success Story in the Making." *Conflict Trends* 1: 10–17.

Index

Abdel-Aal, Ali, 147
Abdelkafi, Badreldin, 81, 82, 105, 179
Abdelliya, 102
Abderrahim, Souad, 104
Abdel Nasser, Gamal, 180
Abul-Fadl, Amani, 221
Adams, John, 42, *see also* democratic theory:
    representative model
Aden, 155, 156, 215–216
Al Bawsala, 92, 93, 111
Al Dhahrani, Khalifa Ben Ahmed, 144
Al Faisal, Toujan, 132, 168
Al-Adl Party (Egypt), 178
Al-Adl Wal-Ihsan Party (Morocco), 129, 131, 169
Al-Ahmar, Sheikh Sadiq, 155
Al-Anbari, Mazhar, 142
Al-Assad, Bashar, 35–36, 141–143, 207, 212,
    239, 241
Al-Assad, Hafez, 141
Al-Awamiyah, 145
Al-Azhar University, 121, 221
Al-Bakhit, Marouf, 131, 132, 134
Al-Bashir, Omar, 242
Alexandria, 165, 174
Algeria. *See also* National Liberation
    Front (FLN)
    authoritarianism, 209, 226
    civil society, 29, 186
    constitution of 2016, 6, 117, 135, 207–208
    constitution-making process, 5, 6, 115, 126,
        137–140, 234, 236, 238
    first national dialogue, 138
    Islamist militants, 139
    protests, 2, 7, 37, 242
    second national dialogue, 138
    term limits, 15, 23, 196

war of independence, 98
Al-Ghad Party, 178
Al-Hirak Movement (Algeria), 242, 243
Al-Hirak Movement (Yemen), 156, 215
Al-Hirak Youth Movement (Jordan), 132, 163,
    168, 173, 176, 235
Al-Islah Party (Algeria), 139
Al-Islah Party (Yemen), 155, 173
Aljanad, 215
Aljazeera, 19, 149
Al-Karama Party, 178
Al-Khateeb, Hamza, 35
Al-Khawaja, Abdulhadi, 190
Al-Masaar Party, 82
Al-Masri, Taher, 132
Al-Masry Party, 178
Al-Sadat, Anwar, 22, 193
Al-Tayyar Party, 178
Al-Thinni, Abdullah, 153
Al-Wa'ee Party, 178
Al-Wasat Party, 178
Al-Wefaq Party, 144
Amazigh
    in Algeria, 37, 207
    in Libya, 152, 153, 188, 218
    in Morocco, 201, 204
    in Tunisia, 98
Amman, 131, 134
Ammar, Rachid, 77, 97
Amnesty International, 111
anti-gridlock institutions, 33, 89, 92, *see also*
    Tunisia: anti-gridlock institutions
April 19 Movement (M-19), 73
April 6 Youth Movement, 49, 124, 136, 163, 173,
    176–178, 180, 189–190, 221, 224, 235
Arab Spring. *See* specific countries

262